An anthropological critique of development

The latest volume in the EIDOS series challenges the Utopian view of western knowledge as a uniquely successful achievement in its application to economic and social development. The contributors, all well-known European professional anthropologists with experience of development, provide an ethnographic and theoretical critique of western knowledge in action. They focus on the importance given in development to 'experts', who often turn previously active participants into passive subjects or ignorant objects.

Making use of detailed ethnographic case studies, from Europe, Africa, Asia and Latin America, the contributors examine the ways in which indigenous knowledges often prove more effective than expert western knowledge and explore the relationships between the two kinds of knowledge. They stress the importance of understanding knowledge in the particular contexts of its use and show how western experts, by dismissing local knowledges in favour of an exclusive scientific Knowledge, contribute to the growth of ignorance rather than the growth of knowledge.

Arguing strongly against the separation of theory and practice, *An anthropological critique of development* bridges the gap between the practical concerns of developers and theoretical interest in the power implications of knowledge in the post-colonial world. It will be of great value to anthropologists and development workers in training and practice, and to geographers, economists, sociologists and political scientists.

Mark Hobart is Senior Lecturer in Anthropology at the School of Oriental and African Studies, University of London, and is a co-founder of EIDOS.

D0308271

An anthropological critique of development
The growth of ignorance

Edited by Mark Hobart

London and New York

First published 1993
by Routledge
11 New Fetter Lane, London EC4P 4EE

Simultaneously published in the USA and Canada
by Routledge
29 West 35th Street, New York, NY 10001

Reprinted 1995, 1997

Typeset in Times by
Intype, London
Printed and bound in Great Britain by
Mackays of Chatham PLC, Chatham, Kent

British Library Cataloguing in Publication Data
A catalogue record for this book is available from the British Library

Library of Congress Cataloguing in Publication Data
A catalogue record for this book is available from the Library of Congress

ISBN 0-415-07958-6 (hbk)   ISBN 0-415-07959-4 (pbk)

Contents

Figures

Contributors

Alberto Arce is Lecturer in Sociology of Development at the Agricultural University of Wageningen. He is author of many articles on rural development. He is currently working on changing patterns of agricultural consumption in the West and the nature of transformations in the third world countryside.

Walter van der Beek is Associate Professor at the Department of Cultural Anthropology, Utrecht University. He is author of *The Kapsoko and Higi of the Mandara Mountains* (1987), co-author of *Symbols for Communication* (1984) and has edited several volumes on African religions. He is currently working in Mali among the Dogon.

Franz von Benda-Beckmann is Professor in the Department of Agrarian Law at the Agricultural University of Wageningen. He is author of *Property in Social Continuity* (1979) and co-editor of *Law as a Resource in Agrarian Struggles* (1992). He is currently working on rural social security and property relations in developing countries.

Richard Burghart is Professor of Ethnology at the University of Heidelberg. He has edited several books on Hinduism and is the author of a forthcoming study of the Maithili language in southeastern Nepal. Among his current interests are the workings of democratic institutions in provincial Nepalese society.

Anthony Cohen is Professor of Social Anthropology at the University of Edinburgh. His books include *Whalsey: Symbol, Segment and Boundary in a Shetland Island Community* (1987) and *The Symbolic Construction of Community* (1985). He is presently writing a cultural examination of Anthropology and Selfhood, entitled *Self-Consciousness*, to be published by Routledge.

Elisabeth Croll is Reader in Chinese Anthropology and Chair of the Centre of Chinese Studies at the School of Oriental and African Studies. She is author of a number of works on various aspects of development in relation to China. Her latest book is *From Heaven to Earth: Images and Experiences of Development in China* (1993).

Mark Hobart is Senior Lecturer in South East Asian Anthropology at the School of Oriental and African Studies. He is academic editor of *Context, Meaning, and Power in Southeast Asia* (1986). He is at present writing a critique of ethnocentrism in anthropological explanation and interpretation entitled *Dwarves Reaching for the Sky*.

Norman Long is Professor of Sociology of Development at the Agricultural University of Wageningen. Among his numerous books are *An Introduction to the Sociology of Development* (1977) and, most recently, with A. Long *Battlefields of Knowledge: the Interlocking of Theory and Practice in Social Research and Development* (1992).

Jan Douwe van der Ploeg is Professor of Rural Sociology at the Agricultural University of Wageningen and Scientific Coordinator of CERES (Circle for Rural European Studies). He is the author of *Labour, Markets and Agricultural Production* (1990). His current research is on the endogenous development processes in European agriculture.

Philip Quarles van Ufford is Senior Lecturer in the Department of Development Sociology and Anthropology at the Free University, Amsterdam. He has edited several works on development. He has also been directly involved in development in several capacities and strongly believes that anthropology is a moral science.

Paul Richards is Professor of Anthropology at University College London and, from January 1993, Professor of Technology and Agrarian Development at the Agricultural University of Wageningen. His publications include *Indigenous Agricultural Revolution* (1985) and *Coping with Hunger* (1986).

Piers Vitebsky is Head of Social Sciences at the Scott Polar Research Institute, University of Cambridge. He is the author of a work on the Sora in India, *Dialogues with the Dead* (1993). His current research interests are on shamanism and environmentalist ideology in Siberia.

Preface

Most of the chapters in this collection were first presented at a workshop at the School of Oriental and African Studies, University of London, in December 1986. It was organized under the auspices of EIDOS (European Inter-University Development Opportunities Study-Group), which was founded in 1985 and brought together British, Dutch and German anthropologists studying discourses of development. Currently the main participating institutions are the Department of Anthropology and Sociology, the School of Oriental and African Studies, University of London; the Institute of Cultural Anthropology/Non-Western Sociology, the Free University, Amsterdam; the Department of Rural Sociology, the Agricultural University, Wageningen; and the Sociology of Development Research Centre, University of Bielefeld, Germany. EIDOS also has a wide network of participating social anthropologists and sociologists from other European institutes.

EIDOS's aim is to bring together anthropologists and sociologists with theoretical interests and those concerned with development studies in different European centres to reflect critically on processes of development, by arranging student exchanges and by providing support for a series of workshops. The purpose of EIDOS workshops is to further understanding of how anthropological and sociological research and arguments are relevant to theories and debates on development, development priorities, patterns and projects, and the social and cultural implications and consequences of new development programmes. The workshops examine new approaches to a number of the more specific and intractable problems of social and economic development. These include practice and policy transformation in development, local knowledges and the creation of ignorance, the analysis of power relations and resource distribution between interest groups, participants and institutions, and organizational linkages and the 'translation' of meaning and policy. Volumes on these topics will include: *Bush Base, Forest Farm; An Anthropological Critique of Development; Policy and Practice; The Traders' Dilemma; African Languages, Development and the State.*

To provide a theme for discussion which linked issues of general anthropological theory and development, participants in the workshop held in December 1986 were invited to consider the nature of local knowledges and ascriptions of ignorance, with particular reference to processes of development. Although the contributors made use of research on topics ranging from agriculture and fishing to mediumship and organized religion in quite different kinds of society around the world, there were interesting convergences. All the participants were critical of the claims of western science to provide the necessary and sufficient 'solution' to problems of development and stressed the importance of understanding knowledge in the particular contexts of its use. Much discussion in the workshop was concerned with the ways in which local knowledges were dismissed by experts, who usually had little idea that there were well worked-out, alternative ways of dealing with the world. A repeated theme was that it was important to consider local knowledges as situated practices. The title of the original workshop was 'Local knowledge and systems of ignorance', and many contributors argued that it was not so much knowledge which was systematic, but ignorance. In different ways the growth of knowledge leads to the growth of ignorance, hence the sub-title of this collection.

The authors wish to thank the School of Oriental and African Studies for funding the workshop, and Sharon Lewis of the Department of Anthropology and Sociology at SOAS for her organizational help.

Mark Hobart

THE SCHOOLMASTER OF THE FUTURE

(And the sooner we get him the better)

BRITISH WORKMAN. "BOTHER YOUR 'OLOGIES AND 'OMETRIES,
LET *ME* TEACH HIM SOMETHING USEFUL!"

Caption to front cover illustration: original
Punch cartoon, November 19, 1887

Introduction: the growth of ignorance?

Mark Hobart

The relationship of Africa, Asia and Latin America to Europe and North America in the post-war period is often couched in the language of development. Something seems to be amiss, however. Granted the vast sums invested in trying to find a solution to what is described as the problem of underdevelopment, by the criteria of the development planners matters should be getting better rather than worse. Instead it would seem that development projects often contribute to the deterioration. A largely neglected aspect of such development is the part played by western scientific knowledge. Not only are indigenous knowledges ignored or dismissed, but the nature of the problem of underdevelopment and its solution are defined by reference to this world-ordering knowledge. Anthropologists have long been among those who have questioned whether such scientific knowledge is as all-encompassing and efficacious as its proponents claim. So it is apposite that the contributors to this collection, who are critical of the workings of scientific knowledge in processes of development, should be anthropologists. The aim is not to offer a solution to the problem of development, which has been notoriously elusive. Development is effectively a synonym for more or less planned social and economic change. So, defining development as a problem susceptible of a solution, or pathologically as a condition requiring a cure, may well be misplaced. In the essays which follow the contributors question the presuppositions which inform much discussion of development and explore the relationship between scientific knowledge and local knowledges in practice. As systematic knowledge grows, so does the possibility of ignorance.[1] Ignorance, however, is not a simple antithesis of knowledge. It is a state which people attribute to others and is laden with moral judgement. So being underdeveloped often implies, if not actual iniquity, at least stupidity, failure and sloth.

SOME INTRODUCTORY OBSERVATIONS

Because the prevailing rhetoric is of altruistic concern for the less fortunate, it is useful to remember that development is big business. Development aid, including loans, probably dwarfs in scale many multinational industries or the Mafia. In one form or another, development is very profitable not just to the western industries involved, but to those parts of governments which receive aid, let alone to development agencies. And the giving of development aid and the extension of markets for manufactured products is more than balanced by the processes of counter-development, by which the countries to be developed make up the major source of cheap raw materials and labour. Less obviously, the idea of 'underdevelopment' itself and the means to alleviate the perceived problem are formulated in the dominant powers' account of how the world is. The relationship of developers and those to-be-developed is constituted by the developers' knowledge and categories, be it the nation-state, the market or the institutions which are designed to give a semblance of control over these confections. The epistemological and power aspects of such processes are often obscured by discourses on development being couched predominantly in the idiom of economics, technology and management. What is signally absent in most public discussion of development are the ways in which the knowledges of the peoples being developed are ignored or treated as mere obstacles to rational progress.[2] In order for them to be able to progress, these peoples have first to be constituted as 'underdeveloped' and ignorant. Conversely, without such underdevelopment and ignorance, the West could not represent itself as developed and possessing knowledge.

Such ascriptions are not, however, self-evident, but are part of a long history of changing western representations of other societies. A striking feature of these representations is that they are often agentive. By this I mean that they depict a state of affairs requiring action or intervention of some kind, usually by the party doing the depicting (see p. 12). At various times the peoples of much of the world have been portrayed as savage, decadent or merely pagan and unenlightened. So they require law and order, effective government or Christianity and civilization. Whatever the rationale, non-western societies have been widely represented as static, passive and incapable of the progress based on rational government and economic activity which the West alone could provide. The difficulties of planned economic and social development are not simply the work of self-interested industries and governments. The social and historical vision of the world order, and the rationality which sub-tends it, has been in no small part constituted and justified by academic writings.[3] In so far as such accounts are adopted by the governments or people of developing countries as constitutive of their aspirations, they are hegemonic in Gramsci's sense (e.g. 1988: 189–221). There are more prosaic difficulties with processes of devel-opment. First, by most standards of judgement, including the pro-fessed goals of the developers, most development projects fall seriously short. For instance, in the much-vaunted project to irrigate the drought-prone Sahel region in Africa, for each 5,000 hectares of land brought under irrigation, exactly the same amount of previously irrigated land was turning into salty desert, because of poor drain-age.[4] An allied problem is the presumption of the priority of tech-nology over social considerations. In Timor, in Indonesia, it rains heavily for some three months of the year, and is very dry for the remaining nine. So a large dam-building project was carried out to bring water to particularly arid areas. When I was there six beautiful ecologically sensitive dams had been finished. None was being used by the population it was supposed to serve. The dams had been built in the best places to build dams. Unfortunately no one lives within many miles. There is a twist to the tale. Coincidentally or otherwise, the dams were mostly near roads. So, if people migrated to where water was, government would be able to keep an eye on them, rather than their remaining in the hills where no one could easily check what they were up to. Such instances abound; and several are documented in the essays below.

However, the problems are not simply the failure to achieve sustainable development, or that technological or economic con-cerns often prevail over social considerations. There is little link at times between the theory of rationally planned development and the implementation of development policies. Such disjunctures are commonly explained as being due to the need to specify theory in practice. They may more accurately be seen, though, as the limi-tations of a paradigm, which combines an idealist theory of ration-ality and a naturalist epistemology. It has proven ill-suited to explain, let alone deal with, processes which are non-natural and involve reflexivity on the part of the human beings concerned. A prime example is the difficulties of coping with unintended conse-quences, the nemesis of so much elegant theorizing, when it encoun-ters practice.[5]

Needless to say these difficulties have little impact on either the formulation of development policy, still less on the paradigm itself. As Quarles van Ufford and Long (forthcoming) note, the rhetorical appeal of policy formulation is aimed at western governments and other donors as the developers' main constituencies, not at the 'targets' of development. For this reason among others, the evaluation of the effectiveness of projects has been slow to develop, where criteria of success are problematic anyway.[6] Further, knowledge, especially technical knowledge, is widely treated as a valued commodity to be sold or otherwise transferred. It would be poor marketing to question its worth, or whether it is a commodity at all. More generally, scientific epistemology, which underwrites development theories, is far less empirical than is supposed (Quine 1953) and, as we shall see, contrary experience can always be accounted for without threatening the paradigm as a whole. A similar point has been made by Winch in a neat parody of Evans-Pritchard's classic study of Zande witchcraft (1937) as a closed system of beliefs impervious to ostensibly contrary evidence, when he notes that the same can be said of western science (1970: 89).

The position adopted by the contributors to this collection, all of whom are anthropologists with extensive field experience of development in some form, is that claims to knowledge and the attribution of ignorance are central themes to development and remain seriously under-studied. Rather than offer yet more generalization to debates on development, they all focus on how kinds of knowledge, western and local, are used in practice. Broadly they treat knowledge not as some abstract conceptual system, but as situated practices. They also take issue with the idea that such practices form 'systems' of indigenous knowledge, although this does not imply that there are not written canons, such as Indian Ayurvedic medicine. I shall consider in detail below how the contributors represent local knowledges. For the moment it should suffice to note that they often appear to be more about 'knowing how' than 'knowing that' (Ryle 1949: 26–60), or 'knowing as' (Cohen). They may perhaps usefully be considered as a 'performance' (Richards), as 'practical, factual, detailed and personal' (van Beek) and sensible to the particularities of place, occasion and circumstance. Contrary to popular representations, such knowledges are subject to testing and modification, involve theory (van der Ploeg) and metaphysical presuppositions, although not necessarily in the senses imagined in western analytical philosophy (Collingwood 1940, Hobart 1985a). Still less can they be dismissed, as often happens, as 'traditional' obstacles to rational progress and convenient 'scapegoats' to explain the failure of development programmes (von Benda-Beckmann).

While each of the contributors sets out to show the under-estimated value of local knowledges, none of them however indulge in the (singularly western) romantic fantasy of the desirability, even were it possible, of a return to native wisdom mysteriously in touch with nature. Rather the stress is on the value of treating local knowledges seriously and examining their potential contribution to peoples' material, intellectual and general welfare. One feature which many of the contributors elaborate is the link of knowledge and agency. Local knowledges often constitute people as potential agents. For instance in healing, the patient is widely expected to participate actively in the diagnosis and cure. By contrast, scientific knowledge as observed in development practice generally represents the superior knowing expert as agent and the people being developed as ignorant passive recipients or objects of this knowledge.

SOME PRESUPPOSITIONS OF SOCIOLOGICAL THEORIES OF DEVELOPMENT

Sociologists and anthropologists have long been critical of attempts to articulate development in purely economic or technological terms, and of the assumptions which underlie them. In this section I shall, however, argue that, despite some well-rehearsed differences, socio-logical theories of development often involve presuppositions drawn from the same rational scientific epistemology. While these theories may be critical of certain assumptions of economists, the effect is to replicate the dominant epistemology in a subtler guise.[7] To the extent that, as I argued above, hegemonic representations constitute the conditions of power, then these critics may unwittingly be caught up in helping to perpetuate what they claim to criticize. My aim here then is not a comprehensive review of theories of development, but a brief examination of some of their presuppositions and the way in which agency is represented.[8]

Development has often been linked to, or equated with, modern-ization; this is the transformation of traditional societies into modern ones, characterized by advanced technology, material prosperity and political stability (e.g. Moore 1963).[9] As elaborated by Smelser (1963), significantly economic development requires *inter alia* the modernization of technology through the application of scientific knowledge and a shift from subsistence farming to cash-cropping and wage labour. Modernization theory assumes a unidirectional evolutionary account of social change and is not based on actual case materials, but is 'an idealization of the main direction of certain social and cultural trends' (Long 1977: 26, citing Smith 1973: 87). It is not just that the categories of 'traditional' and 'modern' are vague and idealized constructions, but the process of development is defined teleologically by reference to the supposed state of the dominant party. The means to this transformation is scientific knowledge. Significantly such knowledge requires the homogenization and quantifiability of what is potentially qualitatively different.[10] For instance, kinds of food become cash crops and human activities become labour. What is lumped together here is often regarded by the peoples concerned as heterogeneous and qualitatively diverse in practice. While the utility of treating human activities *as* labour for certain purposes is evident, such homogenization underwrites a linear evolutionary view of history (of which Marxist histories are as guilty as modernization theory) by ignoring the discontinuities and differences in discursive constructions of land, labour, the units or agents of economic decision-making and the idea of economy itself (Tribe 1978). Whatever its merits, scientific knowledge applied to development is not neutral, as is so often claimed, nor are the implications of its use.

In modernization theory, among others, society or culture is treated, suitably reified, as an 'obstacle' to change, more rarely as facilitating it. What is striking for an epistemology that claims to represent the world accurately and neutrally is the frequency with which abstract and contested notions not only make use of metaphor, but the extent to which metaphor is constitutive (see Ortony 1979). Not only is it inherent in the formulation, as here, of development theories; but knowledge itself is generally constituted around a metaphor, be it knowledge as a mirror, as a commodity, as a space for exploration or expansion (Salmond 1982). If one removes all explicit and implicit references to such metaphorical images, the degree to which many theories require modification or rethinking is remarkable. Society and culture are not obstacles to change, nor except loosely can they be said to facilitate change. Such accounts presuppose society or social relations as some hypostatized pseudo-entity. Arguably change is going on all the time and the problem, if any, is to account for the appearance of stasis. In whatever sense society may usefully be said to exist (on which see Bhaskar 1979, 1989), it is not an object or entity. As Hacking has argued at length (1990), the construction of such pseudo-entities came into vogue with the preoccupation with statistical theorizing in western Europe in the nineteenth century, which was inextricably linked to the extension of control and surveillance of populations. The metaphors implicit in 'development' provide an apposite example. There is a certain entelechy in the notion of something unfolding or growing naturally to the fulfilment of a potentiality, the seeds or programme for which is already established. The refractions of such metaphors may vary between societies and languages. In Indonesia, for example, there are three potential words available. *Perkembangan*, from the root for 'flower', suggests growth which requires little external intervention. *Kemajuan*, 'progress', tends to be linked to western liberal economic and political ideas, with connotations of rationality. The third, *pembangunan*, from the root for 'get up, grow up, build' is the term favoured by government officials and developers because, as Quarles van Ufford points out, 'this process does not realize itself automatically, but needs outside action or encouragement. So, the process of development cannot realize itself if careful guiding and cultivation do not take place' (1985: 57).

For the term 'development', metaphor does not merely illuminate, but is constitutive. The end state and the nature of the process is, partly at least, predefined or prescribed. It does not of course follow that the action prescribed by some account is fully determined. The adoption of *pembangunan* as the chosen idiom neatly combines entelechy with the need for guidance by those with power and knowledge, in this case the government officials who elaborated the notion in the first place.

To return to development theories: a problem of modernization theory is that it omits recognition of wider social and historical processes. This criticism is central to 'dependency theory', according to which structures of dependence are set up by the world capitalist system, which penetrates local societies and economies, and extends down to tie apparently remote workers to the system (e.g. Frank 1969). The use of metaphor to add impact is significant. First, there is a pervasive spatial metaphor of 'up/down', 'metropolitan centre/ satellite', in which capitalism is portrayed as superior and central, or what below I describe as a 'transcendental agent'.[11] This is capped by a sexual metaphor (capitalism 'penetrating'), in which the powerful, superior, male West imposes itself on weak, inferior, captivated (and female) others. Indeed there is a further carceral image (the 'tied' worker) of development as punitive, as against modernization theory's vision of development as reform (cf. Foucault 1975). It is hardly surprising therefore that dependency theory tends to underestimate locally motivated change and other kinds of relationships. Once again, social and economic institutions like 'capitalism' and 'class' are at once reified and abstracted from actual social and historical situations (Laclau 1971).

The corrective to such broad institutional analyses stresses the importance of individual entrepreneurs in economic and social change. Such accounts are almost always transactionalist, the anthropological resuscitation of utilitarianism, in which rational individuals set out self-interestedly to maximize their utility, whether defined as wealth, power or status (e.g. Bailey 1957, 1969; Barth 1963, 1966; cf. Paine 1974). The rejoinder is hardly unexpected. Collectivism and individualism in one form or another are entrenched intellectual positions in a long-running battle.[12] The dispute is somewhat phoney, because the alternatives presuppose and depend on one another more than is often recognized (Bhaskar 1979: 39–47).

Obviously much more could be, and has been, said about development theories. Because of their relevance to the theme of this volume, I am particularly concerned however with questions of explanation, especially the description (or prescription) of the nature of knowledge, rationality and agency, and their attribution. I deal with each in turn briefly.

It would be very convenient if, among rival theories, we could decide which was more or less correct, and also judge the rival merits of accounts based on western as against indigenous knowledge. While theories may sometimes be disqualified by failing to fit facts, often they are not fully verifiable or they account more or less adequately for the available evidence, so that there is no simple empirical method of judging between them. This underdetermination of theory by evidence, as Quine has made clear, is because

> the totality of our so-called knowledge or beliefs . . . is a manmade fabric which impinges on experience only at the edges . . . the total field is so underdetermined by its boundary conditions, experience, that there is much latitude of choice as to what statements to reëvaluate in the light of any single contrary experience.
>
> (1953: 42–3)

Additional criteria are required to decide which theory to adopt (Hesse 1978). For developers, this is likely to be models which are generalizable or appear to offer the greatest predictability or the semblance of control over events. Developers are often asked to complete research and even projects within absurdly short time-spans. So they tend to have to work with pre-established guide-lines and assume that particular conditions fit a general mould. Charming absurdities can result. In the Timorese project mentioned, it is apparently an established rule that piping water should cost no more than 1 per cent of the expenditure on dam construction. That this left taps in the middle of nowhere was neither here nor there. (Were local people to indulge in such thinking, they would be deemed irrational.) Anthropologists, on the other hand, have an obvious interest in explanatory accounts which are as compatible as possible with observable events and with the representations of events by the participants.[13] Incommensurability between accounts of what is going on in development are not just theoretically possible, but are usually the case in practice. For anthropologists, this is part of their subject-matter.

The historical and sociological aspects of scientific knowledge have increasingly been recognized (e.g. Feyerabend 1975; Kuhn 1962). The extent to which such knowledge is a social activity was neatly put by Peirce in 1868:

> the very origin of the conception of reality shows that this conception essentially involves the notion of a COMMUNITY, without definite limits, and capable of an indefinite increase in knowledge.
>
> (1984 [1868]: 239, capitals in the original)

The criteria of what constitutes knowledge, what is to be excluded and who is designated as qualified to know involves acts of power (Foucault 1971). Once more prescriptions of the nature of knowledge and how the knower is constituted are strikingly metaphoric. As Rorty has pointed out, a presupposition in much western epistemology is that the human mind is like a mirror which reflects reality, and problems of accurate knowledge boil down to repairing the mirror (1980). The monopoly on this knowledge is held, in a rather inspecific way, by the West (another significantly imprecise term). Development consists in no small part of knowledge, positivistically conceived as true propositions about the world, being treated as a valuable resource. Both this latter commodity metaphor of knowledge and the mirror metaphor notably exclude the idea of knowing being a dialectical and critical process. Criticism in development tends to be a synonym for telling off the ignorant or lazy natives, not the crucial means to understanding or, more realistically, reducing the degree of misunderstanding.[14]

A related and important metaphorical representation, as Peirce noted, is of knowledge as growing.[15] Apart from treating knowledge as a quasi-natural entity, the implicit entelechy gives a sense of inevitability and so superiority to those who master or are part of this process of growth. Remarkably, it seems to have largely slipped notice that the postulated growth of knowledge concomitantly entails the possibility of increasing ignorance. In development this is manifested practically in local knowledges being devalued or ignored, in favour of western scientific, technical and managerial knowledge.[16] As we shall see when discussing agency, such constructions have implications for power in the way in which people are differently constructed as subjects or objects, agents or patients, according to different kinds of knowledge. Perhaps I should note at this point that these criticisms of representations of scientific knowledge do not imply that it is not, and has not been, of great value and import. It is to note, following Collingwood (1933: 26–53), that scientific and philosophical knowledge (to which I would add historical and anthropological knowledge as well) are dialectically related, such that the latter serve critically to reflect on the implications and consequences of the former.

The idea of development as governed by rational progress has some similar implications to the image of knowledge growing. The whole issue of the nature and relevance of rationality to human action has been the subject of long debate involving philosophers and anthropologists (see Hollis and Lukes 1982, Overing 1985, Wilson 1970). For present purposes, a few observations will suffice. The relationship between theoretical and practical reason is unclear in practice. Advocates of some universal rationality disagree among themselves not only as to what this rationality consists of, but whether it is an a priori necessity of cognition and communication (Hollis 1970, 1982) or is establishable a posteriori from its evident success (e.g. Newton-Smith 1982). Even where rationality is defined narrowly by logic, there is disagreement over whether it is descriptive, prescriptive or a formal condition of thought about the world. Whether everyone shares this vision of the world as ultimately knowable through the exercise of reason, let alone whether they take decisions on this basis, is doubtful. Balinese, for instance, make use of a quite distinct form of reasoning (Hobart 1985a), but recognize both the importance of human feeling and attitudes, and the possibility that some matters may be unknowable to human beings, whose mental capacities are not limitless.[17] Assertions of rationality should perhaps be regarded as *ex post facto* claims in particular situations and as part of social action.

The previous discussion is relevant to a problem which is increasingly being recognized as important in development projects and is often implicated in their failure. This is the nature of the understanding between the parties involved. The desired goal is usually expressed in terms of communication. 'In order to have development and to have people understand how development is to be applied to their particular case, developers need to communicate with "developees"' (Brokensha *et al.* 1980:7). The implication is that, if both sides improve communication a major obstacle (*sic*) will be removed. Such a view is naïvely optimistic. Not only does it ignore the many reasons people may have for not wishing to communicate and indeed to want to dissimulate (e.g. Quarles van Ufford in this volume), it also rests upon a model of knowledge as communicable propositions and presumes rationality to be shared. The mirage of perfect communication presupposes communication to be the relatively simple business of transmitting knowledge as information between sender and receiver. (One might note that there is no obvious antonym of 'information', the antithetical terms being significantly 'misinformation', or even 'disinformation'.) Problems are conceived of mechanically and are held to arise where the code is not shared, there are difficulties in the medium and so on. Wallace has pointed out, however, that all that is required is that the parties concerned can find equivalences of some kind. Not only do they not need to understand each other, but it is questionable how well social relations would work if people regularly did so (1961: 29–44). Such a model of communication assumes a 'conduit metaphor', in which language 'contains' meaning inserted by the speaker and extracted by the listener. Reddy has argued in favour of an alternative image of communication being a matter of degree and the end result of much mutual work (1979). This is close to how I use the notion of understanding, which is inevitably always imperfect, dialectical and critical.[18]

Anthropologists' experience of what goes on in development projects seems better to fit an account of communication as requiring work. The social worlds of developers, whether foreigners or nationals, are almost always far apart from those being developed, as is the nature of their involvement, what is at stake and the perceived purpose of the enterprise (Arce and Long). Even where developers have sufficient command of language to speak and listen, the relationship of developers and developed are usually regarded as hierarchical by both parties. So communication easily becomes the giving of information or instructions by those with expert knowledge. And all too often the only effective means of disagreement is silence or the refusal to engage in enterprises as defined by the superior party, who may treat those to be developed as invisible anyway (van der Ploeg). For these reasons, it is convenient to talk of there being several coexistent discourses of development. By 'discourse' here, I am adapting Foucault's term for the regularities of what is said and done, including, importantly, the conditions of knowledge and power with its inevitable closures (see especially 1972: 21–76). Although discourse is a difficult notion, which seems to work best on grand-scale historical reconstructions, it does draw attention to the differential working of knowledges and powers in practice. This includes notably prevailing metaphors of knowledge and communication, and of the nature of power. In this sense then it may be useful to distinguish for the moment at least three discourses, which may partly overlap. Apart from the professional discourse of developers and the discourse of the local people being developed, the national government and its local officials commonly also have distinctive powers and forms of enshrined knowledge, with their concomitant closure.[19] Just how separate and indeed incommensurable are the respective discourses of developers, developed and governments is a striking feature of many of the essays in this volume.

We have seen how constructions of knowledge may be agentive, in that they indicate who is qualified to know and act, and who is not. They may also indicate the course or nature of the action to be taken. It is instructive briefly to review some of the theories of social development outlined above in this light. Most theories emphasize the need for planned change. In other words, existing organizations cannot achieve the desired goals on their own. So how are these organizations conceived and what form of necessary agency is postulated? In modernization theory the stress is on the deficiencies of traditional institutions which people, treated as passive objects, are incapable of changing. Dependency theory likewise construes people as the passive victims of forces over which they have no control, here the capitalist market economy. According to the former the problem is the absence of agents; according to the latter a nigh omnipotent and alien agent. The agency for change in either case must therefore come from planners, who have a superior understanding of the structures responsible and capacity to change or replace them.

At first sight both theories might seem to aim to make previously passive objects agents. This is however, not so. Closer inspection shows that the diffusion of modern technology is supposed to provide an example (a 'demonstration effect') to 'progressive' farmers. Or, more radically, progressive elements will rise to meet the demands and opportunities of new structures. In other words, the populace is constituted as willing subjects, the planners provide the intelligence about the workings of the modern economy or the will of the revolution, but determine neither. The ultimate agents are therefore transcendental, various groups of humans making up the instruments through which they work. The point is perhaps clearer if we consider the transactionalist approach or its avatar, the New Right's emphasis on the market as the sufficient condition of change. Once again agency at first seems vested in the enterprising individual. But he or she only responds to market forces, the patterns of which are elucidated by economists, planners and others. It is the market itself which determines what happens. Ultimately, you cannot buck the market: it is the market which decides. In different ways, then, agency is attributed to supra-human forces, which certain groups of humans are particularly well placed to know about.[20]

It should be clear that we are dealing with representations of how matters are claimed to be. In practice what happens is far more complex, variable and underdetermined than can be encapsulated in any single account. Such representations, however, play an important part in social action. Anthropologists' subject-matter consists in large part of conflicting representations of actions and events, which directly affect future actions. How knowledge, power and agency are represented and responsibility attributed in different situations are therefore issues of interest; and their relevance to development forms the theme of this volume.

KNOWLEDGE IN PRACTICE

An uncomfortable conclusion of the foregoing argument that theories are underdetermined and consist of representations of events with consequences for power and knowledge is that our own writings are implicated in this process. The work of academics affects what happens in various ways (Fabian 1991). Indeed there is the risk of these writings becoming part of the processes of hegemony, which they ostensibly set out to criticize. While there may be no neutral privileged position from which to capture a timeless truth, it does not follow that all representations are equal, or that nothing worth-while can be said at all. A potentially useful task for anthropologists, as 'priests of humanistic plurality' (Richards), is to discuss critically how the relationship between expert knowledge and local knowledges works out in practice, as we understand it. This task is less easy than it might seem. To construe local knowledge as systematic, or even to classify practices of dealing with the world as 'knowledge', is to domesticate practice by recourse yet again to a hegemonic epistemology. In this Introduction therefore, I neither can, nor wish to, delineate a general account of indigenous knowledges. To do so would be to replicate what I have criticized as the shortcomings of theories which claim such spurious generality and authority. What I can perhaps usefully do, however, is examine how knowledge and agency is attributed, and how local knowledge is represented in the accounts of the contributors for the societies on which they work.

In practice, government officials representing the nation-state play a central role in attributing knowledge, ignorance and agency in the specification of development policy. Croll discusses how this worked in the post-revolutionary period between 1949 and 1976 in China. The example is the more interesting because, in an attempt to reverse the vision of knowledge as stemming from the educated elite, ostensibly it was portrayed as coming from 'the masses' – a term which significantly depersonalizes and diffuses agency. The new officials spoke of government learning from the limitless wisdom of the masses. 'In practice, what this formula demanded was that the scattered and unsystematic views of the masses be collected by the state, carefully studied, co-ordinated, and translated into policy' (see Croll). As problems inevitably emerged in putting this reworked and decontextualized knowledge into practice, local populations came progressively to be defined as backward and ignorant by higher-level administrative cadres. So they became represented not as agents, but as objects to be changed. Croll makes clear that such definitions of agency are a continual and contested process and must be understood in the social and political situations of their attribution.

An important instrument in codifying knowledge and fixing agency in practice is through law. As Benda-Beckmann points out however, although there is ample evidence that it is not so, 'the assumption that local law hinders development and that modern, western law is a prerequisite for development is one of the most deeply rooted ideas to inform development planning'. Modern law becomes a 'magic charm' and local law is represented by developers as the 'scapegoat' for the failure of development. Agency is attributed to legal structures, through 'the idea that legal structures and norms directly cause or determine action and its consequences'. Local law, among Minangkabau in Sumatra, is construed by officials concerned with development as an idealized, traditional system rather than as practices adjusted to changing circumstances. Villagers collaborate in this representation, but for quite different reasons. They make use of their perception of outsiders' ideas of traditional law as a means to articulate and legitimate their opposition to what they judge to be ignorant interference.

The extent to which different discourses are implicated in development is brought out by Arce and Long. In an extended case-study, they examine the fate of a relatively well-meaning agricultural official from the Mexican Ministry of Agriculture, who tried to represent the interests of local peasants, only to land up in a special unit for 'troublemakers'. The farmers concerned lived by growing maize to eat and to feed cattle; this they sold, as they did marijuana, through markets which were not government approved. The farmers petitioned for a baling machine to increase productivity, as part of their negotiations with the official. Such a scheme, however, contravened the centrally planned policy, according to which they had been designated as a region for increased maize production for marketing through official channels. The farmers' 'underdevelopment' consisted in part in their producing what was not officially recognized, and by unapproved means. The difficulties also involved incompatibilities of knowledge in practice. The dictates of scientific agronomy militated against the crop rotation preferred by farmers, based on their experience of land conditions, in favour of the intensive use of pesticides and other chemicals in order to maximize productivity. The farmers objected that this increased crop disease in the long run. The attempt of the agricultural official to aid his clients conflicted with the official policy of maize production and was treated as a challenge to his superior. The outcome was the confirmation of the senior officials' ideas of the recalcitrance and stupidity of the peasants; and their distrust in government. The failure of such centrally-directed planning is explained as the deficiency of the objects of development and of those whose task it is to implement policy.

The nature and difficulties of development are often portrayed spatially. The rejection of 'planning from above' in favour of a 'bottom-up approach' does not, however, necessarily change matters, because the terms and the kind of action expected usually remain defined by 'superiors'. For a project from an outer province of Indonesia, Quarles van Ufford shows how there is a discrepancy between the official language of the development agency – the 'bottom-up approach', and local 'homogeneity' – generating images of an active involvement of the peasants in the project activities, and the virtual absence of any such involvement at the local level as observed by some anthropologists. Expert knowledge is manifested here in a rhetoric of development and planning, which postulates a 'system' and suggests the roles of the various participants are integrated, thereby creating the impression of manageability. The discourse of developers is often resistant to counter-evidence. When a team was sent to evaluate the project and reported that the local organizations set up neither really represented the peasants nor could function effectively, the report had to be buried. Many projects, Quarles van Ufford argues, appear to work because those to be developed are forced to be secretive and compartmentalize their lives. There is an unbridgeable, but largely unappreciated, gap between the neat rationality of development agencies' representations which imagine the world as ordered or manageable and the actualities of situated social practices, an incommensurability tidied away in sociological jargon as 'unintended consequences'. The result is that the overlap of developers' and local discourses does not lead to improved communication, but to strain on those locals who are involved in both, and to techniques of evasion, silence and dissimulation.[21]

In different ways, discursively, some people are empowered to know and decide, others to implement the decisions, yet others not to speak, or not to be heard if they do. It is not just officials and developers who ascribe ignorance to locals; the reverse occurs. Ignorance is also Janus-faced. It may be used actively as a means of ignoring what others say and do. To speak of strategies of 'resistance' or 'denial' on the part of those designated as inferior is to assume that they recognize and submit to the hegemonic representation of them. For this reason I would suggest resurrecting the old English word 'obliviate', which implies an active ignoring of such representations and the prosecution of one's own point of view.[22] Representatives of nation-states may use means of trying to enforce government policies as a claim to or demonstration of power. But, while planners tend to work with idealized, timeless and depersonalized versions of an imagined world which is to be regulated, local people are often clearly aware of the personal, particular nature of the specification of policy or law in practice. Agency is rarely as clear-cut as its ascriptions suggest.

KNOWLEDGE AS PRACTICE

The approach to local knowledge taken by those contributors who deal explicitly with the theme stresses the importance of treating knowing as a practical, situated activity, constituted by a past, but changing, history of practices. Such knowing requires evaluation by some measure like appropriateness to particular circumstances, rather than by its being true as such. The latter is often meaningless, when one is talking of a performance or knowledge which is so local that it could not be authentically codified (see Burghart). The contributors make use of various recent authors who have, in different but related ways, been critical of the dominant approach of systematic epistemological theorizing. Several contributors cite the work of Giddens, whose account of structuration seeks to relate the institutional aspects of structure to action and agency (1979, 1984; cf. Held and Thompson 1989). Another relevant scholar is Bourdieu, who has argued for an analysis of action based on accepted social practices, or *habitus* (1977, 1990). One should note, however, that what the contributors understand by practice differs radically from the term as often used by developers, as the implementation of theory. This dichotomy is misleading, both in the postulated hierarchical relation of theory and practice, and in the failure to consider theorizing itself as a practice with its own history of usage, closure and consequences.[23]

In this sense, the approach of most of the contributions is broadly 'post-structuralist'. A drawback of much post-structuralist writing is that it is often programmatic, polemical and applied on a grand scale, which is ill-suited to fine-grained studies. Also, such writings remain largely Eurocentric and dominated by textual, literary and linguistic concerns, so replicating in subtler form the presuppositions they set out to criticize. The attempt in this collection is to explore how some of the critiques and insights of post-structuralism or postmodernism can illuminate how knowledges are constituted and work as practices.

For these reasons, many of the contributors take issue with accounts which represent indigenous knowledge as systematic. This is a difficulty in different ways with two kinds of recent approach by anthropologists. The first is expounded in the essays in Brokensha *et al.*, significantly titled *Indigenous Knowledge Systems and Develop-*

ment (1980). While the value of pointing out the importance of non-western kinds of knowledge is shared, the assumption that knowledge is systematic is diametrically opposed to the aim of the present work. The second approach is that of Clifford Geertz, elaborated in a collection of essays entitled *Local Knowledge* (1983a). He argues for taking seriously 'local knowledge; local not just as to place, time, class and variety of issue, but as to accent – vernacular characterizations of what happens connected to vernacular imaginings of what can' (1983b: 215). The strength of his argument is in drawing attention to the need to treat what happens contextually in terms of ideas and beliefs in the culture in question.[24] The difficulties include his making use of a pervasive (western) dramaturgical metaphor of social action and assuming sufficient epistemological similarity as to make 'cultural translation' possible (see also Richards's critique of intellectualism below). Such accounts further exemplify their 'modernist' assumptions in ascribing agency to the interpreter and his or her superior understanding. While acknowledging local knowledges is important, whether it offsets the simultaneous, subtle hegemonizing of others is a moot point.

Most of the contributors share the view that the peoples they write about 'seem to work more through a body of practices – knowing how to do things and to react to changes, a set of practical procedures – than through a formal system of shared knowledge' (van Beek), which permits new practices to be adopted easily. Significantly, in many instances, the terms for 'knowledge' are active verbs, as for Dogon who speak of 'knowing the word', which implies knowing both language and its use in accounts of their history. Indeed without realizing how such knowing is historically constituted, including the long-standing threat of slavery, it is hard to understand why they orient cultivation towards optimizing survival rather than large harvests. Land is not treated as a homogeneous area but as finely differentiated; and, gerundively, as manageable, usable or otherwise in varying degree.

The contrast between two kinds of agricultural knowledge in Andean potato farming is clearly drawn out by van der Ploeg. Drawing on Mendras's notion of *l'art de la localité* (1970), he notes that to say that agricultural knowledge works from practice to practice does not entail that such thinking is without theory, rather its syntax 'is not the nomological one of science; the scope is not a presupposed universe', but localized through labour as *savoir-faire*, in a process which 'presupposes an active, knowledgeable actor, who is actually the 'agent' of the unity and constant interaction of mental and manual work'. Whereas the model formally used for scientific plant-breeding starts with an ideal plant type, a genotype, as 'the point of departure for the specification of the required phenotypic conditions', Andean farmers deliberately mix and try out cultivars, so that the given phenotypic conditions are treated as 'starting points for the selection and adaptation of genotypes'. The contrasting kinds of practice involve sharply different ways of representing time, causation, work and knowledge in practice.

Richards expresses a parallel concern with representations of time and intentionality. Farming systems researchers tend to regard intercropping as part of a predetermined design, which 'is to confuse intention and result', because the mix of crops is 'a completed performance', not a *'combinatorial logic'* but *'sequential adjustment to unpredictable conditions'*. For this reason the protected environments of research stations are 'out of time' and 'out of place', because 'cultivation is a performance' in time and in place, not a rehearsal. Attempts to consider situated practices as indigenous knowledge systems therefore involve 'a fallacy of misplaced abstraction: the making of intellectual mysteries out of situations and activities whose practical import is obvious to all but the observer'. Instead Richards argues for treating agriculture – and by extension many other activities – as performances, which is not to invoke a dramaturgical metaphor but a practical image, as in a musical performance.[25] Knowing in this sense is bringing skills learnt through practice and historically derived experience to bear on a particular matter on a particular occasion. (We tend to overlook how much writing articles – and Introductions – is a similar craft skill which has to be learned.) Ability to speak is therefore an important form of knowing, 'a licence to perform'. An implication of this point might be noted by developers, namely that learning to use a language well is not simply a matter of 'communicating' information, but being able to perform adequately.

People may represent what they know as systematic, for instance to express their distinctiveness and to rebuff others' claims to expert knowledge. Ascriptions of knowledge and ignorance involve peoples' perceptions of their social relations with one another and with outsiders, as Cohen makes clear.[26] The islanders of Whalsay in the Shetlands were successful in acquiring and making profitable an exceptionally modern fleet of fishing boats against expert and British government advice. To the locals it is not that outside experts are technically deficient. It is 'less a matter of *what* is known than of *how* it is known'. 'Objective' knowledge must be reworked and considered reflexively in the light of peoples' historical experience and assessment of the present circumstances. If the image of indigenous knowledge as systematic is fallacious, then the 'popular proposition that successful innovation requires the "translation" of an alien idea into an indigenous idiom is revealed as hopelessly simplistic as well as being insidious'. Cohen argues cogently that local knowledges exist as rival versions, which are not separable from the social conditions of their being known, and which make possible a rich and dialectical argument. The fact that outsiders fail to appreciate this confirms their ignorance.

Burghart provides a detailed example of such cultural argument, which involved different versions of knowledge and concomitant ascriptions of agency, on an occasion when he tried to improve the quality of water in a well in a town in south-eastern Nepal. I cannot reproduce the twists and turns of the argument here. Briefly, Burghart shows how the Cobblers, whose well it was, treated him not as a social scientist, but as a Hindu lord 'with the commanding function of mind.'[27] Although the planned cleaning of the well was worked out between Burghart and the Cobblers, when the water turned bitter, he was converted from benevolent lord to a malevolent one. Burghart and the Cobblers were working with different versions of knowledge, which had different agentive implications. He 'went to them with an interest in their health; they were concerned, however, with their well-being'; he took their complaint literally, but they were signalling the 'bitter' quality of their lives to someone they saw as a potential benefactor. There are incommensurabilities between discourses, in which constructions of agency and power are inseparable from representations of knowledge. In this light, the much-vaunted development strategy of relying on 'folk competence' was bound to run into difficulties. 'Rather than implying that successful development projects entailed a dual agency, research on folk competence held out yet again the hope to development workers of their ultimate control of the entire process.'

ON IGNORANCE

In conclusion, what implications might this discussion of local and expert knowledges have for representations of ignorance? In one sense, the seemingly safe image of knowledge as growing entails a corresponding growth of ignorance. Ignorance may be construed in different ways however. It is not just 'not to know' but may suggest decay and the dismantling of a complex structure, or 'something more primordial . . . the cognitive facet of the moral term evil' (Vitebsky).[28] Both knowledge and ignorance, as we have seen, are peculiarly ideal and timeless notions, which, rather than describing unambiguous states, are attributed to some people by others under particular circumstances, often with moral connotations. The relationship between different knowledges, as propounded and used by their adherents, is then often less dialectical than confrontational (or 'eristical', Collingwood 1942: 181–245). In other words, the proponents of one 'system' attempt to eliminate other knowledges, to portray them and those who use them as not just wrong, but as benighted and bad.

What is excluded in such confrontations is the existence of doubt. In his essay Vitebsky considers two ways of dealing with an important phenomenon where doubt and ignorance are inherent, namely death. He contrasts the Freudian psychoanalysis and the use of mediums among Sora in India to show how both attempt to deal with the unknown through dialogue, the former between analyst and patient, the latter between the mourner and deceased. He argues for considering forms of knowing not as true or false, but as appropriate to their knowers and users. 'Yet at the same time local knowledge is often total, by virtue of the very fact that it is local.' By contrast, the more medicalized, scientific and so universalized psychiatry becomes, the less it is able to cope with context 'because it applies to everywhere and nowhere, everybody and nobody'. So ignorance differs in degree and kind according to the presuppositions of different knowledges.

Throughout this Introduction, I have argued for considering knowing, as do many of the peoples discussed in this volume, as an act which involves work as part of one's relationships with others. From this point of view, the use of abstract nouns to encapsulate such processes has interesting consequences. As Vitebsky notes, adjectives and verbs to do with knowing and being ignorant 'belong in the realm of attribute and agency, and the use of the nouns is a denial or diminution of this agency'. The act of nominalizing converts processes of knowing into a commodity, 'knowledge,' which becomes a thing in itself and turns people into objects or patients. 'In development reports, just as in medicine and clinical psychiatry, writers often make the abstract noun usurp the verb and strip it of its agency.' Or 'they turn it round and replace its active voice with the passive and impersonal . . . . In this way, it is not only agency which is diminished, but also causality, and hence responsibility'. Such nominalizing and abstraction are arguably central to the

representation of scientific knowledge as hegemonic. One consequence is to turn people who were at least part agents into a
backward and inert proletariat, the masses, who come to be constituted as passive objects to be developed. It is little wonder that
attempts to develop them so often fail or go awry. The idea that
modern education will solve the problem appears equally ill-
founded. As Henry pointed out, behind the overt pedagogic aims
of enlightening and broadening school children's knowledge lurks a
'hidden curriculum' in which fear and inadequacy are inculcated
(1966: 182–321). Various organizations obviously have an interest
in perpetuating a large population of passive political subjects and
pliant consumers, who have been rendered uncritical, or at least
silently and ineffectually critical. The British government's educational policy for the state sector in the early 1990s stresses 'basic
knowledge,' designed to produce the 'gammas' and 'deltas' of Hux-
ley's *Brave New World*, the new labouring class who will mindlessly
and uncomplainingly man the word processors of the future. 'Underdevelopment' is not a peculiar phenomenon of the evolution of
distant countries, but a continuous process. One aim of this collection is to argue that knowledge is not what it is often represented
to be and to address the problems and implications of the growth
of ignorance.

NOTES

1 I am particularly grateful to Richard Fardon for first pointing out to me
that, as knowledge is usually constituted, the growth of knowledge
entails the growth of ignorance, and for reading the draft of this Introduction. I would also like to thank Lisa Croll, Philip Quarles van Ufford
and Piers Vitebsky for their valuable comments; Ron Inden for a useful
discussion of some of the general themes; Raymond Apthorpe for his
continued interest and enthusiasm; and Nanneke Redclift who read the
manuscript and whose positive comments were a great encouragement.
My special thanks are due to the late Anthony Forge and Cecilia Forge
for their hospitality and kindness in explaining some of the arcane
mysteries of development projects at work.
2 There are of course exceptions, such as Brokensha *et al.* 1980; Chambers
1983. Both works, however, tend to hypostatize local practices into
'indigenous knowledge systems', an approach with which I take issue
below.
3 More detailed accounts of such representations and the role of western
scholars in formulating them are to be found in Alatas 1977; Fardon
1990; Inden 1990; Mason 1990; Pagden 1982; Said 1978. Most of these
authors make use in some way of the work of Michel Foucault
(especially perhaps 1961, 1966, 1975, 1976), whose approach more

implicitly informs the Introduction and a number of essays in this volume.

4 This example is cited by Timberlake 1988: 61. He notes that the vice-president of the World Bank for policy, planning and research, David Hopper, an ex-anthropologist, has castigated 'the anomaly of economic calculus' responsible for the massive damge done in the name of development (1988: 60).

5 Some of the problems of unintended consequences are outlined in Fabian's critique of reason and western epistemology (1991: 189–98). The way such epistemologies serve to distance others, to deny them coevalness and make them objects or victims rather than subjects and agents is discussed in Fabian 1983. Some of the shortcomings of natural scientific and rationalist epistemologies are discussed in Feyerabend 1975; Goodman 1978; Habermas 1978; Hacking 1983; Quine 1953; Rorty 1980; and Taylor 1985.

6 A good example was presented to the original conference by Till Förster. A development agency had undertaken to increase cattle production for marketing among the Poro on the North Ivory Coast. They left, regarding the project as highly successful, because they had succeeded in their aim. Not long after, the Poro with whom Förster worked said they felt it was a disaster. This was both because overgrazing occurred and because the greater number of cattle, which were used in bride wealth payments, brought havoc to marriage arrangements.

7 This is not the place to engage in the substantial undertaking of a critical analysis of the philosophical presuppositions of economic or sociological theory. Just how confused and incoherent the former are is made clear by Hahn and Hollis 1979; and Dilley (1992) offers an excellent critique of economic discourse on 'the market.' Heath offers a straightforward account of the inadequacies of rational choice and exchange theory in economics, which he contrasts with more sensitive sociological accounts. The latter at least allow a measure of context and the recognition of relative, as opposed to absolute, value (1976: 44–50). Both accounts, however, presuppose a model of rationality on which there has been lengthy debate (see pp.10–11 of the Introduction to this volume). I know of no good account of the presuppositions of sociological and anthropological theory, although Giddens 1976 is basic and quite useful.

8 There are already some good clear reviews of the subject, such as Long 1977, of whom I make use in what follows.

9 Granted the scale of destruction wrought in two world wars alone this century by the purveyors of this 'political stability,' such a vision is a remarkable feat of wishful thinking.

10 The trend towards standardization around the notion of 'the average' does violence to observable variation, as in the idea of the fertilizer or pesticide for the average field. On the tyranny of 'averages' and 'norms', see Hacking 1990; and their relevance to development in economic representations of landscape as a homogeneous expanse, see Vitebsky 1992: 242–4.

11 On the widespread use in English of orientational metaphors like height to suggest superiority, goodness, power etc., see Lakoff and Johnson 1980: 14–21.

12 A famous rehearsal is the debate between Durkheim and Tarde (see Lukes 1973a: 302–13). The methodological argument of whether to explain action by reference to collectivities or individuals (see Lukes 1973b) is still alive in Hayek's (individualist) theory of monetarism. Giddens's attempt to combine the two (e.g. 1984) arguably leaves him with two sets of questionable presuppositions, which are additionally partly incompatible, rather than just one.

13 My observations are preliminary, because the whole question of choice between rival theories is complicated and remains underinvestigated. One might note, however, that issues of value are often used in choosing preferred explanations. So a particular political, moral or religious orientation is not necessarily an unwarranted imposition on neutral matters of fact, but one kind of criterion of choice. Anyway, the supposed neutrality of scientific knowledge is misleading.

14 Misunderstanding is not simply explained by poor communication, but is an actively fostered process, often by both sides (Benda-Beckmann). Many of the criticisms of those who are the objects of development involve projections, such as the tendency to think in the short term and the search for magical solutions.

15 Consider the title of the celebrated collection of essays, edited by Lakatos and Musgrave, *Criticism and the Growth of Knowledge* (1970), which criticizes Kuhn's work (1962).

16 There is a long history of western philosophical bias in favour of *episteme*, theoretical knowledge, against *techne*, applied science, art, skill, which is geared to production (*poietike*) with the corresponding need for judgement (*doxa*) and even against the practical sciences (*praktike*) of politics and ethics. For

> Scientific knowledge is judgement about things that are universal and necessary . . . . This being so, the first principle from which what is scientifically known follows cannot be an object of scientific knowledge, of art, or of practical wisdom; for that which can be scientifically known can be demonstrated and art and practical wisdom deal with things that are variable . . . some even of the lower animals have practical wisdom.
>
> (Aristotle 1941: 1027–8)

Even allowing for changing usage of terms, this passage could hardly be clearer.

17 Quarles van Ufford (1985: 53–6) has a good discussion of the importance of feeling, *rasa*, and its link to mystery, *rahsya*, in neighbouring Java.

18 The position which I take is closer to Volosinov's (1973) or Bakhtin's (1986) vision of speech as situated acts. Significantly the word 'knowledge' in English has connotations of 'the passive content of what is known' by contrast to the German *Erkenntnis* and French *connaissance*, which emphasize 'the act, process, form, or faculty of knowing' (Shapiro 1972: 319). I discuss the contrast between knowing and understanding in some detail in Hobart (forthcoming). The trend in development projects towards more direct 'participation' or 'involvement' rests upon the presupposition that this will somehow improve communication, which is questionable. At least 'participation' – if it involves knowing

the relevant languages, and the social and cultural context – does not *preclude* the possibility of less misunderstanding.

19 It may be helpful to consider other major institutionalized discourses, for instance, in Latin America, that of the Catholic Church.

20 In this account I have made use of an unpublished paper by Inden (n.d.) on how agency is constituted in social scientific theories. I elaborate the argument about agency in more detail in Hobart 1990.

21 Over the years, Philip Quarles van Ufford and I have argued amicably over the relationship between theorizing and participation in development, which is one of the constructive tensions of EIDOS. We both eschew the powerful fantasy that there is some notionally neutral theoretical eyrie from which to gaze dispassionately. But, as someone who has been directly involved in development projects, Quarles van Ufford is sensitive to the gap between detached academic understanding and the predicament of the participating 'expert,' who cannot separate theory and practice and who must assume some sort of coherence and system, some rationale for the venture, in order to be able to function. I lack his kind of experience, but am concerned that such a position, far from resolving the relationship of theory and practice, perpetuates it, and its implications, under the name of necessity, involvement or commitment. Theorizing which is not thinking about an object is arguably arid; and the idea that practice does not involve theory is absurd.

22 Finding a suitable term required a bibulous evening with Richard Fardon. One should not confuse silence or the absence of activity, as the two examples from Indonesia make especially clear, with a lack of agency. Not only is ostensible passivity potentially an active strategy, but in parts of the world it may be considered the hallmark of an agent (see Burghart). The efficacy of silence has been picturesquely discussed by Baudrillard, who also makes the point that those constituted as 'the masses' may be part of our own societies.

> That the silent majority (or the masses) is an imaginary referent does not mean that they don't exist. It means that *their representation is no longer possible* . . . . No one can be said to represent the silent majority, and that is its revenge . . . . The strategy of power has long seemed founded on the apathy of the masses. The more passive they were, the more secure it was. But this logic is only characteristic of the bureaucratic and centralist phase of power, and it is this which today turns against it: the inertia it has fostered becomes the sign of its own death.
>
> (1983: 20, 22, 23; emphases in the original)

23 Developers who think that they are dealing commonsensically with theory-free practice in the 'real world' are fooling themselves. As Collingwood remarked, such ' "realism" is based upon the grandest foundation a philosophy can have, namely human stupidity' (1940: 34).

24 Anthropologists often rightly invoke context in situating or explaining action. Quite what context is, however, is elusive (Hobart 1985b). One should also note that essentializing and contextualizing are explanatory strategies with implications for power and are not confined to academics or experts (Hobart 1986: 138–51).

25 Fabian is similarly discontent with existing styles of anthropological analysis and sets out to treat social action, including the process of ethnography, as a complex of performances. He finds in the work of Victor Turner evidence of a move away from performance as dramaturgical to a less metaphoric and fraught usage (Fabian 1990: 16–20).

26 In similar vein, Parkin (1975) has argued that planned change depends crucially on an awareness of social divisions among those concerned. Where there is substantial agreement, it is easier to mobilize people about a specific 'plan'. Where there are serious differences, talk of the need for development becomes a 'symbol' to attempt to minimize the effects of such differences.

27 In societies such as China and India ascriptions of the ability to know are not necessarily egalitarian and are far from fixed (see Croll). Experts may know about or how to do things which others do not. Often knowing is considered a matter of degree and involves a chain of overlapping agency and patiency, whereas when knowledge is professionalized it often leads to those who are not designated as knowing being objects of that objectified knowledge.

28 This last rendition catches some of the implications of the Hindu notion of *tamas*, desire or ignorance (often associated with darkness), which in Bali is often spoken of as one of the three constituents, *triguna*, of human nature (the other two being *sattwa*, purity or knowledge, and *rajah*, passion or emotion; Hobart 1986: 148–51). On their constitution in Indian Vaishnava texts as strands or substrata of all matter, see Inden 1985.

REFERENCES

Alatas, S. H. (1977) *The Myth of the Lazy Native: a Study of the Image of the Malays, Filipinos and Javanese from the 16th to the 20th Century and its Function in the Ideology of Colonial Capitalism*, London: Cass.

Aristotle (1941) 'Nichomachean Ethics', in *The Basic Works of Aristotle*, ed. R. McKeon, New York: Random House.

Bailey, F. G. (1957) *Caste and the Economic Frontier*, Manchester: Manchester University Press.

—— (1969) *Stratagems and Spoils*, Oxford: Blackwell.

Bakhtin, M. M. (1986) 'The problem of speech genres', in *Speech Genres and Other Late Essays*, trans. V. W. McGee, eds C. Emerson and M. Holquist, Austin, Tex: University of Texas Press.

Barth, F. (ed.) (1963) *The Role of the Entrepreneur in Social Change in Northern Norway*, Bergen: University Press.

—— (1966) *Models of Social Organization*, Occasional Paper 23, London: Royal Anthropological Institute.

Baudrillard, J. (1983) *In the Shadow of the Silent Majorities . . . or the End of the Social and Other Essays*, trans. P. Foss, P. Patton and J. Johnston, New York: Semiotext(e).

Bhaskar, R. (1979) *The Possibility of Naturalism: a Philosophical Critique of the Contemporary Human Sciences*, Sussex: Harvester.

—— (1989) 'On the possibility of social scientific knowledge and the limits of naturalism', in *Reclaiming Reality: a Critical Introduction to Contemporary Philosopy*, London: Verso.

Bourdieu, P. (1977) *Outline of a Theory of Practice*, trans. R. Nice, Cambridge: Cambridge University Press.

—— (1990) *The Logic of Practice*, trans. R. Nice, Cambridge: Polity Press.

Brokensha, D. W., Warren, D. M. and Werner, O. (eds) (1980) *Indigenous Knowledge Systems and Development*, Lanham, Md.: University Press of America.

Chambers, R. (1983) *Rural Development: Putting the Last First*, London: Longman.

Collingwood, R. G. (1933) *An Essay on Philosophical Method*, Oxford: Clarendon Press.

—— (1940) *An Essay on Metaphysics*, Oxford: Clarendon Press.

—— (1942) *The New Leviathan or Man, Society, Civilization and Barbarism*, Oxford: Clarendon Press.

Dilley, R. (ed.) (1992) *Contesting Markets*, Edinburgh: Edinburgh University Press.

Evans-Pritchard, E. E. (1937) *Witchcraft, Oracles and Magic among the Azande*, Oxford: Clarendon Press.

Fabian, J. (1983) *Time and the Other: How Anthropology Makes its Object*, New York: Columbia University Press.

—— (1990) *Power and Performance: Ethnographic Explorations through Proverbial Wisdom and Theater in Shaba, Zaïre*. Madison, Wis: University of Wisconsin.

—— (1991) 'Dilemmas of critical anthropology', in *Constructing Knowledge: Authority and Critique in Social Science*, ed. L. Nencel and P. Pels, London: Sage.

Fardon, R. (ed.) (1990) *Localizing Strategies: Regional Traditions of Ethnographic Writing*, Edinburgh: Scottish Academic Press and Washington: Smithsonian Institution.

Feyerabend, P. (1975) *Against Method: Outline of an Anarchistic Theory of Knowledge*, London: Verso.

Foucault, M. (1961) *Folie et Déraison, Histoire de la Folie à l'Âge Classique*, Paris: Plon. (1967) *Madness and Civilization: a History of Insanity in the Age of Reason*, trans. R. Howard, London: Tavistock.

—— (1966) *Les Mots et les Choses: une Archéologie des Sciences Humaines*, Paris: Gallimard. (1970) *The Order of Things: an Archaeology of the Human Sciences*, trans. A. M. Sheridan, London: Tavistock.

—— (1969) *L'Archéologie du Savoir*, Paris: Gallimard.

—— (1971) *L'ordre du Discours: Leçon Inaugural au Collège de France*, Paris: Gallimard. (1981) 'The order of discourse', trans. I. McLeod, in R. Young (ed.) *Untying the Text: a Post-structuralist Reader*, London: Routledge & Kegan Paul.

—— (1972) *The Archaeology of Knowledge*, trans. A. M. Sheridan, London: Tavistock.

—— (1975) *Surveiller et Punir: Naissance de la Prison*, Paris: Gallimard.

—— (1977) *Discipline and Punish: the Birth of the Prison*, trans. A. Sheridan, Harmondsworth: Penguin.

—— (1976) *La Volonté de Savoir*, Paris: Gallimard.

—— (1984) *The History of Sexuality I*, trans. R. Hurley, Harmondsworth: Penguin.

Frank, A. G. (1969) *Capitalism and Under-development in Latin America*, London: Monthly Review Press.

Geertz, C. (1983a) *Local Knowledge: Further Essays in Interpretive Anthropology*, New York: Basic Books.

—— (1983b) 'Local knowledge: fact and law in comparative perspective', in *Local Knowledge: Further Essays in Interpretive Anthropology*, New York: Basic Books.

Giddens, A. (1976). *New Rules of Sociological Method: a Positive Critique of Interpretative Sociologies*, London: Hutchinson.

—— (1979) *Central Problems in Social Theory: Action, Structure and Contradiction in Social Analysis*, London: Macmillan.

—— (1984) *The Constitution of Society: Outline of the Theory of Structuration*, Cambridge: Polity Press.

Goodman, N. (1978) *Ways of Worldmaking*, Hassocks: Harvester Press.

Gramsci, A. (1988) *A Gramsci Reader: Selected Writings 1916–1935*, ed. D. Forgacs, London: Lawrence & Wishart.

Habermas, J. (1978) *Knowledge and Human Interests*, 2nd edn, London: Heinemann.

Hacking, I. (1983) *Representing and Intervening: Introductory Topics in the Philosophy of Natural Science*, Cambridge: Cambridge University Press.

—— (1990) *The Taming of Chance*, Cambridge: Cambridge University Press.

Hahn, F. and Hollis, M. (eds) (1979) *Philosophy and Economic Theory*, Oxford: Oxford University Press.

Heath, A. (1976) *Rational Choice and Social Exchange: A Critique of Exchange Theory*, Cambridge: Cambridge University Press.

Held, D. and Thompson, J. B. (1989) *Social Theory of Modern Societies: Anthony Giddens and his Critics*, Cambridge: Cambridge University Press.

Henry, J. (1966) *Man against Culture*, London: Tavistock.

Hesse, M. (1978) 'Theory and value in the social sciences', in *Action and Interpretation: Studies in the Philosophy of the Social Sciences*, eds C. Hookway and P. Pettit, Cambridge: Cambridge University Press.

Hobart, M. (1985a) 'Anthropos through the Looking-glass: or How to Teach the Balinese to Bark', in *Reason and Morality*, ed. J. Overing, ASA Monographs in Social Anthropology 24, London: Tavistock.

—— (1985b) 'Is God evil?' in *The Anthropology of Evil*, ed. D. J. Parkin, Oxford: Blackwell.

—— (1986) 'Thinker, thespian, soldier, slave? Assumptions about human nature in the study of Balinese society', in *Context, Meaning, and Power in Southeast Asia*, eds M. Hobart and R. H. Taylor, Ithaca, NY: Cornell Southeast Asia Program.

—— (1990) 'The patience of plants: a note on agency in Bali', *Review of Indonesian and Malaysian Affairs* 24(2).

—— (forthcoming) 'The windmills of criticism: on understanding theatre in Bali', in *Political Cultures of Criticism*, eds R. Burghart and V. Das.

Hollis, M. (1970) 'The limits of irrationality', in *Rationality*, ed. B. Wilson, Oxford: Blackwell.

Hollis, M. (1982) 'The social destruction of reality', in *Rationality and Relativism*, eds M. Hollis and S. Lukes, Oxford: Blackwell.

—— and Lukes, S. (eds) (1982) *Rationality and Relativism*, Oxford: Blackwell.

Inden, R. (1985) 'Hindu evil as unconquered Lower Self', in *The Anthropology of Evil*, ed. D. Parkin, Oxford: Blackwell.

—— (1990) *Imagining India*, Oxford: Blackwell.

—— (n.d.) 'Social scientific thinking, or four ideas (and more) of human nature', unpublished paper.

Kuhn, T. S. (1962) *The Structure of Scientific Revolutions*, Chicago: Chicago University Press.

Laclau, E. (1971) 'Feudalism and capitalism in Latin America', *New Left Review* 67.

Lakatos, I. and Musgrave, A. (eds) (1970) *Criticism and the Growth of Knowledge: Proceedings of the International Colloquium in the Philosophy of Science, London 1965*, vol. 4, London: Cambridge University Press.

Lakoff, G. and Johnson, M. (1980) *Metaphors We Live By*, London: University of Chicago Press.

Long, N. (1977) *An Introduction to the Sociology of Rural Development*, London: Tavistock.

Lukes, S. (1973a) *Émile Durkheim: His Life and Work, a Historical and Critical Study*, Harmondsworth: Allen Lane.

—— (1973b) *Individualism*, Oxford: Blackwell.

Mason, P. (1990) *Deconstructing America: Representations of the Other*, New York: Routledge.

Mendras, H. (1970) *The Vanishing Peasant: Innovation and Change in French Agriculture*, Cambridge: Cambridge University Press.

Moore, W. E. (1963) *Social Change*, Englewood Cliffs, NJ: Prentice-Hall.

Newton-Smith, W. (1982) 'Relativism and the possibility of interpretation', in *Rationality and Relativism*, eds M. Hollis and S. Lukes, Oxford: Blackwell.

Ortony, A. (ed.) (1979) Introduction, *Metaphor and Thought*, Cambridge: Cambridge University Press.

Overing, J. (ed.) (1985) *Reason and Morality*, ASA Monographs in Social Anthropology 24, London: Tavistock.

Pagden, A. (1982) *The Fall of Natural Man*, Cambridge: Cambridge University Press.

Paine, R. (1974) *Second Thoughts about Barth's Models*, Occasional Paper 32, London: Royal Anthropological Institute.

Parkin, D. J. (1975) 'The rhetoric of responsibility: bureaucratic communication in a Kenya farming area', in *Political Language and Oratory in Traditional Society*, ed. M. Bloch, London: Academic Press.

Peirce, C. S. (1984) 'Some consequences of four incapacities', in *Writings of Charles S. Peirce: a Chronological Edition*, vol. 2, Bloomington, Ind.: Indiana University Press.

Quarles van Ufford, P. (1985) 'Rationalities and development in Java', in *Development and its Rationalities*, eds C. A. van Peursen and M. C. Doeser, Amsterdam: Free Press.

—— and Long, N. (forthcoming) *Policy and Practice*, London: Routledge.

Quine, W. V. O. (1953) 'Two dogmas of empiricism', in *From a Logical Point of View*, Cambridge Mass.: Harvard University Press.

Reddy, M. (1979) 'The conduit metaphor – a case of frame conflict in our language about language', in *Metaphor and Thought*, ed. A. Ortony, Cambridge: Cambridge University Press.

Rorty, R. (1980) *Philosophy and the Mirror of Nature*, Oxford: Blackwell.

Ryle, G. (1949) *The Concept of Mind*, London: Hutchinson.

Said, E. (1978) *Orientalism*, London: Routledge & Kegan Paul.

Salmond, A. (1982) 'Theoretical landscapes: on a cross-cultural conception of knowledge', in *Semantic Anthropology*, ed. D. J. Parkin, London: Academic Press.

Shapiro, J. J. (1972) 'Translator's notes', in J. Habermas, *Knowledge and Human Interests*, London: Heinemann.

Smelser, N. J. (1963) 'Mechanism of change and adjustment to change', in *Industrialization and Society*, eds B. F. Hoselitz and W. E. Moore, The Hague: Mouton.

Smith, A. D. (1973) *The Concept of Social Change: a Critique of the Functionalist Theory of Social Change*, London: Routledge & Kegan Paul.

Taylor, C. (1985) *Philosophy and the Human Sciences: Philosophical Papers 2*, Cambridge: Cambridge University Press.

Timberlake, L. (1988) 'Sustained hope for development', *New Scientist,* 7 July 1988.

Tribe, K. (1978) *Land, Labour and Economic Discourse*, London: Routledge & Kegan Paul.

Vitebsky, P. (1992) 'Landscape and self-determination among the Eveny: the political environment of Siberian reindeer herders today', in *Bush Base, Forest Farm: Culture, Environment, Development*, eds E. Croll and D. Parkin, London: Routledge.

Volosinov, V. N. (1973) *Marxism and the Philosophy of Language*, trans. L. Matejka and I. R. Titunik, Cambridge, Mass.: Harvard University Press.

Wallace, A. F. C. (1961) *Culture and Personality*, New York: Random House.

Wilson, B. (ed.) (1970) *Rationality*, Oxford: Blackwell.

Winch, P. (1970) 'Understanding a primitive society', in *Rationality*, ed. B. Wilson, Oxford: Blackwell.

1 Segmentary knowledge: a Whalsay sketch

Anthony P. Cohen

In the summer of 1986[1] I took with me to Whalsay, Shetland, the first draft of a book I was writing about the community, intending to show it to some of the people about whom I had written. One man who looms large in part of the book is a controversial figure locally, well known for the single-mindedness and vigour with which he pursues his campaigns. Notwithstanding the regard and affection I have for him, I had tried to write about him 'warts and all', reporting his somewhat ambivalent standing in the estimations of the islanders. I also made reference to several anecdotes which are frequently offered by Whalsay people as evidence of his idiosyncratic behaviour. He did not object to any of this, nor to my account of the extremely contentious manner in which he had campaigned thirty years ago for a harbour development, an argument which caused considerable strife within the community and which still evokes painful memories. He made only one objection: to my description of his brief fishing career as 'inglorious', the judgement of it which was certainly made by the many people who had commented about it to me. Far from being 'inglorious', he said, it had been 'da maist glorious' time of his life. He also explained away in rather prosaic terms the stories which I had proffered as indicating his absent-mindedness and iconoclasm.

The details need not concern us here. I report the incident because it struck me as a prime instance of the partiality of knowledge even in so small and intimate a community of some one thousand people. The stories were of things 'known' about Henry; 'everybody' 'knew' them, 'Oh, aye, we aa' ken wir Hendry'. Yet, what was known 'about' him was clearly not known *by* him, or was known in a quite different way. The knowledge which is assumed to embrace, unite and aggregate the members of a community turns out, like all symbolic forms, to be largely vacuous. It is constituted as meaningful in very diverse ways, yet within the framework of a formulation which is common to the members of the community. I do not suggest that such knowledge is individualized, although I am sure it may sometimes be so. But it certainly varies with the segmentary groups into which the community is divided and which provide the bases for social association within Whalsay (see Cohen 1985). Local knowledge masquerades as an orthodoxy, even as being so monolithic as to be contrastable to 'extraneous' or 'expert' knowledge, or theorized into 'a folk model'. But, just as a multiplicity of meanings may lurk behind a common symbol, so a multiplicity of 'knowledges', which may not easily be reconcilable, informs common 'knowledge'.

The importance of the masquerade is that it is one among many devices which mark the conceptual boundary by which Whalsay people separate themselves from the rest of the world. Such symbolic marking becomes increasingly imperative as geographical and infrastructural boundaries are breached and as local cultures have to respond to the spread of mass media, of national politics and of population mobility (Cohen 1982, 1986). It is not a matter of local people having to *contrive* difference, but, rather, of having to create means of reminding themselves that they do indeed differ from people elsewhere.

The development theorists who dominated the Anglo-American literature until some twenty years ago genuflected to the Weberian assumption that 'traditional' and 'modern' knowledge were incompatible; and that the feasibility of development (or 'modernization') rested on the possibility of replacing the first by the second. The work of David McClelland on 'achievement motivation', though easily dismissed as simplistic, was a stark, but not extreme expression of this position (e.g. McClelland 1961). Social anthropologists who, by the very nature of their discipline, were more closely engaged with developing societies at the grass-roots level, were quick to disown such views. But, ironically, local communities whose members feel themselves to be beleaguered by the inexorable encroachment of 'mainstream' culture, may well feel that they *are* involved in the confrontation of such a dichotomy: that extraneous knowledge does indeed threaten their own knowledge. It depicts itself as 'expert' and is thereby felt to impugn local knowledge as ignorance. Moreover, it appears to be underpinned by power and, therefore, to be even more difficult to resist. Localities thus either capitulate, discard and even, perhaps, repugn their 'traditional' knowledge; or they may make a syncretic accommodation between local and extraneous knowledge; or they may subtly subvert the extraneous. To this observer, Whalsay strategies fall into the two latter categories, and particularly into the last (notwithstanding the judgement of older islanders that their successors have surrendered to 'da sooth'). One of the ways in which the islanders express their distinctiveness from people elsewhere is by suggesting the ephemeral, superficial and usually bogus nature of Expert Knowledge. For reasons which I shall come to later, they do not claim expert knowledge for themselves. Rather, they disparage such claims. When these are made by outsiders about matters which affect the locality, they are discounted and ridiculed: they are 'ignorant'. Such outsiders fall into a generic category labelled variously as 'the authorities', 'the Experts', and 'the powers-that-be'. Outsiders are always wrong – indeed, they must be for, were they to be correct, then the conceptual boundary of 'Whalsayness', to which I referred above, would have been successfully breached.

There is ample evidence to justify the judgement made by Whalsay people that outsiders are usually wrong on Whalsay matters. But the problem is not peculiar to Whalsay. Expert outsiders are almost bound to be wrong, not because they are technically deficient, but because extraneous expertise is insensitive to the modalities of local knowledge. For the Expert Outsider, salient knowledge is substantive: problems may be resolved by having 'knowledge' applied to them. For locals, the disputation with experts may not call into question the *substance* of their knowledge, but its appropriateness. The sense of a discrete local knowledge does not deny that outsiders could know '*what* we know' but, rather, that they could know '*as* we know'. In viewing the world across their conceptual boundaries, Whalsay people argue for a kind of relativity of knowledge, insisting that while facts may well be facts, their interpretations and their implications are culture bound. To be sure, there are certain expert statements which are invariably invalid: those which stipulate where a house should be built; the sea-routes along which submarine telephone or electricity cables should be laid; the capacity of a new reservoir; the appropriate depth of water for the harbour; the basis on which fishing boat subsidies should be calculated. These are regarded, quite simply, as statements of ignorance which are all the more inexcusable because, in formulating them, 'da Experts' have blithely ignored local knowledge, indeed, may even have neglected to seek local advice. Such confrontations are contests for the definition of expertise: 'theirs', or 'ours'? The more intriguing and complicated aspect of the relativity of knowledge does not lie in contesting the expertise but in questioning its appropriateness, less a matter of *what* is known than of *how* it is known. The indigenous modality of knowledge is inextricably tied to the segmentary quality of social relations in Whalsay. A brief example must suffice. During the last thirty years, the one thousand islanders of Whalsay have acquired and capitalized the most modern fishing fleet in the UK. Now worth at least £30 million, the fleet is entirely locally owned. (These figures were correct at the time of field-work in 1986, but will obviously have changed since.) There are no multiple owners; the boats are owned by the crew members in equal share holdings. Whalsay fishermen have made particularly adventurous investments in purse-seiners, designed for fishing the pelagic species of herring and mackerel, although new boats have also been acquired for the lower risk (but lower earning) white fishery. Investment in the pelagic fleet, now in its third generation of boats, and nine vessels strong ranging in length from 90 feet to 190 feet, might well be regarded as economically irrational. Pelagic stocks have proved even more vulnerable to overfishing than white fish and 'industrial' species (caught for processing into fish meal), with the consequence that their abundance from year to year is uncertain and unpredictable. They are subject to continuously revised and politically influenced catch quotas. Some of these boats were ordered during the five-year period when the North Sea was completely closed to herring fishing. The British government ended all its financial support for the construction of pelagic boats; the Whalsay fishermen sought, and found, finance in Norway. The British government designated a very few Scottish ports, excluding Lerwick, Shetland's principal market, for herring landings. The Whalsay fishermen took their catches to Denmark or sold them, sometimes more cheaply, to East European 'klondykers' (factory ships) stationed in Lerwick harbour. The debts which the men incurred in acquiring their boats, and the financial risks of this fishery, gives their investment something of the appearance of a 'deep play' (Geertz 1975).

Why did they proceed in this way, against the advice of marine biologists, of processors and of government? Why did they choose to ignore 'expert knowledge'? Adequate answers require a more comprehensive examination of Whalsay society than can be given here (see Cohen 1987). But one element of them may be stated categorically: they have little to do with fishing, and much to do with Whalsay culture, both as it relates to local perceptions of the outside world, and to social relations within the community. First,

Whalsay people filter the 'objective' ecological and economic considerations through a local interpretive prism which fractures them into a plethora of culturally reflexive questions: what is *our* experience of these considerations? What do they mean to *us* in the light of our historical experience and of our present circumstances? Can *we* overcome the negative indications of the strategy? What might be the implications for the community of our success or failure? Such questions are clearly predicated on Whalsay islanders' perceptions of themselves as different from people elsewhere. The 'knowledge' which they apply in taking their investment decisions is 'local' in the possessive sense illustrated by Vitebski (this volume). If it is not 'theirs', then they would have ceased to be culturally distinguishable from people elsewhere and would thereby have become socially unrecognizable to themselves. Whalsay islanders do not suffer from such an identity crisis; their 'local' knowledge is inalienable (Strathern 1984).

There is nothing contrived or eccentric about this localization of knowledge. It is not a self-conscious attempt to put some cognitive distance between Whalsay and elsewhere. Rather, it is a refraction on a slightly higher societal scale of the disparity of knowledges *within* the community among its segmentary groups. Segmentation in Whalsay should be understood in cultural terms: people think of themselves as belonging to the community through the mediation of their more immediate associations, and think about each other in these terms. 'Formal' associations are based on kinship and affinity; they are expressed in the aggregation of households in crofting *townships*, in membership of fishing crews, and in the treasury of public knowledge about local people. The community does not have the classic structural properties of segmentation noted elsewhere because, both in principle and practice, descent is cognatic and kinship is reckoned bilaterally. Nevertheless, a person is known as belonging for specific purposes to one group; while, for other purposes, he or she may be identified with other groups. These are essentially ascriptive structural associations which people must publicly acknowledge, timeless groups in which the individual's character is held to be rooted even though they may have ceased to provide the nexus of everyday interaction and economic life.

However, the individual's *self*-identification recognizes another, more fundamental notion: 'wir (our) folk . . . yon folk', an opposition sometimes also expressed as between people who are *ken't* (known) and *unken* (see Cohen 1987: 70 ff.). These categories are cognitive and ideal: they are means of discriminating, and of locating, one's chosen associates within a field of potential associates limited only by the geographical bounds of the community. Because this notion conflicts with the dominant rhetoric of local commonality, egalitarianism and homogeneity ('we're all the same here') it has to be expressed in ways which avoid the explicit suggestion of permanent, faction-like sub-community groupings. It is a more subtle form of association than those of kinship, neighbourhood and crew membership, all of which imply inescapable obligations and which compromise individuality. These associations are indeed credited within Whalsay as having idiosyncratic knowledge, but are insensitive to differences among their own members. 'Wir folk', by contrast, implies a greater degree of pliability and voluntarism. Its relationships are reproduced as expressions of choice rather than of ascription. It is not entirely separable from kinship but is a dimension of it, as it is of the other structural forms of close association. It really describes close relationships in practice rather than principle. Identity within Whalsay is thus a process of serial segmentation: the community 'as a whole' *vis-à-vis* 'elsewhere'; its component structural groups (kin, neighbourhood, crews) in relation to each other; 'wir folk' (which may overlap with, and may exclude parts of the former) as social refractions of the self. To each there is a modality of knowledge which, to comply with the imperatives of egalitarianism and communal solidarity, must be expressed through common forms giving the appearance (at least so far as outsiders are concerned) of a shared substantive knowledge, of an orthodoxy. This is to say that within the framework of a common (but possibly spurious) local knowledge, there are many real local knowledges, as in Geertz's use of the term, suggesting differing hermeneutics, ways of imagining and interpreting 'reality' (Geertz 1983: 215).

Relations among the segments are competitive. An opinion venerated within the group, because it was expressed by one of the group's members, may be denigrated by the members of another group. Such opinions are rarely debated across group boundaries for the very reason that they *are* contentious. People try to avoid behaviour which might result in overt conflict. What is actually thought by the members of a group is somewhat irrelevant. They have opinions imputed to them (just as they have identities allocated to them) by the members of other groups on the bases of lore and tradition. Their opinions and claims to knowledge are frequently portrayed by others as expressions of their sectional interests or as products of their idiosyncratic circumstances or histories.

I emphasize that segmentary knowledge should not be regarded as contrived or tactical, even though it has this competitive character. Differences of opinion and of information are not motivated by the mere fact of segmentary confrontation but are, rather, authentic expressions of cognitive diversity within the community. They thereby call into question the existence of a putative indigenous knowledge which contrasts with 'expert' and extraneous knowledge. This has distinct implications for the consideration of knowledge as an issue in 'development'. First (and most obvious) the once popular proposition that successful innovation requires the 'translation' of an alien idea into an indigenous idiom (e.g. Kavadias 1966) is revealed as hopelessly simplistic as well as being insidious. Second, the technical or 'objective' aspects of knowledge are of less significance than outsiders are usually prepared to acknowledge. Third, the integrity of local knowledge and expertise has to be seen as inhering in the segmentary ideology which renders indigenous knowledge into a number of plausible versions, rather than in its *apparent* contrast to extraneous (in)expert systems. Knowledge does not commend itself locally by its intrinsic merit, nor by the subtlety and ingenuity with which it is disseminated (e.g. Paine 1970), nor even by its congruence with what else may be known locally, but rather, by its appropriateness to the ways in which things are known locally.

This difference is vividly illustrated in Feit's account of the contrast between the ecological monitoring of Cree hunting lands undertaken by Canadian government scientists and other white wildlife experts, and as practised by the Cree themselves. Feit shows that Cree knowledge of flora and fauna is infinitely more detailed and sophisticated than those of the Expert Outsiders; but, also, that its association with the customary Cree institution of 'stewardship' makes it acceptable knowledge, *knowable* knowledge, in a way which excludes extraneous expertise as crass (Feit 1982, also 1984).

Outsiders' knowledge of a locality is generalized and imputes to the members of the locality largely undifferentiated views. But by contrast, members' knowledge of their locality is highly particularized, and has a variety of competences. In its *formal* expression as shared knowledge – that is, as a form of knowledge common to members – it has, what Schwartz calls, an 'ethnognomomic' character (1975). It marks symbolically the community's boundary with the outside world, and serves as a 'cultural totem': 'this is how *we* [Whalsay Islanders] know'. But, in internal discourse, this putative collective knowledge, an illusion of shared form, is fractured into knowledge*s* as it is filtered through the community's segmentary boundaries. I think this plurality of knowledges is what Apthorpe has in mind when he urges us, in contradistinction to the conventional wisdom among developmentalists, to assume that there is a 'lack of integration in local knowledges, dissent in local knowledges about meaning, rival tendencies in local knowledges about truth, knowledge and ignorance' (1986: 6).

I stress again that I am not attributing to Whalsay society a segmentary *structure*. Therefore, I do not suggest that these internal boundaries *determine* the modalities of knowledge which they enclose. My argument is, rather, that people make knowledge accommodate their general social circumstances and not just those to which items of knowledge refer specifically. 'Knowing' what qualities constitute the good skipper or the skilful shepherd, the accomplished joiner or the lightsome fiddler depends partly on who is making the judgement, to whom, about whom, excluding whom, and who were the precedents in the judge's experience. To suggest that knowledge is thus variable and contingent does not dispute that to the knower it has the character of absoluteness. But it does entail that in a community like Whalsay in which considerable effort is devoted to the avoidance of conflict and to the continuous reinforcement of local identity, there are peculiar constraints on the conditions of acceptable knowledge. The substantive knowledges of the competing segments must be reconcilable with the communal expressive *form* of knowledge.

In knowledge, as in matters of identity, the culture of segmentation in Whalsay reveals a continuous slide back and forth between the juxtaposed forms of segment and community. Whalsay people are adept at managing these transformations. More remarkably, they can assume and behave in either mode without impugning the integrity of the other. Thus there may be occasions when it is appropriate to stress collectivity and generality: for example, in contrasting Whalsay fishing to that of Burra Isle (the other major fishing community in Shetland) or of Peterhead (a north-east Scottish fishing port favoured by Whalsay crews). But such an idiom does not diminish the claims of any segment to its specialist practices. Like most symbolic statements of collectivity, this idiom would be formulated in terms which are sufficiently vacuous that they may be assimilated to segmentary particularities while appearing simultaneously as a substantive statement of collective interest. This modulation of identity is also replicated in cognitive idioms. People talk about the way '*we* do things here' (i.e. in Whalsay), or about what '*we* know from experience', referring to the community but phrasing the putative knowledge or practice in terms which permit them to be deciphered according to segmentary interests. I do not suggest that this represents a deliberate attempt to balance communal and sectional interests; rather, that it is a form of knowledge and its characteristic discourse.

Modes of knowledge are inextricable from modes of identity. 'Facts', 'knowledge', are not treated on their inherent merits, even if it was possible to establish what these might be. They are assimilated to, and evaluated in the light of the social position of the perceiver (cf. Arce and Long, this volume). Whalsay people are content to concede the plausibility of alternatives and would be reticent about claiming dogmatically the status of fact for their points of view. A Whalsay man will often conclude his statement of an opinion by saying, 'I may be wrong, I likely am, but that's what I think'. Their eschewing of dogmatism is consistent with the powerful theme of cultural rationality which judges that knowledge is acceptable in terms of its appropriateness. Therefore, what makes an investment decision sensible in Peterhead or Cockenzie may be profoundly inappropriate in Whalsay, and vice versa. The same relativity of knowledge is applied also *within* Whalsay. Knowledge is formulated in a way which permits the dialectic of whole and part, with the consequences that conflict is mitigated and egalitarianism protected, both of which help to preserve the collective boundary. In reconciling whole and part, the *form* of knowledge also becomes a condition of knowing, a test of what may be regarded as legitimate knowledge.

The test is applied for the acceptability of extraneous knowledge (does it have this competence?). It also serves as a means of accounting for what may appear to the outsider as ignorance. (Why do people who have sophisticated theories of natural causation continue to sacrifice, ostensibly to produce natural consequences? Why do Dinka continue to practise *thuic*, whilst also taking expedient and practical measures to secure their objectives (Lienhardt 1961)? Why, for that matter, do the Cobblers of Janakpur use, and apparently abuse, their reluctant 'lord', in the purification of their well (Burghart, this volume)?

In Whalsay, knowledge satisfies the conditions of its acceptability by accommodating community and segment. *What* is known is form: a general statement, so articulated that the various groups and members of the community can assent to it without compromising their own interests. *How* it is known, that is, how the form is given substance and thereby made meaningful, is particularistic.

Knowledge is held as *version*, to the extent that people express scepticism about putatively 'absolute' knowledge. That is one reason why the outsider's expert knowledge is bound to be nonsense: in its absoluteness, it is non-segmentary, and therefore fails the test. Moreover, since experts are quite unaware of this dimension of knowledge, they reveal themselves to be ignorant. Their 'knowledge' is as incompetent as the 'legal knowledge' discussed by von Benda Beckman (1986): 'Legal knowledge, as knowledge of conceptions, implies the knowledge of generalities, of abstractions. These do not make sense unless interpreted in relation to a specific context'. It is precisely the segmentary affiliations in Whalsay society that provide the specificities of context through which things can be 'known'.

Segmentary knowledge in Whalsay is thus manifest in disparate interpretations and opinions but, in the interests of communal boundary management, masquerades as orthodoxy and consensus. Segmentary expression is legitimate, so long as it does not expose or subvert the masquerade. The various purser crews offered different explanations for their apparent defiance of financial rationality in purchasing their boats. One crew was said to have done it primarily to minimize its tax liability; another, to provide the basis for the merger of two agnatically-related crews; a third, in anticipation of the development of a new fishery for blue whiting (which, in the event, did not materialize); a fourth, to remain competitive; and so on. If they were to explain their reasons to outsiders, they would do so in quite different terms, offering an account which would appear to be common to all the crews. They would almost certainly defend their decisions on the grounds of community interest, such as maximizing earnings and employment opportunities in order to forestall possible future out-migration. Such an explanation would certainly not be humbug: it would be valid as an expression and defence of the local boundary. However, within Whalsay itself, it would be read differently and with close attention paid to segmentary nuances. The same kinds of sectional cognitive discrimination would be revealed in almost every aspect of life, including such customary activities as the *eela* (small boat handline) inshore fishery, knitting, peat cutting, crofting, and cooking, and extending to knowledge of knowledge ('*we* know; *they* don't; they *think* they know; we *know* they don't').

Of course segmentary knowledge is only one aspect of a segmentary culture whose complexity and diversity belies its solidary and homogeneous appearance. It raises a general question about the aggregative nature of culture. But so far as our immediate purposes are concerned, it obliges us to look sceptically on the idea of an authoritative local knowledge (and at its corollary, local ignorance), a resource on which anthropologists have been inclined to depend heavily. In our ethnographic *naïveté*, we have succumbed to the persuasiveness of indigenous experts: for explanations of the mysteries of ritual, of hunting, of genealogy and so forth. While listening to native erudition from an informant who has been identified to us as 'the one who knows', we must also watch his or her local listeners for the quizzically raised eyebrow and the slightly distended cheek. In our post-modern humility, few of us would claim anything more than 'version' for our own expertise; we should not assume more than that for our informants. In matters of development policy and planning, that may be what makes them, and even, perhaps, us, more reliable as experts than 'Experts'.

NOTE

The author would like to point out that this chapter has not been revised or updated since it was written in 1986.

REFERENCES

Apthorpe, R. (1986) 'Development: styles of knowledge and ignorance', paper presented to the EIDOS Workshop, 'Local knowledge and systems of ignorance', School of Oriental and African Studies, December (mimeo).
Benda-Beckman, F. von (1986) 'Local knowledge of legal pluralism', paper presented to the EIDOS Workshop, 'Local knowledge and systems of ignorance', School of Oriental and African Studies, December (mimeo).
Cohen, A. P. (1982) 'Belonging: the experience of culture', in A. P. Cohen (ed) *Belonging: Identity and Social Organisation in British Rural Cultures*, Manchester: Manchester University Press.
—— (1985) 'Symbolism and social change: matters of life and death in Whalsay, Shetland', *Man* N.S. 20: 307–24.
—— (1986) 'Of symbols and boundaries, or, does Ertie's greatcoat hold the key?' in A. P. Cohen (ed.) *Symbolising Boundaries: Identity and Diversity in British Cultures*, Manchester: Manchester University Press.
—— (1987) *Whalsay: Symbol, Segment and Boundary in a Shetland Island Community*, Manchester: Manchester University Press.
Feit, H. A. (1982) 'The future of hunters within the nation-state: anthropology and the James Bay Cree', in E. Leacock and R. Lee (eds) *Politics and History in Band Societies*, Cambridge: Cambridge University Press.
—— (1984) 'Legitimation and autonomy in James Bay Cree responses to hydro-electric development', in N. Dyck (ed.) *Indigenous Peoples and the*

Nation-State: 'Fourth World' Politics in Canada, Australia and Norway, St Johns, Newfoundland: Institute of Social and Economic Research.

Geertz, C. (1975) 'Deep play: notes on the Balinese cockfight', in *The Interpretation of Cultures*, London: Hutchinson.

—— (1983) 'Local knowledge: fact and law in comparative perspective', in *Local Knowledge: Further Essays in Interpretive Anthropology*, New York: Basic Books.

Kavadias, G. (1966) 'The assimilation of the scientific and technological "message" ', *International Social Science Journal*, 18(3).

Lienhardt, R. G. (1961) *Divinity and Experience: the Religion of the Dinka*, Oxford: Oxford University Press.

McClelland, D. G. (1961) *The Achieving Society*, Princeton, NJ: Van Nostrand.

Paine, R. P. B. (1970) 'Informal communication and information management', *Canadian Review of Sociology and Anthropology* 7(3).

Schwartz, T. (1975) 'Cultural totemism: ethnic identity primitive and modern', in G. de Vos and L. Romanucci-Ross (eds) *Ethnic Identity: Cultural Continuities and Change*, Palo Alto, Calif.: Mayfield.

Strathern, M. (1984) 'The social meanings of localism', in T. Bradley and P. Lowe (eds) *Locality and Rurality: Economy and Society in Rural Regions*, Norwich: Geo Books.

Stuchlik, M. (1976) 'Whose knowledge?', in L. Holy (ed.) *Knowledge and Behaviour*, Queen's University Papers in Social Anthropology No. 1: 1–15, Belfast: Queen's University.

2 Processes and limitations of Dogon agricultural knowledge

Walter E. A. van Beek

INTRODUCTION

In this contribution I try to explore the effect ecological changes and pressures have had on the adaptation of the Dogon in Mali.[1] The general angle will be that of cultural ecology, in which a particular society is viewed from the perspective of its interaction with its physical as well as social environment. This interaction is of a complex nature, and in fact constitutes the subject of this chapter. It bears some features of a system, but the coherence of the variables should not be overestimated. In any case, the interaction is not a homeostatic one. Periodic upheavals of a physical nature (droughts, locusts) as well as of a socio-political nature (slave raiding, demographic growth) periodically upset any survival strategy developed by the population.

A study of adaptation and its fluctuations and changes has to focus on both the internal organization of the group and the specific characteristics of the environment. This has to be couched in a historical framework as much as possible, as the essence of adaptation is adapting to change. Of course, historical sources on the Dogon are few; one has to rely on oral tradition, climatic data over several centuries and the political history of the Nigerbend.

Adaption is, its social apsects notwithstanding, a process involving individual people, who react to their social and physical environment according to their view of the situation, their knowledge of the 'realities' they have to face. This knowledge is usually dubbed the 'perceived environment' (Hardesty 1978) and as such is thought to be the mediating factor between outside change and cultural reaction. I shall try to show that the processes of mediation are of a more complex character, as knowledge of and interaction with environment is less exclusively cognitive. The Dogon seem to work more through a body of practices – knowing how to do things and to react to changes, a set of practical procedures – than through a formal system of shared knowledge. This has consequences for their ways of both resisting and incorporating change; one result is that the main challenge to the Dogon local knowledge is not change in content but in scale.

AN ECOLOGICAL VIEW OF DOGON HISTORY

For the many tourists travelling through Mali, the Dogon villages huddled on the inhospitable scree of the majestic Bandiagara escarpment present both a striking sight (and a substantial income for the Malian state) and a perennial question: how do the Dogon manage to survive in such a seemingly inhospitable environment and why did they choose such a site? Two sets of factors have shaped the Dogon predilection for their 'falaise', historical and geographical. The first was slave raiding. The Nigerbend, where the Dogon area is situated, has been scourged by continuous slave raiding. The empires of Ghana, Mali, Sonrai, the chiefs and kings of the Mossi, Sao and Fulani had a perennial hunger for slaves. For them all non-Muslims were potential slaves. Raiding was usually small-scale and carried out by merchants in a hit-and-run manner. Against this threat, the Bandiagara escarpment offered a fair defence. On the plateau the villages were built behind narrow gorges, and were only accessible on foot; at the foot of the cliff the scree offered some protection against mounted attack and from a high position there was a chance of spotting raiding parties some way off. If the danger was too great, the Dogon could flee into the caverns inside the sandstone cliff.

The second factor is water. The water situation at the plateau rim as well as at the foot is slightly better than either on the plateau or in the sandy dunes of the plains (see the illustrated cross-section). The sandstone rock holds a considerable amount of water throughout the dry season, while the floor of the scree is the lowest part of the area; a rivulet runs parallel to the falaise in the wet season.

So the plateaulands immediately bordering the rim and the valley fields closest to them offered a fair prospect for horticulturalists. The Dogon were by no means the first to settle in the falaise area. Other, prehistoric, groups preceded them, known as the Tellem and the Toloy (Bedaux 1982). Their ecological situation, as far as can be gleaned from the scant data, must have been quite similar. The Dogon arrived at the falaise towards the end of the Mali empire,

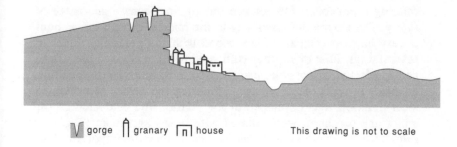

gorge   granary   house   This drawing is not to scale

Figure 2.1 Dogon habitation: a cross-section

somewhere around the fifteenth century. They chased away the
Tellem and settled in their ecological niche, cultivating millet and
sorghum. Periodic droughts must have been part of their collective
experience. The sixteenth to the eighteenth centuries saw at least
three drought periods per century, while the nineteenth century
seems to have been more generous with rain (Bryson and Murray
1977). Though in these periods some rituals may have been generated that bear a close association with drought (van Beek 1986),
oral tradition does not reach further back than the nineteenth
century (with a possible exception for the order of arrival at the
escarpment; see Dieterlen 1942).

From the sixteenth to the nineteenth century the slave raiding
pressure probably increased, as the centres of political activity came
closer to the Bandiagara region. After the distant Ghana, Mali and
Sonrai empires, the Mossi, Fulani and Sao were close and frequent
slave raiders. Their intermediary position as merchants aggravated
matters for the Dogon, as both the intensification of war and the
growth of cities during the eighteenth and nineteenth centuries
increased the demand for slaves in the whole of the West African
Sudan. At the end of the eighteenth century the Fulani jihads,
triggered by a resurgence of Islam, for a large part through Sufism,
put an ever larger premium on slaves for warfare. In the nineteenth
century, the relatively favourable climatic circumstances permitted
large cavalries, for which great numbers of slaves and craftsmen
had to be recruited to enable them to function (cf. Smaldone 1978).
So in the nineteenth century insecurity was at its peak, and the
pressure on the escarpment had gradually increased, when the Europeans arrived on the scene.

The safety of the escarpment was a relative one for the Dogon, offering a possibility for defence but by no means a guarantee of safety. The Dogon did lose many to the raiders, though the amount is very hard to estimate. They coped with the perennial threat in several ways. First of all, they cultivated fields as close to the village and the falaise as possible, using a system of intensive horticulture on fields in sight of the village. Manuring the fields, according to local tradition, was developed at the falaise. The cultivated crops, millet and sorghum, were rotated with beans and fonio (*Digitaria exilis*); the latter crop may formerly have been more important than in recent times, judging by its pre-eminence in ritual. It is well suited for a situation of relative neglect, as sowing is done 'à la volée', and weeding is hardly needed; harvesting has to be done collectively (Paulme 1948). Between these main crops maize and tobacco, introduced long before the Europeans came into Africa, were cultivated; maize served as an early crop (though fonio was more important as a quick harvest in a season of hunger), while tobacco was grown in the river-bed in the dry season, using a version of pot-irrigation.

The social adaptation to the combined need for production and defence was generally an insistence on communality. The size of the villages varied from 500 to 1,000 inhabitants. Smaller villages were hard put to mobilize enough able-bodied young men; in larger ones the land pressure would force cultivation too far from the protecting scree. Work was organized as often as possible in large groups, able to defend themselves against the small bands of horsemen roaming the countryside. Groups of 10 to 20 men were large enough; the farther the fields were from the village, the larger the group needed. Recruitment of groups was done in two ways: the first drew on the extended family, and the second was according to age, that is, the age of men. For the close fields an extended family was usually able to furnish labour-cum-defence, though a combination of two to four extended families, often forming the smallest *gina* (partrilineal segment), was a normal working unit too. The old men of the families in question co-ordinated the work, either having their people work together on one large field, or arranging that families worked on adjoining fields. The old men served as look-outs from the *toguna*, the men's hut built high up against the mountain with an unrestricted view over the plains or the plateau.

For the larger fields, especially those further removed from the village, a larger group was recruited, consisting of men from three to five consecutive age groups. The age-class system of the Dogon had (and has) the regulation of labour as its main goal and *raison d'être*. One age-class of a typical Dogon village consisted of a fixed amount of able-boded males, around 50 in many cases, who gathered whenever there was communal work to be done. Clearing and weeding bush fields were some of the most important jobs. As each group was formed at the age of marriage of the boys, these communal labours also served as bride service, an important aspect of the marriage proceedings (Paulme 1948). If an age class (*kadaga*) worked out in the fields, several old kinsmen served as look-out in the highest *toguna* or – for the villages at the foot of the escarpment – up on the plateau rim. Drums served as a means of communication. The same system served when large-scale communal labour was to be done. A larger task, like digging the village well, setting out the steep paths up to the plateau or reroofing the *toguna*, called for more than one *kadaga*. Then the old men of the wards discussed the task at hand, determined the number of *kadaga* needed and had the town crier call upon the labourers to volunteer in. In large endeavours, beer had to be prepared in advance, as drinking was an integral part of this tye of communal labour. The maximal labour unit consists of all functioning *kadaga* of the whole village (in recent times supplemented with all villagers living in other settlements as well as all in-laws from the village), implying all able-bodied men up to the age of about 45 years.

The co-ordinating task of the old men was facilitated by their general position of authority; theirs was (and still is) a key position, as they control the in-fields, that is, the fields within view of the scree. All fields where permanent cultivation was possible – which were close enough to manure – were assigned to the oldest men of the village and ward, and of the clans and families. The complicated system of land rotation implied that a specific set of fields was assigned to the oldest of the village, another set to the next oldest and so on, for each section of the village as well as for the whole community. So the old men were in a position to co-ordinate and did have a definite interest in the cultivation of their fields. They usually belonged to the same age group, and could base their work on a long-standing tradition of co-operation. During a later phase their task was to be individualized, but in the pre-colonial period they seem to have decided as a body which fields were going to be cultivated, sown with what crop, and how many of what age group were going to participate. Crying out loud in front of the sound-reflecting cliff, they had the village in reach of their voice each evening. As in later phases, and to conform with Dogon standards of interpersonal communication, they played down their own role, extolled the virtues of those who turned out on previous occasions, shamed the lazy ones, throughout stressing the reciprocal dependency of old and young, men and women.

The demographical situation before the European arrival is hard to assess. Probably it would have had a standard pre-transition pattern, with a high natality, a high mortality and little consequent population growth. There is no evidence of natality restriction in that period (there is still hardly any today). Slave raiding would have formed the most important mechanism of population restriction, either by the direct transferral of men and women from the densely populated falaise area, or by a specific institution that developed in response to it: any mother's brother had the right to sell his sister's daughter in slavery. This most often happened when raiders had captured someone's brother, son or wife, captives which could be ransomed for a sister's daughter. From the angle of demography this is highly effective, as the abduction of these nubile young females drastically diminished Dogon reproduction.

THE COLONIAL TRANSITION

The advent of the colonizer brought about some fundamental changes that, at an accelerating pace, transformed Dogon adaptation. The *pax gallica* cut short the slave raiding in the area as well as the (few) skirmishes between Dogon settlements themselves. This resulted in the plateau as well as the plains becoming available for cultivation. At an ever increasing rate the Dogon swarmed out into the newly opened territories, building new farms and founding new villages. Plains and plateau were not exactly empty; some villages had already been established on the plains, as well as on the plateau. Still, in the first decades of the century the Dogon quickly filled in the empty spots on the map, first along the present border with Burkina Fasso with its better soils, then in the sandy plains closer to the escarpment. On the plateau the Dogon drifted in a north-western direction. For the villages at the falaise, on which we are concentrating, this emigration at first resulted in a sparser population. Also, some of the pressure on land was eased owing to the cultivation of distant fields, which were still considered to be village territory. In the falaise villages, new fields at 5 to 10 kilometres from the rim were brought into cultivation. The control of those fields fell to the families that ventured out, first collectively as agnatic lineages but also individually. So, in contrast to control of the in-fields by the gerontocratic structure, these out-fields were owned by families.

At the same time new crops were being introduced. Tobacco had been grown for a long time, but onions came to be cultivated on a rapidly increasing scale. Thus a dry season cultivation developed, in which the onions (and tobacco) were cultivated in the river-bed, irrigated with hand-carried pots and calebashes. Waterholes were dug on several places in the sand, to follow the receding water table during the three months of onion cultivation (December to February). Villages on the plateau grew onions at the border of the few places where an impermeable layer in the rock retained a pool of stagnant water during the dry season. This onion production was the first real cash crop for the Dogon, triggered by the need for money (taxation and the purchase of commodities) and the presence and development of food markets. The onions were readily accepted in the region.

This first colonial phase was characterized by pacification, dispersal and very little investment in the area, and lasted to about the Second World War. Socially, it was a period of moderate fragmentation. The traditional survival strategy of communal labour lost most of its rationale, though it did not entirely disappear. Individual property became more important, though this was not new for the Dogon. The influence of the old men as a body diminished, as their collective co-ordinating role in agriculture dwindled. Yet they remained important in village matters and regulated the large communal tasks for the whole village. However, with the relative privatization of land use and ownership, their importance within the extended family was strengthened, as they gained control over the out-fields through the lineage system. The extended families themselves gained in importance as they grew less dependent on cooperation with other extended families. Besides, the constrained labour the colonizer demanded and recruitment for the army meant a demand for labour that extended families could very well cope with. Production in the onion gardens depended on the individual or the nuclear family. As this production complemented the general subsistence, it left the position of the old men untouched.

The second colonial period, from the late 1940s up to the 1970s, is characterized by a decrease in small-scale and an increase in large-scale migration. While the plains gradually were filled up and the people began to settle in the dune areas closest to the villages, labour migration, after a slow start before the Second World War, began to be quite important. Young men were first allowed and later expected to work a stint in the large cities of the West African coast, such as Accra or Abidjan. Dogon labourers gained a reputation as eager and resourceful labourers, and easily found employment. A work period lasted between one dry season and several years, and brought most of them back to their falaise village loaded with modern commodities such as radios, bicycles, clothes and, of course, money. Monetarily the villages grew dependent on this labour migration.

Onion farming became more important, especially on the plateau, where after a successful start in 1938 an ever increasing number of small 'barrages' (small dams) were built. Dozens of small man-made lakes enabled the plateau Dogon to concentrate on onion farming in an environment where formerly no cultivation – and not even grazing – had been possible, a point to which we shall return later.

Ecologically this is the start of the desertification of the plains. The sandy dunes adjoining the escarpment began to be overcultivated, beyond their carrying capacity. The shifting cycle of the out-fields was gradually shortened and the supply of fire and construction wood became scarcer. Dogon agriculture intensified, concentrating on three focal points: the falaise rim and the out-fields in the wet season, and the waterholes in the dry season. This intensification, combined with the filling up of all ecological niches in the area, put the eco-system under an increasingly severe strain. As the resources were closing, new kinds of limitations appeared. Fertilization of the soils became more problematic, as the onion and tobacco farming demanded ever more manure. The traditional ways of manuring relied on the residue of the subsistence farming on the one hand and on animal husbandry on the other. So an increase in cattle can be noticed in this period, which in turn put the ecology of the area as a whole under pressure and endangered the natural refertilization within the *jachère* system of the out-fields.

Demographic pressure aggravated the situation. The Dogon population rose from an estimated 100,000 at the turn of the century to at least 300,000 in the early 1970s. Outmigration became increasingly important, starting from the strongholds established by the migrant workers in the cities.

Socially this period showed the flexibility of the family structure. The extended family shifted from a patriarchal one to a flexible co-opting of related nuclear families, a community of interests in which the second generation took precedence. During the wet season, when labour was very much in demand, the whole family lived and worked together, cultivating their joint millet fields. The dry season onion cultivation, then, split the family into nuclear ones, on a basis of restricted profit sharing. When the out-fields were too far away from the village, or when one of the sons had settled in a plains village, the extended family remained a single financial unit: both the plains and the escarpment parts of the family contributed to its common fund. This kind of non-resident extended family proved to be very flexible in both arranging labour and meeting expenses as well as profiting from the variegated resources of the region. Most years show a fair difference in agricultural success between plateau, escarpment and plains; so spreading out the family enhanced chances for survival in an ecological system that proved to be less and less dependable.

The old men lost some of their importance, though they retained control over the in-fields, over the finances of their families and over ritual. As onion farming, for example, gave rise to new co-operating groups (like the group of people using the same water-hole) the network of relations in the village grew more diffuse. Still, as kinsmen tended to live close together and peers tended to culti-vate together, the warp and woof of lineages and age groups remained dominant in the escarpment villages.

BREAKING UP THE SYSTEM

Since the late 1970s the pressures on the ecosystem have dramati-cally increased. The drought that set in around 1973 in West Africa hit the Dogon area after 1980, culminating in the disaster years of 1984 and 1985. Though local differences are considerable, even on the small scale of the Dogon region the whole picture is one of gloom. The fact that the good rainy season of 1986 was spoiled by a locust plague in several villages intensified this feeling. Villages that dwindled during the outmigration to the plains are being deserted completely. On the plateau, and especially in the plains, the villages have become the centres of wide circles of desert, where the combined efforts of man and cattle have stripped the soil of its fragile vegetative cover. Migration has started towards the south of Mali, in Bambara country, and towards the Mossi area of Burkina Fasso. This migration, aided by the Malian government and several NGOs working in the region, is, of course, the sign of ecosystem failure.

Still, neither the Dogon nor aid agencies give up that easily. Aid is pouring into the Dogon area from various sources in several ways. Food aid is one form, the construction of 'barrages' another. Before going into this problem, however, we have to glean some insights into how the Dogon construct the ecological reality, how they view their environment.

DOGON AGRICULTURAL KNOWLEDGE, GENERAL AND SPECIFIC

Dogon agricultural knowledge is the result of a long interaction with their physical environment, both with those aspects that remain more or less constant and with the changes that their ecological history has brought about. Their perception of the ecology can be described as a general perspective on their relation with their environment on the one hand, and on the other as a set of procedures to obtain highly specific local knowledge through interaction with that environment.

The general view is one of unlimited resources. There is no scarcity of land according to the Dogon: 'there is plenty land in the plains'. The people living on the escarpment in particular view the plains as long stretches of bush more or less empty of habitation. The same holds for wood, another increasingly scarce resource. Trees are still considered to be available in relative abundance. If one cannot easily find a field, or trees, it is simply a question of going a little bit further, walking another hour. That this view does not correspond with the way the plains nowadays are filled up with villages and hamlets, and with the rapid disappearance of substantial trees (the firewood zones of the villages start overlapping each other) is not relevant. The old image from the falaise, from the times of the slave raiding, is that of a seemingly endless emptiness, a sea of uninterrupted yellow or green gently undulating land, dangerous because of human and supernatural beings, but waiting for the human hand to exploit and cultivate it. An area to be colonized, in short.

Thus an important opposition is the one between the village habitat and everything else: *ana* (village) versus *oru* (bush). One is safe in the village, while never fully at ease in the bush. The bush is the old raiders' territory, and before even that, was the region of spirits. Though most of these are not thought to be malevolent, their very presence is eery and annoying. Besides, evil humans (van Beek 1993) such as witches (*yadugonu*) and sorcerers (*dudugonu*) roam the bush after dusk. At night one should be protected, isolated from the influences of nature, within the village, sleeping not on top of the roof (a bird might pass over the sleeping figure, possibly causing harm with its spirit), but safely within the confines of a house or under a lean-to. In the Dogon view the village in which one is safe and secure is surrounded by an inhospitable vastness of bush. This *oru* can be cultivated with a lot of exertion but in itself it stays untamed. Beyond the village perimeter things are not domesticated, but have to be 'tamed' over and over again. The dangers of the bush are not evenly divided over the area: places near water are dangerous, and so are stands of trees. The way to tame the bush is to build houses, grass lean-tos at first, more permanent houses later, if possible within sight of other settlements. Fellow humans are preferred as companions over the 'things of the bush'.[2]

For the Dogon it is the humans that are in short supply, not the fields. Their system is an expansive one, in which more people are always needed, more fields have to be taken into cultivation, more cattle raised. Fertility is highly valued. In their yearly work-cycle this notion of labour shortage is understandable: during the cultivation season, especially when weeding, labour in fact *is* in short supply, and every hand is needed. The rest of the year, however, this is not the case. Onion farming, of course, with its heavy demand for labour, has served to reinforce this attitude. Like humans, animals are in short supply, and with animals, manure. For the Dogon manure is one of the limiting factors in agriculture, and most cattle are seen primarily as dung machines. So increase in animals means new opportunities for cultivation.

This general view of environment in a way presents a cultural lag, as we noted, but one that is more than simply a time lag in understanding new conditions. This vision of availability of resources is central to the Dogon attitude towards their survival, and in itself has been instrumental in their relative success so far. Tied in with the vision of the wide open spaces, is a special version of a frontier mentality, a vision of riches waiting to be explored and put to use. The specific way in which this is crystallized in Dogon culture is through a set of expectations and practical procedures in dealing with that environment.

Given this notion of open resources, the question is whether they can be mastered, and secondly, how. Consequently, the Dogon view of their environment stipulates two criteria: whether parts or aspects of their surroundings are 'manageable' or not, and whether they are 'usable' or not. The first criterion decides if – in the opinion of the Dogon – one can 'do something about' it, if one is master of this part of the environment. This does not always imply that production should result from the human interference; any kind of change will do. The hand of the Dogon should be visible. The environment is sized up as to whether one can 'make something of it', or as the Dogon expression goes, if one can *yegere*, arrange matters, put things straight. The difference between an environment brought into harmony with the people living in it, and one where this is not done, is crucial.

The second criterion, 'being usable', decides whether something productive can be done with the environment. If a stretch of land, a field for instance, can bring about a substantial crop, it is usable. If a similar stretch of land would not yield much crop at all it is unusable. The Dogon terms for this distinction are simply 'good' and 'bad'. The same holds for rocks that can be used for building, and those boulders that cannot be split up, or put to any other use.

The first criterion is crucial. On the whole the Dogon consider their environment manageable: if people work, if they truly exert themselves, they can shape their own basis of living, their survival, subdue the untamed bush. A strong work ethic is part of this view: one who works, survives. Thus they can perceive a much larger proportion of the environment as manageable than would be expected by an outsider. Of course, the basic elements, the escarpment, the plateau, the scree and dunes are given entities, but within this large cadre most things are not given. For an ascent up on to the plateau, for instance, the Dogon are not content to be dependent on nature; where there is no ascent, they make one, shattering larger boulders with their self-fabricated gunpowder into medium-sized rocks, and installing ladders and ropes. Building houses on the scree involves shattering large rocks, shaping them into convenient sizes, before even starting to build. Another, individual, example: someone who needed water for his cattle asked where he could find water. The answer was that he could find it at a depth of 60 metres. His reaction: no problem, that is just two months' digging (1 metre a day). Likewise, according to the Dogon any field can be cultivated, if only people exert themselves in manuring it.

The second criterion, whether a particular part of the environment can be used or not, is of course partly dependent on manageability, but not wholly so. For instance, the stretch of land just beyond the in-field zone is not used for cultivation, because, according to the Dogon, the land is not good. Manuring would help, but that is not possible because of lack of cattle. In their view the land has hardly ever been used at all. Still, research on aerial photographs and soil composition reveals that the fields have been used very intensively, in fact have been overused, in the past. Their depletion has made regeneration very slow. Another, quite spectacular example is onion farming on the plateau. The Dogon are justly famous for it. When water is trapped behind a barrage, the Dogon have the immediate border of this small man-made lake to cultivate. Often this is just naked rock. From kilometres away they bring in soil to lay on the rock. Then small stones are sought, cut and lined up in order to mark out the cultivation squares. Manure and fertilizer are added to the soil, and finally the bulbs are planted. Then the actual work starts, watering the fields by carrying pots or calabashes from the well or lake to the field, each full morning for three months. It is a Herculean task, but one deemed normal for the Dogon. So even the inhospitable rock is in principle usable, and – if so defined – the Dogon will *yegere*, manage, too, in order to make it usable.

Within this framework, the agricultural knowledge of the Dogon is practical, factual, detailed and personal. Their knowledge includes a detailed distinction between many minute varieties of the main crops, especially millet. They distinguish on the basis of smell and taste, as well as adaptability to specific terrain, even specific fields. In the in-fields mixed cultivation of several crops is guided by a detailed view on what crops should go together and which definitely not. Rotation in the out-fields follows a distinct pattern (beans, millet, millet, fonio). The start of the cycle, the end of the fallow period, is indicated by specific grasses appearing on the fields. The end of the cycle is shown by the emergence of specific weeds between the millet or sorghum. The start of the cultivation season is known by both counting moons, watching the exact spot of the sunset and waiting for the migration of a specific bird (*ana sasa*). During the cultivation season, the Dogon farmers are guided by a detailed knowledge of manure, both for the millet fields as well as for the onion patches.

This knowledge is practical. As subsistence farmers the Dogon are survival oriented, aiming at – in western terms – an optimization of the chances for survival, not at a maximization of the harvest. They do so by spreading risks; sowing several sorghum varieties, maize, groundnuts, fonio, sesamum, even rice, with their main crop of millet they are sure that though certainly some crops will not yield a harvest, some will. For the millet, their mainstay for survival, which is best adapted to dry conditions, they choose several varieties with differing drought resistance; some will yield. Agriculture is to do with survival, not profit, a tendency which does not make them rich, but has the great advantage of keeping them alive, as it has done throughout the past centuries.

Knowledge is factual and detailed. The Dogon have a crystallized view of the general characteristics and exigencies of each of their crops: what amount of rain is needed, the dangers they run from crop diseases and parasites, the amount of manure needed, the way in which one crop combines with others, etc. In even more detail, Dogon farmers know from the look of each field what has been grown on it, what the yield was, what manure serves best and how much weeding is needed. They know what plants should appear before starting cultivation in general, and where to expect those grasses on that particular field. They know the slight depressions in the dunes where they can bury a pot to catch some rain for drinking when out in the fields for days. When tending their onion gardens, they know at what stage of growth what type of manure is to be used (they distinguish between at least eight different types of fertilizer, ranging from goat dung to termite mounds, from guano to pounded phosphate-holding rocks), and they know when the bulb is mature by judging the state of the flowers.

Knowledge is personal. A farmer has this knowledge about his own fields, the fields he uses. When the fields change hands, the former user is expected to indicate the best use of the field to its new 'owner'. As the fields fall into well-definable categories (scree, valley floor, in-field dune, out-field) this personal knowledge consists of some details per field, on top of the general knowledge pertaining to that particular terrain.

The above mentioned qualities make for a very open system of local knowledge. Though some generalization as to categories of fields, crops and other resources are made, the focus is on the individual and his or her knowledge of his or her personal environment. Local knowledge, at least in agriculture, is less dependent on 'tradition' (whatever that may be) than on personal experience; it is a process of information selection and evaluation, more than a body of ready-made notions and values. Trial and error is much more important than fixed ideas, as the system of acquiring knowledge is definitely non-scholastic.

Thus, local Dogon knowledge quickly incorporates new elements. The precise knowledge gained on crop rotation and soil refertilization can serve as an example. Out-field cultivation started this century and the related detailed, practical knowledge must have been generated in that restricted time span. Characteristically, the Dogon emphatically state that they have 'always known it', a statement indicating – in my view – the social value and respectability of that body of knowledge (they use the same expression when describing new rituals that have been incorporated). A more recent example is onion farming. The know-how, which is considerable, has been built up in decades, not in centuries. Thus a relatively new problem with onions – storage – has not been resolved yet and still is in the first trial-and-error phase. Finally, a totally new crop, such as the water-melons grown in a falaise village for three years, presents a new problem for the Dogon: determining when the melon is ripe is difficult, and the Dogon have as yet not found the clue (the people in the inner delta of the Niger have no problem at all in this respect).

The Dogon expression for knowledge is just as flexible: 'knowing the word'. On the one hand this points to the function of words in traditions, for knowing the stories of migration and strife that led to the existence of the Dogon at the falaise. On the other hand it means simply 'knowing the language', that is, knowing the ways to formulate new thoughts. Both aspects, the traditional as well as the everyday are about equally important in Dogon society. There is, however, some notion that women focus more on the practical, flexible words (*sò*), and men more on the traditional, fixed words.

So two aspects of Dogon agricultural knowledge can be discerned. They view their ecosystem as stable, even if geared to a situation of the past. Rituals and some myths form part of this collective memory, this fixed knowledge. This part of the Dogon view of the environment is part of a long-standing historic process. In the paragraph on history we sketched the main challenges on Dogon society up to the present. They have lived for centuries in a situation where resources were visible but out of bounds, where the main restriction on adaptation was manpower. The Dogon answer was to collectivize labour and to privatize knowledge. Within the general framework of their overall view of their environment, this specific and privatized knowledge in combination with the joining of labour forces proved highly adaptive. It enabled them to fill effectively all possible niches in their environment, as individuals ultimately decided on the use of any particular resource. This combination, which is just the opposite of the course western society has charted, also allows for a very flexible input of labour. It was essential that this privatization was founded not on a body of fixed knowledge but on a system of permanent information assessment, a procedure to gather, evaluate and implement practical, detailed and small-scale information. One cost could have been that this practice allowed some things to be forgotten, such as the results of past trials and errors. However, the collectivization of labour might have mitigated this tendency somewhat. Still, the gap between the inflexibility of the general view and the flexibility of the privatized knowledge is apparent, and there seems to be no intermediary between these two fields of knowing. The traditional general knowledge is not confronted with the personal, flexible information and remains unchallenged. This fits in with a general characteristic of Dogon thinking, as exemplified in their religion, namely its cumulative, non-systemic character (van Beek 1982). Diverging notions are not reasoned out, and new elements can be introduced without change in the whole system. Just as there is no theology in Dogon religion, there is no systematization of Dogon ethno-science. This may put a question mark over some fundamental anthropological ideas on cultural integration.

One major problem is that of scale. The combination of private knowledge and public work works well in small-scale society, with a reasonably slow rate of change; there, personal experience not only seems but often in fact is the most reliable source of information, and the personal experiences of the various members of society do not diverge too much. Up into the late colonial period the Dogon villages were pretty much autonomous units, where the ecology of one village (especially the scree villages) was the microcosm of the ecology of the whole group. This system is breaking up, as we explained before. Foreign aid has built at least fifty-five barrages on the plateau, and many more are under construction. This, combined with the difficulties in growing cereals in the dry years of the recent past, has changed the ecology of the plateau villages. Quickly, they are becoming onion farming villages. No longer does the money gained from onion farming serve as a financial supplement for a subsistent unit. Now cereals, millet and sorghum have to be bought at the market in order to feed the family. In onion farming, fertilizer, bought through government channels, replaces manure. The result is that wherever barrages are present villages are built. The plateau attracts a population at a level well above its present carrying capacity in subsistence. The farmers become wholly dependent on the external onion market and on the supply of fertilizer. They no longer have control over their fields, as these are provided for by foreign aid, for the construction as well as major maintenance of the dams. This process, which I have called cultural proletarization elsewhere (van Beek 1986) is easily discernible in the larger settlements. The smaller villages with restricted water storage still have a more mixed economy.

The subsistence food for the plateau has to come from the plains. There villages concentrate on growing millet, and in the good years do so with good results. The development of a market for millet, formerly only produced and consumed within the extended family, has led to extensive millet production. More land has come under cultivation, fallowing periods are being shortened, so the strain on the environment is growing, and the desert is close.

It is on the escarpment that both parts of the Dogon ecology still are in some balance: subsistence cultivation-cum-onion farming; this may be due in large part to emigration. Another reason may be that the escarpment is out of reach of motorized transport, which stimulates cash-crop farming. However, here drought (and locusts in 1986) have struck more often than among the other villages. Thus, present Dogon villages no longer are a microcosmic representation of the whole area. Most of them represent one variation in an interdependent system with specialized parts. The problem then is, that the fixed knowledge of the general view of environment as well as the specific systems of knowledge have no way of coping with the larger scale of Dogon society. Within the local situation the traditional attitude may be adequate, but it can be destructive for the system as a whole.

This implies that ignorance in Dogon agricultural knowledge has at least three aspects. First, several parts of their environment are not stipulated as part of the (agri)cultural process and, as such, may be irrelevant, and are kept out of the information-processing. For some period the zone between the in-fields and the out-fields remained beyond attention: people simply did not bother about it. Second, new elements are still in the trial-and-error stage; the cultivation of water-melons may serve as an example. Finally, the most important lack of information is the inability to cope with information beyond the community level. For development purposes all three causes of ignorance are relevant, though the 'ignorance of scale' is by far the most important.

It is this problem of scale that leads towards destruction of the ecosystem in the plains, and a very rapid one at that. On the plateau the Dogon general view and local knowledge stimulate an ever increasing and intensifying onion culture, to the detriment of their own chances for long-term survival. At the falaise it leads to the desertion of those villages where the conditions for survival actually may be best. Thus, the very survival value of Dogon knowledge processing leads towards a strategy in which the means for present survival endanger their existence in the long run. This sacrifice of the future for the sake of the present is a typical feature of peasantification and of cultural proletarization.

NOTES

1 Research among the Dogon has been carried out in 1979–80, 1982, 1983, 1984, 1985, 1987, 1989 and 1991 and made possible through grants of the National Foundation for the Advancement of Tropical Studies (WOTRO), the University of Utrecht, Time-Life, Agence Aigle and Dutch Television (VPRO).
2 For a more extensive treatment of the Dogon view of their environment see chapter by W. E. A. van Beek and P. M. Banga in E. Croll and D. Parkin (eds) (1992) *Bush Base: Forest Farm – Culture, Environment and Development*, London: Routledge.

REFERENCES

Bedaux, R. M. A. (1982) 'Tellem, reconnaissance d'une civilisation préhistorique', *Journal de la Société des Africanistes* 23 (2): 113–34.
van Beek, W. E. A. (1982) *Spiegel van de mens: Religie en Antropologie*, Assen: Van Gorcum.
—— (1986) 'L'état ce n'est pas nous: cultural proletarization in Cameroon', W. van Binsbergen, F. Reyntjens and G. Hesseling (eds) *State and Local Community in Africa, ASDOC Studies* 2–3–4: 65–88.
—— (1993) 'The innocent sorcerer: coping with evil in two African societies (Kapiski and Dogon)', in T. D. Blakely, W. E. A. van Beek and D. L. Thompson (eds) *Religion in Africa: Experience and Expression*, London: J. Currey.
Bryson, R. A. and Murray, T. J. (1977) *Climates of Hunger*, University of Wisconsin Press.
Dieterlen, G. (1942) *Les Ames des Dogons*, Paris: Presses Universitaires de France.
Hardesty, D. (1978) *Ecological Anthropology*, New York: Wiley.
Paulme, D. (1948) *L'organisation sociale des Dogon*, Paris: Presses Universitaires de France.
Smaldone, J. (1978) *Warfare in the Sokoto Caliphate: historical and sociological perspectives*, Cambridge: Cambridge University Press.

3 Cultivation: knowledge or performance?

Paul Richards

AGAINST LOCAL KNOWLEDGE

It is a characteristic feature of the oneness of the modern world that indigenous cultivation should have come to be thought of as grounded in local knowledge. To technologically-minded improvers this local knowledge is often or mainly outmoded, and something to be replaced. Anthropological romantics, by contrast, in establishing their credentials as priests of humanistic plurality, are apt to celebrate it. Both groups are thereby liable to credit local knowledge of agriculture with a spurious epistemic independence, as if it were the regular outcome of a process of 'peasant intellectualism' parallel in some way to the processes of intellectualism operating in North American or European academic life. Intellectualist movements arise from time to time within communities of small-scale cultivators (Feierman 1990, Richards 1992) but their achievements are dangerously undervalued by assuming that small-scale cultivators *necessarily* abound in agro-ecological wisdom. This assumption seems to me to run the risk of ethnocentricism. Stephen Marglin (1991) has drawn attention to the historically localized peculiarities that led to a rather strict segregation between *episteme* and *techne* as forms of knowledge in western society. Nineteenth-century Victorians, for example, had good reason to try to insulate the reflective privileges of intellectuals from the authority claims of builders, plumbers and other purveyors of practice in a world undergoing rapid material transformation (cf. Galton's statistical work on the absent-mindedness of professors, gaze averted from the contents of their breakfast tables, their attention devoted to higher matters). But I see no reason why anthropologists should continue to stigmatize cultivators with an intellectual dichotomy redolant of the class-based parochialism of later-Victorian imperialists.

What I try to suggest in this chapter is that much of the material that gets woven by the anthropologist (or other observer) into a satisfyingly complete, free-standing 'indigenous agricultural knowledge system' is often nothing of the sort, but rather the product of a set of improvisational capacities called forth by the needs of the moment. It is hard for observers to appreciate what is often obvious (and therefore hardly worth stating) to performers. This leads academic bystanders into a fallacy of misplaced abstraction: the making of intellectual mysteries out of situations and activities whose practical import is obvious to all but the observer.

Among a number of reasons for deploring the prevalence of misplaced abstraction in anthropological accounts of local knowledge two stand out. First, the resultant over-interpretation tends to obscure important, if probably quite rare, cases of genuine 'local knowledge' arising from real but place- or epoch-specific differences in the way the world works (Hacking 1982). There are a number of such particularisms in agro-ecology (Richards 1985) even if the historical examples are at times hard to interpret owing to an accelerated pace of recent environmental change (Richards 1991). Second, misplaced abstraction tends further to cramp our (already limited) understanding of human improvisational capacities. Why is it that some people can pick up an instrument and play where others struggle half a lifetime to coax from it a reasonable tune? How is it that some people seem to be good at finding their way through unfamiliar terrain or coping with unprecedented circumstances that would leave others hopelessly lost or panicked? Through the exercise of what talent or instinct is it possible for some people safely to negotiate political minefields or moments of great social awkwardness where others would achieve nothing more than embarrassment or acrimonious confrontation? Why can some people make frail plants flourish where others only have to raise a watering can for them to die? We tend to talk in vague terms about having a musical 'ear', a 'talent' for diplomacy, a 'sense' of the situation, a 'feel' for the problem, a 'golden touch' or 'green fingers', but without much apparent idea of how, if at all, the skills thus invoked are related to 'knowledge systems' more conventionally defined.

The purpose of this chapter is to direct attention to the need for more precise ethnography of these kinds of performance skills, as a necessary antidote to the fallacy of misplaced abstraction, if the anthropology of knowledge is to progress beyond the by now well-rehearsed limits set by the rationality debate on the one hand (Hollis and Lukes 1982) and an anti-scientific, post-modern, culture theory on the other (Geertz 1983). I focus in particular on a number of agricultural examples from West Africa, and apologize in advance for a chapter that still bears the marks of its origins as a contribution to a conference specifically concerned with agricultural experimentation (a summary of the original paper appears in Chambers, Pacey and Thrupp 1989). My concern now, as then, is to understand how farmers cope with difficulty and *do well*, rather than with the more usual dualism – technical correctness versus social expressiveness – at issue in many debates concerning local knowledge.

I ought to add (though it will soon become clear) that in calling attention to the importance of performance skills as an element in the debate about local knowledge I see this as quite separate from 'performance studies' in anthropology as developed by Victor Turner and others (e.g. Turner 1974). There, the focus is placed upon the dramaturgy and interpretation of ritual – with (in effect) purpose, content and outcome of the specific genres of performance commanding the lion's share of attention. My primary concern is with improvisational capacities in the technological arena. More generally (in the larger project to which this chapter is a preamble) I am interested in the 'musical' skills and 'embodied' capacities that permit continuous flow in human performance of all kinds. With some surprising exceptions (Needham 1967), anthropologists interested in ritual performance have tended to shy away from the issue of bodily capacities, perhaps fearing the influence of the cruder forms of biological reductionism. There are recent welcome signs, however, that the strict anthropological Cartesianism that has so far rendered embodied skills intellectually suspect (Geertz 1983, Rouget 1985) is beginning to come under effective critical scrutiny (Ingold 1991).

PERFORMANCE IN WEST AFRICAN RICE FARMING

In the rice-growing zone of West Africa agricultural research effort since the 1930s has concentrated upon varietal selection. Encouragement to farmers to grow improved varieties has been a key component in a number of rural development initiatives. But in upland farming conditions, and with uncertain supplies of fertilizer, the yield of improved varieties rarely outstrips local cultivars by more than 10 to 20 per cent.

In the Mende village of Mogbuama in central Sierra Leone, where I first carried out field-work in 1982–3, no farmer used any improved varieties (apart from in a few small plots for which I had supplied seed). In that year, and leaving out of account total failures, rice yields on the best five upland farms in Mogbuama exceeded yields on the poorest five by about 50 to 60 per cent (Richards 1986). The sample (thirty household farms) was not greatly differentiated by size or social status. The major constraint determining success or failure was timely access to labour (and most especially access to the skills of co-operative labour groups during the planting season). Each farm would be ready for planting in its own time, depending on soil type and when the farmer had opted to set fire to the felled vegetation. But the window of opportunity for planting is restricted. A cleared farm left too long before planting is choked by weeds, or seed is lost before it germinates on account of the heavy rains. Hence the need for a large labour group to ensure the bulk of the farm is planted in one go at an auspicious moment.

To secure the timely services of a labour group it is necessary both to command a range of social skills (to know how to talk to convenors) and to be in a position to offer the right kind of food and other perquisites. Labour groups will down tools if the food is considered inadequate. The rules are explicit. The group must be offered rice, and the sauce must contain fish or meat and sufficient salt. Some groups have a 'company doctor' who tests the food on offer to decide whether the work should proceed. Alcohol, cigarettes and cola are additional inducements to timely and careful work.

It is often tricky for the farmer to raise the necessary resources. The assistance of a labour group in making a household upland rice farm is needed when stocks from the previous harvest are running low and food and cash are in short supply. One way to cope with this difficulty is to convert 'spare' labour time during the dry season into an asset encashable during the period of pre-harvest hunger. One such asset is *omole*, a local liquor distilled from palm wine. This stores well, commands a ready market for cash, and can be used as an additional inducement in recruiting labour groups. A Mogbuama woman who distilled large quantities of the stuff frequently had a largish informal work group of (somewhat hung-over) young men helping on her farm, to clear off their previous evening's drinking debts. The process of putting together an agricultural work party, therefore, is not totally unlike the throwing of another kind of party that regularly enlivens Mende village life: informal dancing on moonlit evenings after the harvest. The parallel is especially striking in the case of those labour groups that work to musical accompaniment (Richards 1986). In this case the drummers map out in beats the steps of the young men hoeing in the rice after it is broadcast, and a singer praises the swift and chides the tardy, much as the musicians for a dance cue, and comment upon, the perfectly-timed changes of step that so delight the lively snake of participants in the moon-lit conga around the village square.

Agricultural researchers spend much time measuring rice yields, and perhaps (like anthropologists – cf. Little 1967) not a little time enjoying music or dance under the harvest moon. But I have come across few measurements relating to the significance of music in agricultural production. What, for example, is the impact of drumming on the efficiency of agricultural labour? I made some measurements of this while taking part in rice planting in Mogbuama. This resulted in several sets of figures relating to areas planted and hoed by a labour company working separate stints with and without music. Per hour, 20 per cent more ground was covered by the same group of people (on the same soil type, a crucial factor in determining the efficiency of planting work) when accompanied by drumming than without it.

This figure is intriguing, since it suggests that the difference between getting *performance factors* right and wrong in African hoe agriculture may have the same order of magnitude of impact on productivity as might the adoption of new varieties, or other research station inputs, in typical small-farmer circumstances. By and large, however, agricultural research seems to have ignored performance as an area for systematic enquiry – but surely not for want of basic evidence. The ethnographic literature is rich in relevant instances, including accounts of the part played by music in agricultural production or of the connection between brewing and labour organization (Ames 1959, Bassett 1988, O'Laughlin 1973, Saul 1983, Sharpe 1982). It is the significance, not the existence, of this material that seems to have eluded agriculturalists working on tropical small-farmer cultivation systems. I was once asked to participate in a conference on the contribution of anthropology to farming systems research, organized by one of the international centres for tropical agricultural research. But the paper a colleague and I submitted on agricultural labour groups in Nigeria and Sierra Leone was rejected on the grounds that it was 'too anthropological' and of insufficient practical interest to agricultural researchers. Why? Why should the performance of agricultural work seem irrelevant to applied scientists interested in improving small-holder farming systems?

Some of the fault, surely, must lie on the social science side of the fence. Anthropologists, and others interested in social agency, tend to set up their arguments and analyses as if they are offering an alternative (contemplative, interpretive) way of looking at the world, a vision opposed to that vouchsafed by science with its commitment to intervention as a test of understanding (Geertz 1983). But an adequate theory of performance must be based on an understanding of the way in which theory and practice (including theory and practice in science) intertwine. Bourdieu (1978) points the way, but even he seems unconcerned with the implication that an adequate theory of practice may have important practical implications, that it should facilitate *better* performance. This seems perverse. Is it not a contradiction in terms to posit a contemplative theory of practice – to posit silent music? Unless the anthropologist aspires to the role of the talentless music critic, unable to play a note, an interest in the ethnography of performance carries with it an implicit commitment to a valid 'applied' anthropology, capable (in the present case) of influencing policy and practice in agricultural science. (Perhaps a better guide in this regard than Bourdieu is Jacques Attali's remarkable book *Noise: a Political Economy of Music* (1979), an intriguing cultural manifesto by the economist now in charge of the international bank for the economic reconstruction of eastern Europe!) My purpose, then, is to suggest that the search for an adequate theory of agricultural performance is an essential complement to applied agricultural research. In particular, I want to press the point that 'local knowledge', when it seems incomprehensible from a technical point of view, is sometimes 'performance knowledge' rather than (so-called) 'indigenous technical knowledge' (Howes and Chambers 1979), and to point to the confusion liable to stem from their conflation.

INTERCROPPING: PLAN OR PERFORMANCE?

Let me try further to clarify what I mean by 'performance knowledge' with an example that will at the same time illustrate how distant normal agricultural research sometimes is from performance thinking. The example draws on Michael Watts' discussion (in his book *Silent Violence*, 1983) of the way in which farmers in a village in Katsina, northern Nigeria compensate for the effects of poor rainfall. Hausa farmers make a series of rolling adjustments to drought. If the rains are late or stop unexpectedly the first planting of sorghum may fail. The farm is replanted as many times as is necessary to secure germination, or until the farmer no longer has any seed left. At each replanting a different seed mix may be tried, better to fit available resources to changing circumstances. As need arises or resources permit the farmer may then hedge or criss-cross the main plot with various back-up and insurance crops.

Farming-systems researchers might imagine themselves to be on familiar ground at this point (cf. Norman 1967). They would tend (so Watts argues) to treat each of these resulting cropping patterns as a predetermined design, as if in effect each farmer had said, 'This year, to minimize the risks from drought, I will plant so much sorghum, so much millet, so much cassava'. But this is to confuse intention and result, to misunderstand what has *happened*. The crop mix – the layout of different crops in the field – is not a design, but a result. It is a completed performance. What transpired in this performance, and why, can only be interpreted by reconstructing the sequence of events in time. Each mixture is a historical record of what happened to a specific farmer on a specific piece of land in a specific year. It is not the outcome of a prior body of 'indigenous technical knowledge' in which farmers are figuring out variations on a local theory of inter-species ecological complementarity.

In the circumstances of the case described by Watts, researchers interested in intercropping are looking at the wrong problem. They are looking for the *combinatorial logic* in intercropping where what matters to the Hausa farmer is *sequential adjustment* to unpredictable conditions. To understand the register within which the farmer works it is important, in this instance, to distinguish between spatial and temporal logic. It is necessary, in thinking about intercropping, to separate plan and performance. But here we come up against a major difficulty. If conventional agricultural research is not good at coping with performance issues this is for (understandable) methodological reasons. Trials are carried out under experimental controls in which the realities of time and place are 'frozen' to allow for replication and comparison. This is the logic behind setting up and endowing research stations as 'protected' environments. To this extent, they can be described (quite properly) as 'out of time' and 'out of place'. By contrast the issues at stake in performance only become apparent *in time* and *in place* – when, in fact, cultivation is a performance not a rehearsal.

To be fair, plant breeders are fully aware of the need to test for genotype-environment interactions (GE), but generally only screen for biological not cultural factors, and certainly not for sociogenic contingencies as components in that cultural environment, since it will be assumed – perhaps wrongly – that these will be randomly distributed across the population. Even so, GE effects are difficult to pinpoint without sophisticated and complex biometric analysis: the work is sometimes skimped to the detriment of the released innovation (Simmonds 1979). I suspect anyone proposing the addition of a further order of complexity derived from cultural factors to the experimental design for GE would receive a fairly dusty response, not to mention a searching and sceptical scrutiny of her or his statistical competence.

THINKING ABOUT AGRICULTURAL PERFORMANCE

Musical analogies

If agricultural research has so far failed to take on performance issues, where might we look for models and inspiration? Musical performance is potentially a helpful starting point, not only because of the integral role in agricultural performance in many societies, but because it provokes some useful questions about the link between analyst and performer. A parallel can be drawn between musical analysts (critics and scholars) in western concert music and agricultural scientists. Both are high-status intellectuals concerned to understand how their subject-matter works. This analogy breaks down (in a useful and thought-provoking way) when we take account of the performer. Concert artists are at least the equal of musical analysts in power and social standing. The connection between 'research' and 'performance' is open to negotiation between equals: some performers find analysis helpful and interesting, others are openly sceptical about what musicology contributes to their success as performers (Kofi Agawu, personal communication). The sceptics are liable to stress that it is not necessary to understand the physics of the violin (for example) to play the instrument well.

Agricultural research for impoverished small-scale farmers is different. Here the performers are all of low status and little influence. They too may be sceptical about whether research helps, but they have little scope for voicing this scepticism: agricultural researchers are powerful individuals whose confidence that performers would perform better if they hearkened to analytical advice is hard to query. Musicologists approaching concert artists would tend to be more circumspect, and less confident that their insights are in any way relevant to the solution of performance problems.

Robert Chambers (1983) has addressed this crucial issue of the asymmetry between analysts and performers in rural development in poor countries, and has suggested ways of dealing with it by a series of conscious inversions and role reversals directed at trying to get researchers to assume the farmer's standpoint, including a much greater emphasis on on-farm trials and with-farmer research programmes (Chambers, Pacey and Thrupp 1989). Trying to run a farm with the resources available to the typical peasant farmer is doubtless a salutory experience. I would argue, however, that role reversals and running experiments in 'real time', useful though they may prove, will not by themselves be enough. A sustained programme is needed to capture a sense of the way in which farming operations are embedded in a social context with its own cultural logic and imperatives (reasons of the 'last week we had to sell the cow to pay for granny's funeral' kind).

This is a problem with which musical performers are familiar. They study the notes, and practise hard, in order not to make mistakes. They plan ahead how to phrase a melody, co-ordinate entrances, pace the various sections of a piece. But much of this planning may go awry on the night. Faced with the realities of an audience, and the contingencies of a temperamental instrument, or hall with uncertain acoustic, it suddenly seems different. A good musician needs additional skills, therefore: how to overcome nerves, how to avoid panic, how to recover from mistakes. No one, however talented, plays perfectly all the time. The capacity to keep going, and to avoid complete breakdown, is always an important musical skill, however hard to define or teach.

It may be of interest, therefore, to agricultural researchers to pay some attention to the coping skills of musical performers as a prelude to thinking about the coping skills of agricultural performers. An initial survey suggests the range of strategies is unusually wide (Grindea 1978). Some techniques are based on common sense and experience. Others depend on medication or advice from psychologists. A most interesting category comprises 'indigenous' theories developed by performers themselves (Havas 1978). Much of the material in the last category is likely to appear to outsiders to verge on pseudo-scientific mumbo-jumbo. It might seem to serve the same kind of psycho-therapeutic, confidence-boosting, ends as the charm against thieves made by the Azande householder locking up his isolated compound prior to dry-season hunting expeditions (de Schlippe 1956). To the performer grappling with anxiety, stage-fright or nervous tension, scientific respectability is of little significance compared with whether the nostrum works or not.

This helps, I think, put much of what is counted as 'indigenous technical knowledge' in the agricultural field (especially the local knowledge that at times seems closer to magic than science) into a new and useful light. Much of it should be judged and valued not by the standards of scientific analysis, but as self-help therapy through which farmers put their mistakes and disasters behind them without the performance grinding to a halt. Gell (1988) suggests that Trobriand 'garden magic' (as interpreted by Malinowski) takes on a renewed significance if viewed from a performance perspective. Gell's notion is that Trobriand garden magic is a way of conceptualizing and rehearsing ideal outcomes. In effect we are being invited to view magic as pro-active performance therapy (the ritual equivalent of a Beta Blocker!), not a botched theory of natural causes, or a displaced moral philosophy, as some anthropologists would insist. But to treat indigenous technical knowledge (including magic) as a patch-and-mend philosophy in this way is not to diminish its importance. Outsiders tend to undervalue the capacity to keep going under difficulties, and to treat the coping strategies as 'muddling through', not skilled achievements. But in truth – in the appalling, and rapidly deteriorating, environmental and economic conditions faced by many small-scale farmers in the African tropics – even to reproduce the status quo is oftentimes a brilliantly innovative achievement.

Perhaps the gap between farmers and researchers could be closed if those on the formal side of the fence reflected upon one further lesson from the musical field. Technical perfection is no guarantee that the performance will succeed in stirring the imagination of an audience. Conversely, technically imperfect performances are sometimes great performances. The composer Gustav Holst (reflecting upon musical performances by amateurs) was fond of quoting Chesterton's aphorism that 'if a thing is worth doing at all it is worth doing badly'. This comes close to pinning down the essence of what it is about performance that is otherwise so elusive to those whose perspectives are based entirely on an overconfident reading of the claims of 'normal science'.

Social theory: actors and agency

Performance has until recently also eluded social theorists. The field is polarized. Perhaps in response to the overemphasis given by historians to the role of the individual actor or agent in shaping events, economists and sociologists long tended towards an opposite overemphasis on macroscopic structures, in which time and agency were neglected, excluded, or rendered irrelevant by the guiding actions of the 'hidden hand'. An important exception is to be found in the work of the economist and statistician G. L. S. Shackle. Shackle's book *Decision, Order and Time* (1969) queries decision-making orthodoxy as the reduction of possibilities to probabilities, and explores an alternative conceptual framework in which performance concepts (e.g. a notion of surprise in keeping with the Bayesian tradition of statistical reasoning) substitute for approaches to the future based on 'timeless' distributions of statistical orthodoxy.

Other social theorists have made similar journeys. Performance – a focus on the social agent, and how agents achieve results – is a central focus in ethnomethodology, for example. Historically inclined sociologists are in the process of recovering time from the grip of the nineteenth-century epochal Grand Theorists. In this new historical sociology (cf. Peel 1983) social change is a performance enacted upon a stage with carefully delimited socio-economic characteristics, but it is a real performance for all that. The Ijeshas in Peel's account were not simply absorbed into the new colonial order of southern Nigeria. They did more than discover and react to a system imposed by the march of global capitalism. Peel shows how the agents of Ilesha history held their corner in an improvised dialogue that helped make the system to which we now recognize they belong (for a comparable Liberian example, see Breitborde 1991).

The theoretical tendencies behind this kind of account are most thoroughly developed in the work of Anthony Giddens. Giddens (1979) provides a sophisticated analysis of the links between performance (agency), structure (invariant or slowly varying features of institutions) and power (control of resources, capacity to act). Giddens's achievement is to bring the 'power' orientation of Marxian social science, the concern with pattern and meaning in structural-functional and structuralist sociology and anthropology, and the performance concerns of ethnomethodology into common focus. Although power and structure have a great influence on what can be achieved, the stage is dead without the actors. There is overriding significance therefore in the fact that social life is 'the skilled performance of lay actors'. A central point modern social theory requires us to grasp is that social life is simply not corrigible by outside observers. Outsiders may be able to rebuild the set (or to mix a metaphor, move the goalposts) but they do not make the action.

Giddens, like Shackle, moves the debate away from planning (the world of social engineering) to the much more subtle (and perhaps nebulous) world of performance, and how to enhance the capacity of given agents and groups to perform under difficult circumstances (how, for example, to cope with the challenges of a harsh or deteriorating environment). But in this case is there a role for outsiders in assisting at such events? To what extent can and ought outsiders try to influence the directions taken when poor people improvise in the face of drought and famine, for example? Can social agents be intensively coached and trained to perform better under such circumstances? Or, alternatively, if local creativity is decisive in social action, are outside interventions best restricted to psychological and promotional assistance? What (in short) are the prescriptions for agricultural research policy under an agency-oriented theory of social action?

HOW ETHNOGRAPHY OF PERFORMANCE MIGHT HELP

This change of emphasis in social theory has large implications for the way policy-makers conceive of interventions in agriculture and the purpose of agricultural research. Agriculture as a performance is part of the wider performance of social life. It is an obvious characteristic of small-scale resource-poor farmers that there is little scope (however orthodox economics might wish otherwise) to insulate the farm from other aspects of existence. This embeddedness is a feature of all people-intensive small-scale farming systems, irrespective of whether output is for market or household subsistence. Members of the farm household in these circumstances judge the success of their on-farm actions by whether they further their social projects more generally. This in turn means treating seriously the argument that agriculture, as a component within the broader field of social action, is an expert performance of lay actors, and that as social action it is not corrigible by outsiders.

How might agriculturalists begin to understand agriculture as social action, and so determine new (though inevitably more modest) targets for assistance to agricultural activities inextricably bound up in larger social processes? One interesting possibility that I wish to explore in conclusion is the case for giving much greater prominence than hitherto to so-called ethnographic methods in agricultural research. Ethnographic methods (notably participant observation) allow some access to and understanding of performance issues in agriculture. The approach was pioneered in the 1940s by the Belgian agronomist de Schlippe, working among the Azande in southern Sudan. De Schlippe was an agronomist who re-trained as an anthropologist, and wrote what is still one of the best books on performance in African agriculture. One of the great achievements of de Schlippe's *Shifting Cultivation in Africa: the Zande System of Agriculture* (1956) was to show that aspects of life totally alien to the outside viewpoint (e.g. Azande ideas about witchcraft and magic) became much more understandable in the context of the kind of risks engendered by agricultural performance. In this respect his book is an essential complement to the much more famous account by Evans-Pritchard of Azande witchcraft, oracles and magic. He was also one of the first observers to describe explicit agricultural experiments undertaken by African farmers (women in particular) and to present these as coping strategies in the aftermath of system failures.

The attention paid to participants' own theories of performance is a central feature of the ethnography of performance. Ruth Stone's book on the organization of the music event among the Kpelle of Liberia (*Let the Inside be Sweet*, 1982) is a fine example of the genre. In it she pays attention to the way in which sponsors of musical events, and the musicians and audiences, first negotiate a performance, and then to how they understand the business of performing well. This introduces the reader to a range of performance skills, as understood by the Kpelle: timing, turn-taking, how to begin and end, how to cue entrances and exits, how to cope with mistakes, and broader notions of harmony, togetherness and the social and spiritual auspices under which music takes place.

Stone's study is especially interesting when read alongside the work of Bellman (1984) on the social uses of secrecy in Kpelle society. Working within the ethnomethodological tradition, Bellman is concerned with the way the Kpelle use ideas about ritual secrecy to segregate and demarcate distinct discourses. The ability to speak in Kpelle is far from simply a question of possessing relevant knowledge. 'Speaking' is having a licence to perform. Such licences are gained through membership of appropriate closed associations (secret societies). The Bellman study is an immediate corrective to any naïve belief in the power of 'dialogue' to facilitate communication between farmers and agricultural scientists, or in the capacity of such dialogue to achieve generally beneficial results. Researchers would first have to examine the auspices under which any participatory debate took place, and how those auspices were interpreted both by participants and bystanders. Since it is not obvious without careful prior empirical investigation that Kpelle notions on these points would in any way coincide with those of agricultural researchers, the possibilities for cultural mis-communication must be considerable.

So accounts of agricultural performance informed by critical insights of the kind deployed by Stone and Bellman are badly needed in agricultural research. As my material at the outset suggests, one place to start would be the process of labour negotiation. Another is how 'household' farming units are put together. Farm households are not given in social structure. To a large extent they are the result of specific social negotiations (e.g. marriage transactions). In some cases, they are negotiated and renegotiated on an annual basis (Richards 1986). This brings into question the tendency among agricultural economists and farming systems researchers to treat the farm household as a unit of analysis for sampling purposes. Another obvious area for further work is performance under duress. Coping skills in agriculture are often especially difficult to pin down systematically and describe, but there are good accounts in, for example, the work of Michael Watts (1983) on coping with drought and Barbara Harrell-Bond (1986) on refugee resettlement. This latter study is especially noteworthy for having demonstrated the extent to which refugee survival is a skilled social achievement. By describing the contrast in fortunes of self-settled refugees and those in camps run by agencies, Harrell-Bond demonstrates the need above all to sustain that sense of vision and purpose through which social groups retain their capacity to act in a creative and cohesive manner.

CONCLUSION

It is the grounding of this creativity, then, that is, or should be, a central concern in any anthropology of local knowledge. How, in specific ethnographic contexts, are curiosity and inventiveness first kindled in children? What factors are conducive to their maintenance in later life, especially under duress? Are there systematic differences between rich and poor, young and old, men and women, in these areas? What, if anything, can outsiders do to help? The Mende in Sierra Leone are fond of a proverb, 'Say half, leave half unspoken', which says a good deal about their theory of knowledge. It is only too easy, through loose or excessive talk, to paint yourself into a corner. Life and folk are unpredictable. It is generally wise, and almost certainly better tactics, to underspecify a problem, or to reserve some aspects of your case against the day when circumstances change. Flexible performance requires options to be kept open. Life is bogged down by elaborate rules. In difficult circumstances the intellectualization of peasant thought as a fully specified 'local knowledge system' may be more hindrance than help. A celebration of the virtues of dancing might be more to the point. It is here that we are more likely to find appropriate training for those skills of balance, rhythm and articulation necessary to cross life's tightrope in good order, and, with luck, to add a twirl or two as we go.

POSTSCRIPT

This chapter originated in a short (intentionally polemical) essay written for presentation at a conference on complementary methods of agricultural research organized by Robert Chambers and held at the University of Sussex in 1987 (Richards 1989). It was intended to make the case for an ethnographic (even ethnomethodological) approach to agricultural research in a forum largely sympathetic to participatory and dialogical work with farmers, but inclined (as is evident in the published proceedings, Chambers, Pacey and Thrupp 1989) to treat 'local knowledge' in rather straightforward, even naïvely positivistic, terms. Mark Hobart was kind enough to suggest that the paper might be equally relevant to the discussion in his workshop on anthropological approaches to 'local knowledge'. Having struggled to revise it to fit these new requirements I am conscious that I have failed to eliminate the signs of its original purpose, and that (for an anthropological audience) I will surely be judged guilty of re-stating the obvious in a number of respects. I ought also to add that in 1987, whereas I knew something about the impact of agricultural research on farmers, it was only subsequently that I studied an agricultural research community at first hand. I now know it is a mistake to take the propaganda of bio-technology at face value. Some plant breeders are quite sceptical about the extent to which their discipline will be transformed by these new procedures. Simmonds (1979), in his well-known and highly regarded textbook on plant breeding, treats the methods of bio-technology as useful additions to the breeder's armoury of technique, but evolution is likely to have the last word on those who imagine they have unlimited powers to design and redesign successful plants at will. Simmonds is explicit that only part of plant breeding is an exact science based on the manipulation of major genes according to Mendelian principles. Important attributes such as durable resistence to pathogens often turns out to be under the control of polygenes 'captured' by breeders only through a combination of sophisticated biometrical analysis and what Simmonds refers to as 'general experience, instinct and "eye" '. One of the purposes of my argument above is to suggest that there may be benefit in allowing the breeder's 'eye' to be schooled by a thorough knowledge of local performing traditions.

REFERENCES

Ames, D. W. (1959) 'Wolof co-operative work groups; in W. R. Bascom and M. Herskovits (eds) *Continuity and Change in African Cultures*, Chicago: University of Chicago Press.

Attali, J. (1979) *Noise: a Political Economy of Music*, trans. B. Massumi, Manchester: Manchester University Press.

Bassett, T. (1988) 'Breaking up the bottlenecks in food-crop and cotton cultivation in northern Côte d'Ivoire', *Africa* 58: 147–74.

Bellmann, B. (1974) *The Language of Secrecy; Symbols and Metaphors in Poro Ritual*, New Brunswick, N. J.: Rutgers University Press.

Bourdieu, P. (1978) *Outline of a Theory of Practice*, trans. R. Nice, Cambridge: Cambridge University Press.

Breitborde, L. B. (1991) 'City, countryside, and Kru ethnicity, *Africa* 61: 186–210.

Chambers, R. (1983) *Rural Development: Putting the Last First*, London: Longman.

Chambers, R., Pacey, A. and Thrupp, L. -A. (1989) *Farmer First: Farmer Innovation and Agricultural Research*, London: Intermediate Technology Publications.

de Schlippe, P. (1956) *Shifting Cultivation in Africa: the Zande System of Agriculture*, London: Routledge & Kegan Paul.

Feierman, S. (1990) *Peasant Intellectuals: Anthropology and History in Tanzania*, Madison, Wis.: University of Wisconsin Press.

Geertz, C. (1983) *Local Knowledge: Further Essays in Interpretive Anthropology*, New York: Basic Books.

Gell, A. (1988) 'Technology and Magic', *Anthropology Today* 4 (2): 6–9.

Giddens, A. (1979) *Central Problems in Social Theory: Action, Structure and Contradiction in Social Analysis*, London: Macmillan.

Grindea, C. (ed.) (1978) *Tensions in the Performance of Music*, London: Kahn & Averill.

Hacking, I. (1982) 'Language, truth and reason', in M. Hollis and S. Lukes (eds) *Rationality and Relativism*, Oxford: Blackwell.

Harrell-Bond, B. (1986) *Imposing Aid: Emergency Assistance to Refugees*, Oxford: Oxford University Press.

Havas, K. (1978) 'The release from tension and anxiety in string playing', in C. Grindea (ed.) *Tensions in the performance of music*, London: Kahn & Averill.

Hollis, M. and Lukes, S. (eds) (1982) *Rationality and Relativism*, Oxford: Blackwell.

Howes, M. and Chambers, R. (1979) 'Indigenous Technical Knowledge: analysis, implications and issues', *IDS Bulletin* 10(2): 5–11.

Ingold, T. (ed.) (1991) *Human Worlds are Culturally Constructed?* Group for Debates in Anthropological Theory, Manchester: Social Department of Anthropology, University of Manchester.

Little, K. (1967) *The Mende of Sierra Leone*, London: Routledge.

Marglin, S. (1991) 'Two essays on agriculture and knowledge', *Proceedings*, Workshop on 'Agricultural knowledge systems and the role of extension', Institut für Agrarsoziologie, Universität Hohenheim, Stuttgart, Bad Boll, 21–4 May 1991.

Needham, R. (1967) 'Percussion and transition, *Man*, N.S. 2: 606–14.

Norman, D. (1967) *An Economic Study of Three Villages in Zaria Province*, 1, *Land and Labour Relationships*, Zaria: Institute of Agricultural Research.

O'Laughlin, M. B. (1973) 'Mbum beer parties: structure of production and exchange in an African social formation', Ph.D. thesis, Yale University.

Peel, J. D. Y. (1983) *Ijeshas and Nigerians: the Incorporation of a Yoruba Kingdom 1890s–1970s*, Cambridge: Cambridge University Press.

Richards, P. (1985) *Indigenous Agricultural Revolution: Ecology and Food Production in West Africa*, Hutchinson: London.

—— (1986) *Coping with Hunger: Hazard and Experiment in a West African Rice-farming System*, London: Allen & Unwin.

—— (1989) 'Agriculture as a performance', in R. Chambers, A. Pacey and L.-A. Thrupp (eds) *Farmer First: Farmer Innovation and Agricultural Research*, London: Intermediate Technology Publications.

—— (1991) 'Mende names for rice: cultural analysis of an agricultural knowledge system', *Proceedings*, Workshop on 'Agricultural knowledge systems and the role of extension', Institut für Agrarsoziologie, Universitaet Hohenheim, Stuttgart, Bad Boll, 21–4 May 1991.

—— (1992) 'Landscapes of dissent: Ikale and Ilaje country, 1870–1950', in J. F. A. Ajayi and J. D. Y. Peel (eds) *Peoples and Empires in Africa: Essays in Memory of Michael Crowder*, Harlow: Longman.

Rouget, G. (1985) *Music and Trance: a Theory of the Relations between Music and Possession* trans. B. Biebuyck, Chicago: University of Chicago Press.

Saul, M. (1983) 'Work parties, wages and accumulation in a Voltaic village', *American Ethnologist* 10: 77–96.

Shackle, G. L. S. (1969) *Decision, Order and Time*, Cambridge: Cambridge University Press.

Sharpe, B. J. (1982) 'Group formation and economic relations amongst some communities in Kauru District [Northern Nigeria]', Ph.D. thesis, University of London.

Simmonds, N. W. (1979) *Principles of Plant Improvement*, London: Longman.

Stone, R. (1982) *Let the Inside be Sweet: the Interpretation of Music Event among the Kpelle of Liberia*, Bloomington, Ind.: University of Indiana Press.

Turner, V. (1974) *Dramas, Fields and Metaphors: Symbolic Action in Human Society*, Ithaca, NY: Cornell University Press.

Watts, M. (1983) *Silent Violence: Food, Famine and Peasantry in Northern Nigeria*, Berkeley, Calif.: University of California Press.

4 His lordship at the Cobblers' well

Richard Burghart

In 1984 I travelled to the eastern Tarai region of Nepal in order to investigate the contexts in which a culturally specific knowledge of hygiene and sanitation could form a basis for primary health care in the region.

My interest in a culturally specific knowledge had been awakened by a cursory reading of the literature on the public health movement in nineteenth-century England. A scientific, and perforce retrospective, reading of this movement reveals that significant public health improvements were not implemented on the basis of modern medical knowledge. The idea of variolation against smallpox, using smallpox lymph, predated Jenner by several centuries. Even the use of cowpox lymph, which Jenner tested under controlled conditions throughout the late 1790s had been developed earlier by a Dorset farmer who inoculated his wife and two sons during the smallpox epidemic of 1774. His inspiration came from a West Country idea that cowherders do not get smallpox. From the early nineteenth century certain ports in England began to organize municipal sanitation systems and a public drinking water supply. The aim was to decrease the risk of illness by improving the quality of the environment; the medical understanding of this risk was cast in terms of the theory of contagion, and later, of miasmas. All this preceded by several decades Pasteur's 1864 lecture at the Sorbonne on the germ theory of life (which was later more agreeably called the germ theory of disease). In sum, the epidemiological data show that smallpox, cholera, typhus, and diptheria were well in decline by the time medical scientists discovered the nature of these pathogenic organisms and hence understood how their forebears had been able to bring these diseases under control, using 'erroneous' ideas.

I found our collective past of interest when thinking about the way in which Eurocentric health workers have tried to organize the collective future of others. The more missionary side of development has sought to 'change people's minds' merely by superimposing ideas more in accordance with scientific consensus. Such an approach is indefensible on various grounds, but it was not until the 1970s that the experience of enough failures encouraged development workers to think that such a policy might also be impracticable. A new strategy emerged in which development workers were to take into account the pre-existing competence of local people to act. The term 'folk competence' was a call to arms of such ambiguity that it was bound to become the next important, uncontroversial idea in development planning. On the one hand, the word competence evoked the spirit of professionalism and legitimated the knowledges of untrained, even illiterate peoples. Development projects could succeed only in so far as they were based on what people already knew, and much of this knowledge might in some sense be 'right'. The legitimation of cultural knowledge fitted the post-colonial rhetoric of the decade: of 'development dialogue', of 'participatory projects', 'collaborative ventures' and so on. On the other hand, the word competence evoked the search for Chomskian deep structures, which would enable the development worker to predict and control the multifarious performances of actors at the local level. Rather than implying that successful development projects entailed a duel agency, research on folk competence held out yet again the hope to development workers of their ultimate control of the entire process.

Although the charitable posture of folk competence advocates affected the style of my own research, I remained a man of little faith as far as competence itself was concerned – either that of the so-called experts or of the so-called people. In the former case my faith was weak because the wisdom of the ages is that the knowledge of one age becomes the ignorance of another. In the latter case I doubted the possibility that 'folk competence' could be codified by social anthropologists. Much knowledge is so local in its construction that it could not be authentically codified. Other forms of knowledge, such as proverbs are fixed, but their application to particular contexts remains indeterminate. Both the sayings 'he who hesitates is lost' and 'haste makes waste' have an intrinsic plausibility; the wisdom lies in applying the code to the appropriate context. Rather than attempt to codify 'folk competence', my aim was merely to investigate the contexts in which local understandings of hygiene and sanitation were 'adaptive' on bio-medical terms. Should certain practices put a people at risk, I would then want to investigate whether this risk might also be expressed in local terms.

Research was carried out in the provincial town of Janakpur, situated some 11 kilometres north of the Bihar frontier in the Tarai region of south-eastern Nepal. The natives of the region speak Maithili, making a language group of some 'twenty million people all but one million of whom live on the Indian side of the frontier. The Tarai is a low flat land, 100 metres above sea level, from which abruptly rises the Siwalik range of the Himalayas. The water table is high, varying from 3 to 10 metres below ground surface, although during the monsoon the table rises almost to a level with the ground. Janakpur has a population of 15,000 people, but it is Nepal's second fastest growing town with a 60 per cent increase in population in the last decade. Like many English towns of the early nineteenth century, its sanitation system and drinking water facilities are still largely rural; as such, they are increasingly inadequate for the town's present size.

Until the 1950s most residents of Janakpur drank water from open wells; at present very few people do. Most prefer handpump water, simply because of its convenience in collection. None the less they complain about its quality. There is too much iron in it, which is said to cause constipation and degenerative liver disease. Women are also suspicious of the film that it leaves on the inside rim of the cooking pot after boiling rice. But despite the litany of complaints about tubewell water, there are only a few families who still drink open well water, mostly on the principle that they have been drinking the water of that well all their life. They feel that a sudden change of habit would harm their health and well-being. I was keen to observe how such people used their well, what they thought of its water, and how they kept the water pure. To this purpose, I canvassed the northern side of town – together with Brikhesh, my research assistant – in search of open, masonry wells that were still in active use.

THE BENEVOLENT LORD AT THE COBBLERS' WELL

'The water from our well used to be sweet.' This was the message Brikhesh reported to me from the Cobblers' hamlet. For several days he had been working his way through the neighbourhood, testing their drinking water. The Cobblers' wives washed their clothes at the open, masonry well in the centre of their hamlet, but they collected their drinking water from the handpump in the adjacent Khatuwe and Muslim hamlets. Either way, the distance to the handpump was a mere 30 metres, and it was probably faster anyway to collect the water from the handpump at that distance than to raise the water in pails from the open well in their own community. But they were irritated by the backbiting of Khatuwe and Muslim women, who treated them as outsiders, blaming them for the queue which formed at the pump. What's more, the handpump, even though a public resource, was a neighbourhood responsibility in that its upkeep – say repairing the handle or renewing the washer – was maintained by neighbourhood collection. The Cobblers had all the benefits, but none of the responsibilities. It was good, there-fore, for each community to have its own well, or handpump.

When I heard that the Cobblers no longer found their well water to be sweet, I thought that this might give me the opportunity to observe the way in which they purified their well water. Together with Brikhesh I went to visit the Cobblers. Their hamlet comprised some twenty thatched homes, built of mud plaster on bamboo wattle, situated beside a brick-paved track which led to the two main commercial streets in the new bazaar nearby. Their open, masonry well was situated in the heart of the hamlet. I explained to the Cobblers my purpose, saying that I had come to their country to test the purity of their water and to look at what kinds of illnesses people sometimes got by drinking bad water. Everyone knows, I asserted, the importance of having pure water to drink, and I wanted to learn what the people of this country thought of their water. When I heard that their water was no longer sweet, I wanted to learn from them how it had lost its sweetness and what they proposed to do about it.

As I explained my interests, a crowd began to form around the Cobblers. By the time I had finished there were others just arriving who wanted to have everything repeated to them. The Cobblers turned and explained to the newcomers on the outer circle that the government had told the sahib to tour the country to see the con-dition of common folk and that my government was going to help the Cobblers clean the well.

As soon as I caught the drift of the conversation I hastened to set matters right. I would be happy to help them clean their well, but I had never mentioned anything about the government. Now everybody thought that I had been sent by some Nepalese ministry. I quickly corrected them, saying that I had not come from Kathmandu. The Cobblers were confused. But if the Nepalese government did not send me then who did? I said that the Nepalese government had approved of my research, but that I was not from Nepal; rather I had come from London. (In Nepal the political capital gives its name to the realm such that *landan* means Great Britain and *khās landan*, or 'particularly London', means London). Everyone seemed relieved. The inner circle explained to the outer that I had been sent by the London government to tour Nepal to report on the condition of common folk. Now the British government was going to help them clean their well. Some even lapsed into hyperbole about how great and compassionate was the British government. This also disturbed me. If such a story were to reach the district commissioner, that an agent of the British government was out helping Nepalese subjects, he might feel that Nepalese sovereignty had been violated. So I hastened to correct them once again. No, I had simply come from London to look into these matters on my own account; later I would submit reports to the Nepalese and British governments, but I was not under any specific instructions from them. I was still my own man. Here I attempted to explain my ethical neutrality, political impartiality, indeed the objectivity of the social sciences. Again confusion spread in the crowd.

Later, on reflecting upon this confusion, I realized that the Cobblers were scripting me for a more lordly role than that of the social scientist. In Hindu society a lord possesses a domain and commands the people who derive their livelihood from that domain. The people whom the lord commands are the instruments of his will. There is a dual movement in the relation of agent and instruments. On the one hand, the lord subjectifies the entire polity in the notion of the body politic, incorporating ruler and ruled. On the other hand, the lord objectifies the polity by casting the instruments as his physical body – the organs of perception and action – while reserving for himself the commanding function of mind. Agency is expressed in passivity. The lord speaks softly and briefly, issuing commands to his subjects – likened to 'limbs' – who enact the instructions. The position of agent and instrument are relative; a man may be lord of his household, but an instrument of his landlord's will who, in turn, may be an instrument of the district commissioner's will. In brief, there is a hierarchy of lordship, which is structured by relations of *sors aiṇḍ fors* ('source and force' as the Nepalese-English expression goes), which are seen to stem ultimately from the political centre of the realm.

The polity is also a moral society, whether this be the polity of Nepal or Britain, or the micropolity of the village or household. The subjects are in some sense dependent upon their lord for their livelihood and well-being. The lord is duty-bound to protect his subjects. Should anyone go hungry, or naked, or should any brahmin be unable to perform a sacrifice for lack of firewood, the lord may be accused of negligence. One of the traditional duties of lordship is the provision of drinking water for the people on his domain. As for the dependents, they are expected to serve their lord with faith and devotion. Since the lord is the mind of the polity and the subjects its limbs, there is no place for criticism, for that would imply that some other mind is at work. Rather the subjects should praise their lord in speech, thereby magnifying his *naim aind phaim* (name and fame) as well as making the world an object of his pleasure.

In the lordly polity there are, however, several persons who disturb orderly relations. There are, of course, lords of adjacent domains who may be either one's enemies or one's allies. Neighbouring lords may send spies to discover what goes on in the 'mind' of another polity. A spy is respected for his principles, but is thought highly dangerous because of his different loyalty and the concealment of his intentions. More despicable than a spy is a man without principles. They come in two role-types: the first of these is the sycophant (*darbārī, camcā*) who praises his lord's 'good name' in society, but behind his lord's back sows intrigue among courtiers and spreads suspicion. The second person is a broker (*dalāl*) or contractor (*ṭikādārī*), who profits from information, making deals on what should be matters of principle. He operates between micropolities, professing no loyalty but to his purse. The term broker (*dalāl*) is a term of political abuse in Maithili.

I soon realized that my attempt to establish the autonomy of the social sciences among the Cobblers was doomed. By stating that I was the instrument neither of the British nor of the Nepalese government, I had succeeded in creating the impression that I was that most cursed of political impresarios, a broker, who had come to Janakpur to play the two governments off against each other. Faced with a choice, I opted for lordship. Admittedly I was but a minor lord when compared with my sovereign Maharani Ailizabet and my patron in Nepal, Maharaja Birendra, but for the Cobblers I had the virtue of being a more accessible presence than the great lords of London and Nepal. My complicity was sealed when I stopped 'correcting' the Cobblers about my position, and ceased to object when they referred to me as 'his Lordship'. My research assistant Brikesh, who was also rapidly becoming my friend, became from the Cobblers' point of view my *diwān* or *mainajar*, who oversaw my daily affairs. In this respect I realized that by having dispatched

Brikhesh to the Cobblers' hamlet to collect water samples, I had –
by virtue of my manual passivity – already taken on the role of
'lord'. So there we were – anthropologist, assistant and informants
– as a micropolity of lord, *mainajar* and people. As one excited
Cobbler said, 'His Lordship has come to us, and now our well has
started up again. So we will all drink the well water.' By my grace
the water would soon taste sweet.

THE COBBLERS' KNOWLEDGE ABOUT CLEANING A WELL

Neighbourhood wells are identified with the people who draw water
from them, not only because the water nourishes and sustains the
community but also because women gather to bathe, wash clothes
and scour their cooking pots at the well. Being untouchable, and
of rather low caste even among untouchables, the Cobblers have
always had difficulty in procuring drinking water, for higher caste
neighbourhoods have been reluctant to grant them access to their
own caste-community water source. Moreover, being ever mindful
that the reputation of a caste is, in part, bound up with the reputation of its women, many caste communities want to have their
own neighbourhood well so that they are in a position to protect
the public arena of their women.

The Cobblers are proud of their open, masonry well. They had
it dug in the 1930s after having raised sufficient funds by public
suscription. According to their accounts, it was dug to a depth of
about 10 metres and is 2.15 metres in diameter. At the turn of the
1980s, in the course of the town council electoral campaign, the
Cobblers promised their votes to a candidate who undertook, if
elected, to have the council supply bricks and cement so that the
Cobblers might improve their well. Everyone delivered on their
promises. At present the well has been completely renewed at the
top and is encircled by a raised brick and cement platform, some
five feet wide, which provides a clean surface, free of mud, on
which to bathe and wash. Their open well is one of the finest in
town, although it must be borne in mind that most people still use
handpump water.

I asked the Cobblers what they needed to make the water sweet.
They replied that to clean their well they would need to pump out
all the water. A few said that lime would also be needed. Another
suggested that *gur* be added. *Gur* is unrefined sugar which is sold
in blocks, having been boiled down from the cane sap. Everyone
understood the purpose of the lime, but when a quizzical look was

cast at the man who suggested *gur* he said that lime makes water bitter. The *gur* would serve to settle the lime at the base of the well so that the water at the top would lose its bitterness. The other men did not catch his point, for they understood instead that the water would lose its bitterness by becoming sweet. I assumed that when the Cobblers had told me earlier that the water was no longer 'sweet' they were not thinking that several kilos of *gur* would do the trick. But everyone responded with enthusiasm to the suggestion that *gur* be added. 'Now the water will really be sweet,' one man said. His neighbours laughed at the idea; and the children looked up intently at the prospect of having really sweet water to drink from now on.

I had this meeting with the Cobblers in March, some weeks before the festival of Jur Sital. My business in anthropology was not to restore 'tradition', but I knew from other informants that neighbour-hoods used to clean out their open wells once a year on the occasion of Jur Sital. The festival of Jur Sital is in honour of the goddess Sitala and her sidekick Jwar. Sitala (ironically the 'cooling one') is the goddess of pox (smallpox, measles and chicken pox) and her assistant's name means, literally, 'fever'. Local perceptions of the seasonality of illness concur with those of epidemiologists, who note that the incidence of pox increases from March and peaks in June after which time the rain-filled paddy fields and muddy roads keep people at work in their fields, thereby breaking its human chain of transmission. But in the hot, windy summer, just before the mon-soon breaks in June, Sitala is said to roam the countryside, astride an ass, accompanied by Jwar who scatters lentils (an icon of pus-tules). Jur Sital being traditionally the well-cleaning day, the Cob-blers rose to the suggestion that the work be done on that day. We arranged to meet at the well at dawn: I with a pumping set, lime and *gur*; and they in sufficient number to clean the well.

On the appointed day we all met at the well. The well was deeper than people had thought, so that the pipe, connected to the pumping set, was not long enough to reach to the bottom. Drawing out the remaining metre of water by bucket took about a half hour, almost as long as the time required to pump out the initial 7 metres of water. Then one of the Cobblers lowered himself into the well by rope and began to fill buckets with the odd things found at the bottom. This included a lot of fallen bricks and stones, one rusty bucket which had been lost when its rope had broken, some cooking implements, one 18 cm long fish, and about twenty buckets of mud. When the mud was brought up, the children were delighted to find in it some of their marbles that had fallen into oblivion. It took about three hours to clean out the base of the well. I asked them about adding the lime and *gur*, but was told that the water was not yet 'done'. We would have to wait one day until the water had risen.

With the well being 'dry' people were curious to peer into its depths. The women noticed that water was already starting to trickle between the gaps in the bricks and slide down the sides of the well to the base. 'That was the reason why the water was not good', they said. The good water comes up from the base of the well, from deep within the earth; but the water which comes in from the side is surface water which brings dirt from the ground into the well. A man took up the theme, suggesting that some cement be used to seal the interior of the well so that the bad water might not come in. Another bystander countered this proposal by asserting that it is the water which trickles down the side of the well which gives the illusion that the water fills the well from the base. If one were to seal off the side of the well then no water at all would come in. But the women seemed concerned mostly by the water that trickled in from the north side of the well. This was the side on which there was vacant land (which women often use for defecation under cover of darkness); another suggested that a house be built on the land to cover it so that the dirt there could not seep through into the well. If the well were completely surrounded by houses, the water that came in from the side would have to come from a greater distance.

By dawn the following day the water had risen to a depth of about 3 metres. I returned to the well with my *mainajar* to watch the Cobblers finish the job. It was difficult, however, to mobilize the 'people', all of whom were recovering from hangovers. Apparently the community spirit awakened by the cleansing of the well was sustained by other sorts of spirits until late at night. After four return visits we finally found a Cobbler who had awoken, and was searching for some medicine for his headache. It was about noon; the sun was bright overhead and it was the time of day most people go to sleep in the shade. The women, however, were up and about, and in their senses. They were also on our side. They egged the man on to call a few others and to finish off the job. The children were also eager that work got underway, hoping that there might be some left-over *gur* for them to eat. A half hour later work was resumed on the well.

We had provided two and a half *paserí* of lime (about 10 kilograms), for that was the amount they thought necessary. About a kilo at a time was taken, and mixed with water in a large cooking pot. When the lime was dissolved, it was thrown into the well. While more lime was dissolved, others lowered empty buckets into the well and by raising and lowering them in the depths, they stirred the well water, mixing the lime with the water. After about half the lime had been used, the water was gaining a milky appearance and concern was voiced that the water would become bitter. One man urged still more lime be added, but most thought that it was enough, and a few thought it was already too much. One more kilo was added, but the proponent of additional lime was unable to defend his position after that. The *gur* was then added in the same manner, first mixed with water in a bucket and then stirred into the well water. The children were not disappointed either.

THE MALEVOLENT LORD AT THE COBBLERS' WELL

Throughout the period of purifying the water I collected samples to measure the extent to which the Cobblers' method was effective in bio-medical terms. One common method of assessing the extent of contamination is to count the number of faecal coliforms. These are a class of coliforms which inhabit the intestinal tract of warm-blooded animals. They may in themselves cause diarrhoeal disease, but they are used in epidemiological research as an indicator of faecal contamination in general. If faecal coliforms are present then one might suspect the presence of other excreted pathogenic agents in the water supply, including viruses (e.g. poliomyelitis, hepatitus), bacteria (e.g. salmonella, shigella, cholera), protozoa (entamoeba, giardia) and helminths (ascaris). In principle, no faecal coliforms are present in treated water, but this is not the case with untreated water. Current WHO guidelines recommend a maximum of 10 coliforms per 100 ml for drinking water and 100 coliforms per 100 ml for bathing water. Third World governments in tropical countries find it difficult, if not impossible, to achieve such standards; and indeed the validity of the standards (and the cost of maintaining such standards) is contested. My citation of these figures is intended as a guide to the guides. In my research I measured the extent of faecal contamination by counting the coliform *Escherichia coli* in 100 ml samples, using a portable water laboratory.

For three days before the Cobblers' cleansing of their well and for three days afterwards I visited the Cobblers' hamlet four times a day to take a water sample. If the men were about, they greeted

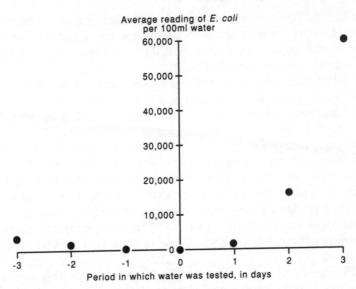

Figure 4.1 First purification of the well: *Escherichia coli* readings before and after

me respectfully; the older women told me that the water had never tasted sweeter. They said they now drank it all the time. The younger women would briskly veil themselves and disappear out of my path. The world was being formed as an object of his lordship's pleasure; and apart from the behaviour of the younger women, which ensured that I would not take this state of affairs too literally, the Cobblers were doing their best to present a picture to me of my personal potency and grace.

But by the third day, when the samples collected on the second day had been incubated, I already knew that something had gone seriously wrong: the coliform count had shot up (see Figure 4.1). The fact that the mud on the platform of the well was still dried and caked assured me that the Cobblers had not been telling me the truth. No one had been bringing up pails of fresh water, or at least not in any amount. The water was definitely foul, and I assumed that the Cobblers had been guided by their sense of smell. But when would the Cobblers tell me that the water was not 'sweet'?

Eleven days after the purification one of the Cobbler spokesmen saw me in the bazaar and, with palms joined together, beseeched me to return to the well. Something had gone terribly wrong. I followed him back to the hamlet and, peering over the parapet, saw the blackish, lifeless water. A pail was lowered and as it broke the surface of the water a fetid smell wafted upwards that caused everyone to turn away. One woman said that the water was so bad not even their livestock would drink it.

I asked them what had gone wrong. One man offered the theory that people from another hamlet had become envious of their well. They had probably come in the night and thrown in a dead animal to turn the water foul. He was clearly more interested in blame than in reasons. Not living in the hamlet I could not determine whether there had been any fault-finding amongst the Cobblers themselves; or whether they all, like this one man, preferred to make allegations about their neighbours, with whom they had long-standing grudges. I took more water for tests, and promised to let them know the results the next day. This was purely an academic exercise, but it did give me some time to think about the best course of action.

The results of the test were virtually uncountable. My estimate was about 760,000 faecal coliforms per 100 ml. The next day I told the results to the family opposite the well and urged then to spread the word not to let anyone use the water until it had been properly purified. Rather than set them against their neighbours, I also told them that the *gur* was the source of contamination. They were disheartened, and in some sense humbled. I told them I would supply whatever materials they would need to reclean the well, if their hamlet would contribute the labour.

The next day Brikhesh and I returned to the hamlet to arrange a date and to ask how they thought this time the well ought to be purified. As we entered the hamlet, we overheard people telling others that the well water used to be sweet but then a sahib came and caused the water to become foul, so that not even animals would drink it. He had told the people to put *gur* in the well. Everyone did that in good faith, thinking that it must be right. And now the community no longer even had a usable well.

From these comments, I realized that the scene had changed. His lordship was now being cast in a malevolent mode. The lord is the fount of justice, compassion, liberality. He is also seen to be the supporter of society, the father of the fatherless, the benefactor of the poor who cannot look after themselves. This is *dharma*. But not all lords observe the *dharma*. Some close their eyes, ignoring the suffering of their people. But worst of all is a lord who subverts the social order. He is duty-bound to establish order and justice; but instead he creates disorder and then abuses his authority in such a way as to re-establish order on terms favourable to him. He will set two honest men against each other, and while they are distracted by their rivalry, he will plunder their property. He will cause suspicion to surround the honest and oblige them to bribe their way out of their difficulty. This is not *dharma*. This is *ulṭá dharma*, the perversion of the moral order.

From the comments buzzing around me, I realized that the Cobblers were fairly much agreed that the contamination had been caused by the *gur* and that I was to blame: not because I had let them go ahead with their own idea but because the idea had been mine in the first place. Having recorded all our discussions in connection with the well, I felt that I was in a position to correct them on this matter. I reminded them that one of their number had suggested that *gur* would cause the lime to settle to the base of the well, and that everyone accepted the idea. They completely disagreed with me, forcing me to realize that we were not in a courtroom. The Cobblers were unable or unwilling to assign individual responsibility within their community for their decision to use *gur*, for that would have divided their neighbourhood. They preferred to assign blame to their malevolent lord. My search for culturally specific knowledge had gone awry. They were disowning their own 'knowledge' and saying that it had been mine instead. I assumed from their allegations that my 'people' were blaming me in the hope that I would assume responsibility. For no matter whose fault it was, it was still my duty as their lord to enable them to clean their well. I told them that I would provide the pump and the lime; and we fixed a date.

AN ANTHROPOLOGIST'S KNOWLEDGE ABOUT PURIFYING WELL WATER

Everyone agreed that the well had been correctly cleaned the second time. The foul water had been pumped out and fresh water rose in the well; it was then mixed with lime. But can it be said that the lime purified the water?

For lime to be an effective sanitary agent it must form a 1 per cent solution with the water. It works by changing the pH value, rendering the water too alkaline to support certain forms of microbial life. Using buckets to measure the water, one could arrive at the correct proportion. For every one hundred buckets of water taken out, one bucket of lime must go in (with some extra allowance made for the water which seeped into the well while drawing it out). But the Cobblers were not going to resort to buckets when a pump was available. At any rate they judged the proportion rather like a chef adding salt to the soup, sensing the appropriate amount. By continuously raising and lowering the bucket at various depths, they churned the water, thereby mixing in the lime. When the water turned milky, they began to worry that the taste of the water might be seriously impaired. My estimate was that only about a 0.6 or 0.7 per cent solution was reached. This would account for the fact that the water was not entirely free of contamination; on the other hand to make the water so bitter that people do not drink it would not have been a solution either.

By the time the well had been cleaned a second time, people were generally satisfied that it had been done correctly. One day before the second decontamination the faecal coliform count was estimated at 20,000 per 100 ml; five days after the decontamination the mean count was estimated at 10,000 per 100 ml. In short, there was a 50 per cent reduction in faecal contamination over a six-day period using lime. These results might seem impressive were it not for the fact that the 20,000 count took place only five days after the count that had estimated the contamination at 760,000 per 100 ml; in other words, without human intervention a 97 per cent reduction took place over a slightly shorter period. Thus most of the faecal coliforms in the well, nourished on the *gur*, had died a natural death before the lime had been added a second time. For comparative purposes further readings were later taken over a fifteen-day period; it began with a prolonged heavy rainfall that brought the well water nearly to ground level. At the end of the fifteen days, when the well water had subsided to about 1.2 metres below ground level, the contamination was reduced by 95 per cent. No lime had been added in this period. These figures suggest that the ecology of the well, not the use of lime, is central to understanding the purification of the water.

Very little is understood about the micro-environment of an open masonry well (more is understood about ponds), but it is certain that a well is, quite literally, a self-contained universe, supporting a rich aquatic life. In the case of the Cobblers' well the water sustained countless microbes, plus mosquito larvae, crustacea and molluscs, and at least one *jírá* fish 18 cm long. The Cobblers understood how the well could become polluted, but their only notion of decontamination entailed the use of lime. There were, however, two other important ways in which the well was constantly being purified. First, solar radiation kills off bacteria to a depth of about

45 cm. Admittedly the depth of the water and the rim of the well prevent complete daytime exposure, and the efficacy of solar radiation on turbid water is uncertain. But even two hours of overhead sunlight across the top of the well would have been of some benefit, especially in view of the fact that women collect water from the surface of the well. Second, there is a rich microbial life in the water, some species of which are predators of faecal coliforms.

This then posed a second question. The lime is an indiscriminate killer: it kills not only the faecal coliforms but also their predators. If micro-invertebrate fauna were more lethal than solar radiation and lime then the addition of lime would not necessarily be beneficial because it would kill both good and bad bacteria. Indeed this is what seemed to happen in the first cleansing of the well when the lime presumably killed both coliforms and predators, and then the *gur* fed the coliforms until they multiplied exponentially. Was the lime not necessarily beneficial?

These preoccupations drew me back to the Cobblers' hamlet a third time. The pretext, however, was to have a conversation with a Cobbler woman whose house adjoins the well. She told me that the water was not quite good. She hastened to add that she drank it all the time; moreover, the water 'worked' like good water should. When she cooked lentil soup, the lentils 'melted' quickly in the boiling water. Moreover, there was no reddish-brown stain in the pot after cooking rice. And after the meal, when she drank the water, the food in her stomach was quickly digested. But still the taste was not quite right. She wondered whether the reason might have been using rock lime, rather than *situwá* lime. This other kind of lime is made from the pulverized shells of local fresh-water molluscs and snails; it is thought to be superior in taste to rock lime. *Situwá* lime is used to mix in with chewing tobacco, or spread thinly on betel leaves. I was struck by the woman's tact in describing the quality of the water. Criticism indicates the presence of another mind at work; and there is only one mind, that of the lord who commands his dependants. It was highly unlikely that the woman actually drank the water; but by saying she drank his lordship's water, she was affirming her personal loyalty. I also doubted that she used the water for cooking, but she probably did use it for washing herself, as well as clothes and pots and pans. And, as she had noted, the water was not really fine.

So I returned again to the well, and asked the Cobblers if they would mind my purifying their well a third time, but this time with *situwá* lime. Not much work would be involved, for it did not seem

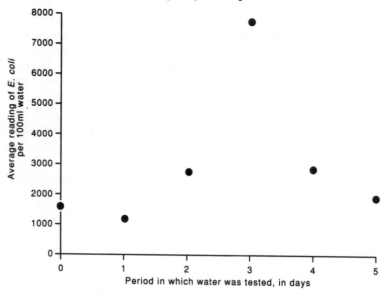

Figure 4.2 Third purification of the well: *Escherichia coli* readings shortly before purification and on the five days thereafter

necessary to clean out the well, only to add the lime. With the help of a Cobbler I added the lime. The faecal coliform count immediately beforehand and thereafter is shown in Figure 4.2 (samples were taken at two collection points; the figures show the mean). The data seemed to bear out my hypothesis about the lime. Going again on taste criteria, an inadequate amount of lime was probably added. The faecal contamination was diminished during the initial twenty-four-hour period, but then increased higher than before for two days before returning roughly to the level prior to purification.

Upon reflection, however, my hypothesis seemed odd. If lime indiscriminantly kills all bacteria then why should the faecal coliform rate later go up disproportionately, for both the coliforms and their predators would have succumbed to the high pH value. And if the coliforms increase suddenly then so should their predators, which would then brake the increase. These doubts, however, fail to account for two factors. The first, of unknown value, stems from the fact that the (presumably inadequate amount of) lime was concentrated in the upper 2 to 2.5 metres of water and not in the depths of the well where anaerobic reactions take place. The second factor is that by lowering buckets into the well, people were actively adding bacteria. If they added more faecal bacteria than predators one would expect in the first few days that the faecal coliforms would artificially increase at a rate that outstripped the natural increase of their predators. Further tests, with rigorous experimental controls, might sort out the relative importance of these two factors. At present one can only conjecture that solar radiation and other forms of microbial life are a more effective means of purifying well water than are insufficient amounts of lime.

But where then did the idea of using lime come from? The only other local instance of using lime for decontamination is by the sweepers, hired by the town council, who spread lime on the road-sides and at public places where visitors to Janakpur defecate. I suspect that this public health practice was introduced by the British a century ago in northern Bihar, India, just 11 kilometres to the south of Janakpur. The only virtue of lime, in cleaning a well, would be if the well harboured one particular pathogen that was a public danger. For example, in a cholera epidemic it would be beneficial to add sufficient lime to kill all the *Vibrio cholerae*, even though the effect of this would be to kill other forms of bacterial life, some of which might be beneficial. But if there is no epidemic, the benefit of adding lime lasts for no more than a day, the harmful consequences may last for several days, and the long-term value is neutral.

A further curiosity in all this, however, is the procedure of pumping all the water from the well and then adding lime to the incoming fresh water. To pump out the water and remove the detritus made sense if one were cleaning the well. To add lime made sense if one were decontaminating the water. The former action focuses on the container. One cleans by throwing out 'dirt' and re-ordering the environment. Just as women clean their homes, so men clean the community well. The Cobblers did not scrub the sides of the well (although other informants told me that this should have been done), but still they did clean the container by removing all the mud and detritus from the base. The latter action, however, focused on the contained. The lime was used to kill the 'bugs' in the water. But since the new water, like the old, was not likely to be completely pure, there would seem to have been no advantage in their pumping out the old water and adding lime to the new. One could have simply added lime to the old water. The Cobblers linked two practices together, that of cleaning the well and that of decontaminating the water. Taken together, they did not necessarily make bio-medical sense in ordinary, non-epidemic conditions.

LOCAL KNOWLEDGE AND THE PROMOTION OF PUBLIC HEALTH

If Cobblers cleaned wells as often as they repaired shoes or their wives boiled rice, then there would have been a regular enough testing of practices for them to have taken for granted the purification of water. But this was not the case; hence the procedure for cleaning a well became a community problem-solving activity. In this activity the heads of households who thought the well to be in some sense 'theirs' participated. The knowledge of the procedures of purification was local in its construction. A different set of circumstances might have produced a variant procedure. It had presumably been some time since a Cobbler had thought to add *gur* to the well. Alternatively, someone had hit upon a new idea which made sense and gained acceptance in the neighbourhood. It would be difficult, if not impossible, to systematize such locally constructed knowledge. At best one might expose the ideas on which the problem-solving was based or the values to which it was oriented so that one might be better equipped to forecast how such problems might be decided.

With regard to water purification the Cobblers had various ideas, most of which converged with mine. We knew that one could decontaminate water by adding 'medicine'. We knew that to clean the well one could remove its contents and scrub the container. We also recognized that water becomes impure through improper use (e.g. allowing things to fall into the well) or by surface contamination from adjoining land (although they thought good water rose from the base of the well, not from the water which had been filtered by the earth). What I knew, and they did not, was that solar radiation and predator bacteria also purify water. For them water could become impure, and fresh water, correctly handled, was pure, but stale or impure water could not become pure again. One threw such water away, returning it to the undifferentiated water of the universe. Our ecological knowledge did converge, though, in our understanding that wells are kept fresh by their regular use. When water is removed from the well, naturally filtered water enters, restoring the well to its previous volume. If water is not regularly removed then it stagnates and becomes unfit for drinking. Of course, it is also use which contaminates the well. If the buckets lowered into the well are not clean, then the well becomes contaminated. But everyone recognized that the well must be used for it to exist in any usable way.

In addition to these ideas about water, the Cobblers valued water for its taste, its sustaining power and its digestive capacity. As for considerations of taste, my encounter with the Cobbler community began with their complaint that the water of their locality had lost its sweetness. In the narrow sense of the term their water was not pleasant to taste. This sense was important in that they wanted their water to taste sweet (pleasant, agreeable). Lime makes water alkaline (bitter, unpleasant). The Cobblers never added sufficient lime to make a 1 per cent solution, for that was contrary to their aim that the water taste sweet.

In a wider sense, however, the term 'sweet' referred to a general pleasantness, 'bitter' water to pain. At the start I missed the meta-phorical nature of their complaint and picked up only on the literal. Later I realized that in complaining about the water's quality the Cobblers were also complaining about the quality of their life. The Cobblers recognized that water sustains life. I went to them with an interest in their health; they were concerned, however, with their well-being. Their complaint about water signalled to prospective benefactors a complaint about life. They were looking for a patron to raise them up, to sustain them. When my lordly persona was cast in a benevolent mode, the Cobblers no longer said that they drank the water of *their* well, but that they drank their lordship's water. At the start of the encounter I missed the ontic basis of the political economy.

Finally, the Cobblers were concerned about the digestive capacity of the water. Digestion is likened to an act of cooking whereby the stomach is a pot, heated by the body's digestive 'fire'. One does not drink during a meal; rather one eats and then literally pours one or two glasses of water into the stomach. The proficient do not even swallow. Ingested food, to which water has been added, is then 'cooked' in the stomach. Waters are evaluated according to their digestive capacity. Good water should facilitate digestion, caus-ing neither diarrhoea nor constipation. The former affliction is a personal inconvenience: the latter is a health problem because impurities are retained within the stomach diffusing their influence throughout the body. The digestive capacity of water varies from locality to locality, according to the trace elements found within it; it also varies according to the type of materials (e.g. the iron-cased tubewell or brick-lined open well) that contains the water.

Such an understanding of ideas and values enables one – be he Cobbler, anthropologist or public health worker – to anticipate the sorts of decisions underlying a people's handling and treatment of their water. In my case it also helped me formulate hypotheses about the adequacy of Cobbler hygienic practices, when measured with micro-biological instruments against bacteriological criteria. Yet my adequacy-testing was not the sum of everything I learned around the Cobblers' well. Other things I came to realize in retrospect only after I had reflected upon how I had been drawn into the Cobblers' community. Herein lies the moral of my tale.

Throughout my field research I tried to maintain a certain passivity in observing the Cobblers making their water taste 'sweet'. Only in this way could I trust that I was observing a sort of behaviour that would have existed were I not there to observe it. With regard to the meaning and aims of the purification procedures used by the Cobblers, I sought to structure my investigation as an exchange of information about our respective knowledges. Assuming from the outset that hygienic practices were culturally variable, objective and discussable, I asked questions of the Cobblers and from their answers sought to construct their knowledge of hygiene and sanitation. Meanwhile families from various neighbourhoods sought the results of my tests on their drinking and bathing water. This was especially the case with women who felt their children were weak, illness-prone or underdeveloped, and who suspected the local water supply to be at fault. The results of my tests were made known to all the families concerned. In sum, I saw myself as being either a detached observer of other people's practices or a learner who, in turn, questioned what he learned and reciprocated with his own knowledge. Our exchange of information was symmetrical.

Although there is some sense in which an item of information may be understood as a mental fact, a body of knowledge is not so much a summary of such items as a decision about their internal arrangement. This knowledge was constructed by the Cobblers as a community, for their open, masonry well was a collective responsibility. Critical to the construction of this knowledge was the power to make one's voice heard and to work things in the environment. The words of three respected Cobblers were particularly heeded. Yet power was also in some measure verbal. The pun that the water from the well would now really be 'sweet' was decisive in securing the idea that *gur* be added to the water; in other words, the pun also produced an effect. Finally the power was collective in that the collective voices of the Cobblers eventually put an end to one respected Cobbler's attempt to add yet more lime to the well.

In all these encounters my voice was also heard, although when played back to me, it did not seem to be the real me. But it was in this playback that I realized my encounter with the Cobblers had not been solely structured by my own intentions. Through their passivity, not mine, the Cobblers localized my general interest in hygiene and sanitation into a particular interest in the quality of the Cobblers' water. By further providing the Cobblers with lordly visions and the necessary materials to make their water 'sweet', I enabled them to take action in their own community. The Cobblers placed their trust in my benevolence and attributed to me the power of agency. The Cobblers' water became his lordship's water; and by drinking their lordship's water, they affirmed our union in a common body politic. They had their own ideas about water purification, but it was by my grace that these ideas would work. Hence their knowledge became my knowledge.

In sum, my detached observations and my respect for their own 'competence' assumed their knowledge, like mine, to be theoretical. I then tested their knowledge for its adequacy. Yet they also tested my knowledge, if not for its adequacy, at least for its results. They found it inefficacious in bringing about the intended result and immoral in its disturbance of their community. The Cobblers wanted me to be involved and practical where I was expecting them to be autonomous and theoretical. Our encounter took place in a mismatch of raised expectations in which, at the end of it all, the Cobblers' own ideas and values remained intact. They are probably even now saying to one another, 'The water from our well used to taste sweet'.

ACKNOWLEDGEMENTS

I am grateful to His Majesty's Government of Nepal for permission to carry out research on the socio-cultural parameters of hygiene and to the Overseas Development Administration, the Nuffield Foundation and the London School of Oriental and African Studies for its financial support. My debt to the Cobblers of Janakpur and to Brikhesh Chandra Lal in the collection of my field material is obvious. Further acknowledgement is due to Sandy Cairncross at the London School of Hygiene and Tropical Medicine and to Mark Hobart for their detailed comments on a previous draft of the paper.

5 Is death the same everywhere? contexts of knowing and doubting

Piers Vitebsky

Can ignorance 'grow', and if so, does it grow out of the decay of its supposed opposite, knowledge? I should like to move from these categories towards a consideration of the processes which appear to give them meaning. Certainly, it is a commonplace that knowledge is something which 'grows', both in popular speech and in critical philosophy (Lakatos and Musgrave 1970). This image comes from notions of organic processes in which ever more complex forms arise out of simpler ones, all the while preserving or enhancing an intrinsic mathematical order and perfection. A tree grows, putting out ever more branches; an embryo grows from a single cell to a fully-formed human. Whether the impulse comes from within, as in the concept of genetic code, or from without as in the concepts of entelechy and of morphic field (Sheldrake 1981), the imagery of organic growth makes the growth of knowledge seem tantamount to a growth of order, a defiance of entropy in the realm of cognition.

However, this understanding of knowledge leaves ignorance as a very murky opposite. In reverse, the parallel with organic growth cannot be pushed very far. It would be unfortunate to say that ignorance grows like a tree, since this would be to ascribe to it that same increase in structure and order which is the hallmark of knowledge. If ignorance is discussed at all in terms of structure, its increase may be represented as the senescence and decay of a perfectly-formed creature, in other words, as the dismantling of a complex structure (as in the images of 'decline and fall', of barbarians invading the empire). But often, ignorance appears as something more primordial, dark, heavy and formless. Here, 'ignorance' is not simply a category of cognition, as would be required by any philosophy of knowledge (the opposite of which could simply be a state of not knowing), but is the cognitive facet of the moral term evil. If it grows organically at all, it does so like a biblical tare, a triffid or a cancer.

Ignorance is generally ascribed to someone as a mark of their moral failure. In the encounter between societies and cultures, this failure is one of an entire world-view. People in the tropics may be too ignorant to use fertilizers properly, until instructed by development workers; in the Arctic, they may be too ignorant to become vegetarian until taught better by animal-rights activists. Knowledge and ignorance, then, are not so much cognitive as evaluative terms. That is, they are not part of the world as it would be if human actors were detached and positionless, but depend on those actors' involvement with the world and with each other. Rather than being categories of any absolute philosophy, ignorance and knowledge can be little more than folk categories of the people who use these words.

As such, they denote states which are ideal but which are not inhabited by real people. These states are timeless, in the sense that real people and real communities are constantly changing their minds about what they and others know. They live under conditions of flux, reform and revisionism. To the extent that ignorance and knowledge can be taken seriously as cognitive categories at all, people live with a high level of doubt.

'Development' is classically concerned with agriculture. The argument that follows is one I have begun to sketch out elsewhere, in relation to the move from mixed subsistence cropping to market-oriented monocropping in a region of Sri Lanka (Vitebsky 1984, 1986). 'Development' is also concerned with health programmes: other people can be too ignorant to boil their water, or to limit their families properly. But ultimately, even in these arenas, the question comes down to one of metaphysics, that is, of underlying assumptions about reality (Collingwood 1940). I shall therefore discuss this problem in relation to a subject about which it is perhaps hardest of all to feel absolute certainty: what happens to people we know when they die? There is an obvious sense in which we do not know what happens; yet in another sense we seem to have very specific ideas about it. The history of human cultures is full of the most elaborate accounts of the state of being dead, along with highly technical explanations which link the nature of this state to the principles and processes of the cosmos.

Do these accounts amount to systems of knowledge or of ignorance? Let us for the moment think of them simply as expressions of awareness, or as ways of conceptualizing the dead in order to apply these concepts to one's own needs. I shall consider two such conceptualizations. One is Freud's model of the process of bereavement (Freud 1957 [1917]), cast within the framework of psychoanalysis. The other is one which I have distilled from the daily life of the Sora, a 'tribal' people in eastern India (Vitebsky, 1993), cast within a kind of shamanism. Both these conceptualizations, with their accompanying practices, are very similar in formal terms since both are variants of a 'talking cure' for the bereaved person. Yet in their metaphysics, that is, in their fundamental presuppositions about reality, they are starkly opposed.

Freud lays out his model in a paper called 'Mourning and melancholia'. This paper represents the most coherent and influential secular theory of the mental processes of bereavement in the industrialized West. Whether acknowledged or not, it lies at the root of a wide range of current traditions in psychotherapy and bereavement counselling (e.g. Volkan 1981, Worden 1982). The basis of Freud's model and practice is the certainty that a person who has died has, in a profound ontological sense, ceased to exist (1957: 244). This person can have no subjective being and any continuing attempt by the bereaved person to interact with the deceased is therefore based on an illusion. In the early stages, this illusion forms part of what he calls normal 'mourning'. It can be normal to think you hear the dead person's voice, or to imagine that he or she is sometimes still in the room with you.

However, 'reality testing' (1957: 244) soon convinces the mourner that the dead person no longer exists, and it is the recognition of this, the acceptance of the 'verdict of reality' (p. 255), which starts the process of recovery. If the bereaved person does not accept this verdict of reality, he or she enters the pathological state of melancholia. This is a retreat into a 'hallucinatory wishful psychosis' (p. 244) in which the existence of the dead person is 'psychically [and erroneously] prolonged' (p. 245), to excess. The patient's dialogue with the analyst (or psychotherapist) must eventually help him or her towards the recognition of this error.

The Sora would not accept this view of reality. For them, the dead remain fully existent but have been qualitatively transformed. Where Freud contrasts normal and pathological states of mind in the bereaved, Sora contrast benign and aggressive states of mind in the dead. They locate these in various features of the landscape. The dead reside in these locations according to their mood of the moment and the living encounter them and become involved with them by moving across this landscape. In certain aspects or moods, the dead nurture their descendants and ensure lineage continuity; in others, they attack their descendants and cause in them the same illnesses from which they themselves died. The shaman provides a channel through which the living and the dead engage each other in dialogue. These dialogues are held at divinations, healing rites and funerals. Here the living and the dead explore each other's moods in order to modify them. To be healed, you invite your dead attackers to a dialogue in order to find out how they feel about you and why they have attacked. You then try to persuade them into a different, less aggressive state of mind, while they in turn may persuade you to change something in yourself.

The insights offered by each of these two ways of thinking about the dead, and the avenues which they open up for healing, are strikingly similar. Freud shares the Sora's understanding that close personal relationships contain an ambivalence between tenderness and violence; and that a person who clings too closely to the memory of a dead person may suffer from an identical illness. One's own melancholia, like an attack from the aggressive aspect of the deceased, can be fatal. Yet his different understanding of reality leads him to reverse what the Sora see as the direction of this attachment. For Freud, the power to initiate the relationship and to dominate its emotional tone lies with the bereaved person, who remembers the deceased. It is not so for the Sora, for whom the deceased remains attached to the bereaved person. I have discussed elsewhere the contrast between these views and their implications for the societies in which they are used (Vitebsky 1993).

It would be hard – at least for an anthropologist – to find a meta-standpoint from which to say, crudely, that either of these understandings of death is an example of 'ignorance'. Indeed, such a proposition seems meaningless. The difference here is one not of observed fact, nor of empirical evidence, but of inferred explanation.

In their metaphysics, practitioners in both traditions seem very certain about what they know and even reinforce this conviction through procedures of verification. Freud talks of 'reality-testing' leading to 'the verdict of reality', which is that the deceased 'no longer exists'. The Sora likewise have ways of interrogating the dead in order to be sure that they are really who they say they are and not just impostors who have come along to feed on a free sacrifice. In both cases, one could argue from outside these beliefs that they are mistaken. Freud's 'reality-testing' does not actually test reality, but rather, tests propositions against a preconceived notion of reality. Similarly, the entire practice of dialogues with the dead could plausibly (though I believe thinly) be interpreted on the assumption that these dialogues are no more than a theatrical stunt.

And yet for those who use them, both systems are enormously powerful. In order to understand this, we need to move a long way from any truth-value theory of knowledge (to say nothing of ignorance) towards notions of adequacy, appropriateness and context. Knowledge now appears as a collective term for thoughts about the world which give to their thinkers the conviction of commanding that area of experience to which those thoughts refer. These thoughts remain part of 'knowledge' for as long as they continue to exert this command and to satisfy this conviction. Yet under certain circumstances, experience can move away from the certainty of knowledge, defy it, slip out of its grasp. An entire system of knowledge, or parts of it, come to appear ineffectual in the face of reality. This is the area of doubt. This is not because the knowledge was bad knowledge (like Frazer's interpretation of magic as bad science), but because the scope and expectations of its application have changed. Examples are the gradual, painful abandonment of the pagan gods in late antiquity, or of the Russian Orthodox Church and of Siberian shamanistic spirits under Communism. The fragility of any existing system of knowledge is especially obvious in the realm of death, but the same processes can be seen or predicted in the destinies of monocropping for the market in Sri Lanka (or of social forestry in India, or of the saturation of the land around the Aral Sea with pesticides). These abandoned ideas, whether about death or about agriculture, are more than simply fashions. They appear later as the hulls of burnt-out knowledges which are then seen as merely 'beliefs', and sometimes foolish beliefs at that.

This involves asking under what circumstances the practitioners of either of two contrasted systems of 'knowledge' could be in a position to declare the other a form of ignorance: shamanism or psychoanalysis, subsistence mixed cropping or monocropping for the market; and, further, under what circumstances they would want or need to do so. Conversely, how could the practitioners of the other system of knowledge acquiesce in this, or be plunged by it into doubt?

To the extent that the abstract nouns 'ignorance' and 'knowledge' have any meaning at all, they are unstable and unreal because the realm of experience to which they refer resides in persons, that is, they are attributes of persons in the context of their relations to other persons. These persons are judged or assessed, not so much by means of these nouns, as by the adjectives 'ignorant' and 'knowledgeable'. They are the subjects of the verb 'to know' and of various attempts to construct its negation ('not to know', 'to be ignorant'). These adjectives and verbs belong in the realm of attribute and agency, and the use of the noun 'ignorance' is a denial or diminution of this agency. It is not that something called ignorance 'grows'. It is that 'ignorance' becomes a more convincing imputation, becomes reified and systematized, as the awareness of various actors is modified. Some persons have their agency diminished to the point at which they no longer count as knowledgeable and at which their awareness is no longer 'knowledge'. Persons who previously knew something, withdraw or are pushed out from faith in their own competence to know, in relation to others who 'know' better.

In industrial society as a whole, this takes the form of leaving, or being forced to leave, many matters vital to oneself in the hands of experts or professionals. Lay persons cannot participate in these experts' knowledge very actively, but only as its patients, objects or clients. As the lay person is excluded from exercising an area of knowledge or participating in it from any angle except a passive one, so knowledgeability becomes less of an attribute, knowing becomes less of an action and knowledge becomes more of a thing in itself. As the adjectival and verbal forms are squeezed out, the nominal form of knowledge hardens, this reification appears to take on a reality, and knowledge becomes a commodity, alienable and subject to hoarding and trading. I once read a sci-fi comic in which aliens explained to the American public that on their planet people paid for what they wanted, not in money, but in 'knowledge'. Everyone agreed that this was an ideal system because the more you spent, the more wealth you created: knowledge passed on to others was not knowledge lost to oneself. The catch, which emerged only later, was that these aliens were earthling con-men in disguise who merely pretended to disdain money in order to lower security at a bank which they were planning to rob.

This parable shows the hopelessness of the fantasy which tries to overcome the paradox of knowledge: if only it could simultaneously be both a commodity and yet not privative of others, if only it could be given away freely without being alienated. The knowledge in which the 'aliens' dealt was not knowledge as certainty, understanding, or wisdom, which can be derived only slowly and cumulatively through experience and inner effort. It was the most commoditizable form of all, knowledge as information or as the instant application of technique. In this understanding of the word, knowledge is a means to an end, a sort of magic. The vision with which they enticed the American public first equated knowledge with money by making it the material of wealth, and then used this to abolish poverty of knowledge – that is, ignorance.

In Sora life, this equation would not stand. Wealth differentials can be acute; there are headmen and moneylenders, and Sora villages suffer from normal factionalism. But no one is a knowledge-pauper, like the ghetto kids in Philadelphia who have no idea why it gets dark at night and light in the morning (Ken Gordon, personal communication). This is true of outsiders, too. Sora recognize a plurality of knowledges, all equally valid, through their notion of custom (*ukka*). Why should others want to feed my ancestors and to be correspondingly vulnerable to their attacks? Why, indeed, should I want them to? Tribal Khonds, Hindu Oriyas, Brahmins, English people, all do it their own way. Dead Christians (including Baptist Sora ones) do not even go to the Underworld at all, nor do they talk to the living. So where Sora emulate outsiders, for example when their shamans use high-caste familiars who can write and command armed retinues, they see these as having other powers rather than other knowledges. Their Baptists, similarly, say not that the coming of Jesus has made other comparable beings less real, but that he is a bigger and better being.

If we choose to interpret these as alternative systems of knowledge, then despite their relative strengths, none of these knowledges is seen to render the others ignorant. Each 'is appropriate to' (*tamte*) its own knowers and users. It is profoundly local. The Sora concept of 'knowledge', then (for which there seems to be no word), is not totalitarian, in the sense that – to reify and animize it for a moment, as one is obliged to do in English – it does not seek to impose itself on other knowers. Yet at the same time, local knowledge is often total, by virtue of the very fact that it is local. All Sora illnesses and deaths must be accounted for, and responded to, within this idiom. When a meteorite crashed into a field, it was given a pastiche of a human funeral, I think because it had entered sufficiently into the Sora world to become at least partially subject to their knowledge. Similarly, I once fell ill after running across the mountains on a hot day hunting a peacock to offer to the goddess Durga. In the divination, it turned out that my illness had been caused by the goddess herself, who had been impressed at the sight of an Englishman taking part in the hunt and had raped me. Again, I think that I was not far enough inside the Sora world to be attacked by a Sora ancestor, but sufficiently inside for my illness to have a

Sora kind of cause. Similarly, it was widely believed that I was immune to sorcery; but some of the perceptive Soras also understood that if I stayed for a longer time I would gradually lose this immunity.

Yet this kind of knowledge is not totalitarian, because it is total only within its avowedly circumscribed arena. When, however, a knowledge is exported beyond the limits of this area, it can survive and be sustained only by some sort of claim to universality. Often in 'world religions' and the secular successor ideologies of Christendom such as Communism, Nazism, Thatcherism, or monetarism (it is significant that shamanism is not an -ism in this sense), this is done militantly. Then it must annihilate, degrade or subsume other ways of knowing, seeing these as rivals in a colosseum of mutually negating knowledges. This can be seen in the stories from Amazonia of missionaries demanding that dying and uncomprehending natives carried in from the jungle for treatment confess their sins on their deathbeds; or in the triumphalism among the western right over the collapse of Communism, as though the Russians were finally open to the realization that 'democracy' and the market as America understood them were the only possible ways to live – or, indeed, that the collapse of Communism actually went to prove this.

Knowledge commoditized, then, is knowledge which is separable from context and situation, and thus easily separated. Ignorance 'grows' only in someone whose knowledge and context no longer fit each other. Such a person is not alone, but lives inside a drama which contains various roles or positions. One can slip into the role of client and victim, or else of tutor and victor. For the triumphant party, one's own knowledge is no longer local; for the defeated, it is no longer knowledge. Within these, there are many degrees of resistance, coercion and collusion. The destruction of local knowledge creates a class world whose overlords require a proletariat: since there are the landowners of knowledge, there must also be the landless labourers and the unproductive beggars.

To be a landowner, one must push one's own knowledge outwards on to others. The local paradigm is declared universal and must be propagated; the Good News must be proclaimed. This is because it is now seen as a cognitive achievement which is valid independently of context. A missionizing attitude is almost inevitable: one seeks out people whom one constitutes as ignorant, in order to teach them. One may not always force them to convert at gunpoint, but they would be foolish not to follow one's glorious lead. The missionary sets up a dispensary in the jungle to entice dying Indians for medicine, in order to save their souls; having won the Cold War, the Free World must now win the peace by converting the Russians to their own particular version of the market.

The very essence of 'development' is to declare an essence in someone else, in order to end their previous state of knowledge by transmuting it into ignorance – a sort of reverse alchemy. If local traditions are allowed to survive, they do so only as 'beliefs' and are encapsulated as 'folk' or 'little tradition' and put into quotation marks. This is a secular version of the process by which monotheism converted local gods into saints, spirits and demons. There is created a great chain of being, of life-forms or awareness-forms. At the lowest level are people who cannot even fill out a form or sign their name, or who even orally answer a questionnaire not in the categories required – truly ignorant people. This hierarchy appears to be cognitively based, but is actually one of a quite different kind of power. The value of this knowledge itself, so soon to be annulled, is clearly reflected in another chain of being, with its life-forms evaluated according to their salaries: from the expatriates, who terminate this knowledge; via their local assistants, who know the language and supply them with most of their information about the knowledge; to the locals themselves, who have been thinking practically about the issues for centuries, are paid nothing and will live with the consequences of the project for generations after the others have gone home. For them, the project does not end with the final report.

Significantly, the natives may not even be genuinely consulted, or at any rate, not in their own idiom. They may be asked in surveys to put a figure on their income and expenditure, or an 'acreage' on their forest clearings, when they themselves do not think in these categories and may even realize that their acreages are illegal (Vitebsky 1986: 7). The tabulation of informants' 'replies' into elaborate models may then consume more thought, money and manpower than did the collection of the data in the field; but this work is done safely within the framework of the questioners' own categories. In one agricultural research institute where I worked, there was even talk of devising the ultimate questionnaire which could be used unchanged in any project, regardless of what it was about.

And so a report is written about what the natives do and even think, by those whose model is so un-dialogic that it even presumes to pre-empt experience. In development reports, just as in medicine and clinical psychiatry, writers often make the abstract noun usurp the verb and strip it of its agency. If they do keep the verb, they

to arrive by mutual negotiation at an intersubjective consensus about the form of the person's death and its meaning for themselves. This consensus is reinforced by the way it is mapped on to the physical landscape over which the living walk, work and dispute every day of their lives. For Freud, and for the western secular tradition generally, the structure of this kind of experience is based on the structure of the mind which does the experiencing, so that experience is essentially private; while for the Sora, the mind seems to have no inner structure and so the structure of experience is based on that of the outside world which the mind experiences. Experience is essentially consensual.

Sora knowledge is perhaps no more than local knowledge, yet at the same time, within its own field of operation, its scope is total. The key to this is the socially embedded nature of Sora ways of knowing. Whereas Freud offers a mere psychology of death, the Sora enjoy a psychology, a theology and a sociology of death. Freudian therapy already has difficulty taking social context into account. Even further along the scale into 'pure' medicine (remembering that in some countries, one cannot be a psychiatrist without a medical qualification), the knowledge is very limited in scope but within this domain, it is universal in its claims. It applies to a more and more restricted area of life, but demands a more and more total control over it. This is shown in Figure 5.1.

Reading it from left to right, the diagram represents a progressive separation of the body from the soul or mind and the emergence of the category 'medicine' as a readiness to treat the body on its own. At each stage, nothing has been changed or even challenged within the realm of cognition. What is at issue in comparing them is not the substance of knowledge, but its appropriateness. It is the context, scope and expectations which have changed. What is hived off at each stage is not simply a spiritual aspect of the person being treated. The inclusion of the soul towards the left-hand side means not just that the body is seen as related to the soul, but that the person is seen in relation to other persons. What is hived off is also a layer of integration in the social dimension within which the whole encounter takes place – that is, a degree of dialogicality. The three stages in the diagram can be characterized as follows:

1 Sora psychotherapy is highly dialogic, with the dialogue taking place between the mourner and the dead person on whom his or her attention is focused.
2 Freud's technique is fairly dialogic, but the interlocutor is dimin-

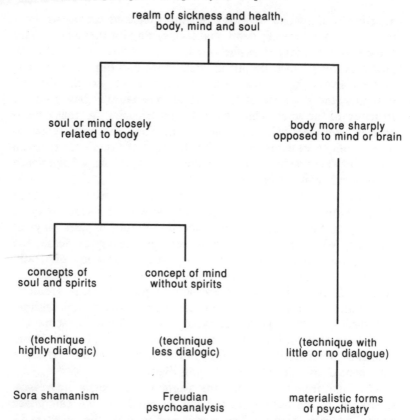

Figure 5.1 Degrees of dialogicality in Sora shamanism, psychoanalysis and clinical psychiatry

ished because the important person has ceased to exist and the analyst can play the role only of a pale substitute.

3 Clinical psychiatry, which in its techniques using tranquillizers and shock therapy is completely de-dialogized.

Part of the process whereby knowledge can become totalitarian is to draw its interlocutors away from this active mode and to convert them into objects: to diminish their agency and consequently their awareness. Within the healing practices of industrial society, there may be a greater or lesser degree of this. Psychoanalysis is rather close to the Sora is its emphasis on speaking, but the material-ist metaphysics of its secular tradition which denies the existence of the dead means that the role of the analysand's interlocutor is drastically modified: instead of talking *through* the specialist *to* the deceased, the mourner can only talk *to* the specialist *about* the deceased. Consider the same patient if he or she embarks on the path of clinical psychiatry or electric shock treatment, perhaps under a doctor who considers psychoanalysis (let alone shamanism) to be mystical nonsense, or a patient being clinically treated before Freud 'unseated physicalism from its pride of place in the treatment of nervous illness and located all therapeutic power in the doctor–patient couple' (Forrester 1980: 1).

To participate in any dialogue or quasi-dialogue, a speaker must be a subject or agent. By this token, even when they see themselves as victims of the dead, the Sora have a high degree of agency since dialogue informs the way in which they perceive and act out their encounters with the dead. The Sora shaman's client participates in the shaman's specialist knowledge in what may be called a very knowing way, that is, in a complementary, active role which gives him or her a high awareness-status.

What remains of ignorance and knowledge in all this? If one is concerned more with technique than with context, then the highly contextualized, technically local methods of shamanism (or subsistence cultivation) may seem ignorant; if one respects context, then the de-contextualized, technically universal methods seems effective, but crass and thus just as ignorant in their own way. There is no growth of ignorance, only the possible *appearance* of ignorance from certain viewpoints looking over to others, all of them constantly shifting their positions in the encounters of history and society.

This appearance of ignorance depends on a denial or annihilation of dialogue. In the encounter of European development programmes with the rest of the world, one can perhaps trace the influence of a certain late medieval development of scholasticism:

> Ramist rhetoric has lost all sense of Socratic dispute . . . . The Ramist arts of discourse are monologue arts. They develop the didactic, schoolroom outlook . . . the speaking is directed to a world where even persons respond only as objects – that is, say nothing back.
>
> (Ong 1958: 287, quoted in Fabian 1983: 114–15)

Consider, for example, the aggressive language of many development projects, with their 'strategies' 'aimed' at 'target groups' who must be vaccinated, sterilized or converted into producers for the market. This is not even the paternalistic language of continuing colonial rule, with its dialogue between unequals. Rather, it is a new, post-colonial language shorn even of this sense of parental responsibility: the language of zapping aliens in a video game. There is a disturbing analogy between an enemy villager whom one bombs, and a friendly villager on whom one wages a health programme or irrigation. The informal interlocutor of the Sora (or the stylized encounter with a royal or chiefly personage in many other highly dialogic societies) gives way to a non-encounter. For the developee, project administrators are akin to the 'faceless' bureaucrat, someone with whom one can have no dialogue, not even an obsequious one. The losers are made ignorant in the sense that they cannot reply or challenge the other person: the game has moved from the debate or the duel to the blanket techniques of high-tech war.

Ignorance is knowledge denied or denigrated, and its apparent 'growth' is really a growth in the knowing party's power to denigrate other knowledges and to refuse to engage in dialogue with their knowers. What is so dangerous when other knowledges are dismissed as ignorances, is that a manichaean terminology which properly belongs in the realm of power relations, is perverted into the idiom of cognition. No cognitive battle has taken place, yet it is part of the folk wisdom of the 'developed world' to believe that it has done so and that the battle has been decided in these terms.

NOTE

I am grateful to Mark Hobart and Ron Inden for comments on an earlier draft of this article.

REFERENCES

Collingwood, R. G. (1940) *An Essay on Metaphysics*, Oxford: Clarendon Press.
Fabian, J. (1983) *Time and the Other*, New York: Columbia University Press.
Forrester, J. (1980) *Language and the Origins of Psychoanalysis*, London: Macmillan.
Freud, S. (1957) [1917] 'Mourning and melancholia', in Standard edn, vol. XIV, London: Hogarth Press.
Gorer, G. (1965) *Death, Grief and Mourning*, London: Cresset Press.
Lakatos, I. and Musgrave, A. (eds) (1970) *Criticism and the Growth of Knowledge*, Cambridge: Cambridge University Press.
Ong, W. J. (1958) *Ramus: Method and the Decay of Dialogue*, Cambridge: Cambridge University Press.
Sheldrake, R. (1981) *A New Science of Life: the Hypothesis of Formative Causation*, London: Blond & Briggs.
Vitebsky, P. (1984) 'Policy dilemmas for unirrigated agriculture in south-

eastern Sri Lanka: a social anthropologist's report on shifting and semi-permanent cultivation in an area of Moneragala District, Cambridge: Centre of South Asian Studies (cyclostyled).
—— (1986) 'National discussion and local actuality: the 'stabilisation' of shifting cultivation in southeastern Sri Lanka, *Manchester Papers on Development* 2(2): 1–12.
—— (1993) *Dialogues with the Dead: the Discussion of Mortality among the Sora of Eastern India*, Cambridge: Cambridge University Press.
Volkan, V. (1981) *Linking Objects and Linking Phenomena: a Study of the Forms, Symptoms, Metapsychology, and Therapy of Complicated Mourning*, New York: International Universities Press.
Worden, J. W. (1982) *Grief Counselling and Grief Therapy: a Handbook for the Mental Health Practitioner*, New York: Springer Publishing Company.

6 Scapegoat and magic charm: law in development theory and practice

Franz von Benda-Beckmann

We must view with profound respect the infinite capacity of the human mind to resist the introduction of useful knowledge.

Thomas Raynesford Lounsbury,
quoted in Macarov, 1980

INTRODUCTION

Ever since I first read the above *aperçu* I have been thinking of it in relation to law-related planning and analysis of social and economic change in developing countries.[1] Law-related development planning – and there is little development policy and implementation which does not involve law – but also large parts of what goes under the name of development theory, seem to prove the above statement. The idea of legal engineering, of achieving social and economic change through government law, still ranks foremost in the arsenal of development techniques. Law, as 'desired situation projected into the future' (F. von Benda-Beckmann 1983a), is used as a magic charm. The law-maker seeks to capture desired economic or social conditions, and the practice supposed to lead towards them, in normative terms, and leaves the rest to law enforcement, or expressed more generally, to the implementation of policy.[2]

If projects fail, law is an easy scapegoat. Sometimes this role is given to state law, particularly if the law in question had been made by a previous government. As a consequence, new law has to be enacted, better law, a more powerful magic charm, but it is usually with no more success. Another explanation for the failure of state law-based projects is that state law does not fit in with local laws and customs. Social scientists, legal anthropologists in particular, tend to blame this upon the legal planning of state governments, which do not take sufficient account of local law. For governments and development planners it is usually local law and customs, or in Indonesia, *adat* which are framed as the scapegoat. The assumption that local law hinders development and that modern, western law is a prerequisite for development is one of the most deeply rooted ideas to inform development planning. It continues to inform development planning despite the fact that it has been repeatedly shown, first that the large-scale introduction of so-called western law has led to deteriorating social and economic conditions for most of the rural population rather than to development, and second, that local law can be sufficiently flexible in its adaptation to social and economic changes.

In short, basic ideas about the function of state law and traditional law have repeatedly turned out to be mistaken. Yet this insight, although quite widely disseminated, somehow does not seem to be acceptable and is hardly ever taken as a point of departure for policy making and project planning.

For those interested in development studies it is not sufficient to stand still and marvel at the capacity of development planners to resist the introduction of useful knowledge. We must try to understand it. If we examine the assumptions mentioned so far we see one common strand: both the magic charm and the scapegoat vision of law are based upon structuralist-functionalist assumptions, the idea that legal structures and norms directly cause or determine action and its consequences. This structuralist-functionalist assumption, which underlies the introduction of state law as a tool of development, has been criticized by many social scientists, in relation to development policy, to the law and development movement, and in social theory.[3] These critiques, however, have largely been directed against the assumptions underlying to state law policy. They have not been systematically extended to the analysis of the social significance of traditional law. Legal anthropologists have criticized legalistic interpretations of customary law and have pointed out that customary legal notions are quite different from western law, being – for instance – more negotiable and flexible.[4] Traditional laws, they showed, therefore frequently adapted easily to changing economic and social conditions. There is also a growing number of analyses showing how local legal notions have been transformed by their interpretation in western bureaucratic courts, and it has even been asserted that customary law was created by colonial state agencies.[5] But the failure of state law and projects based upon it has often been explained in terms of their lack of fit with local law. Thus the structuralist notion here is similar to that held by state bureaucrats. It is only the scapegoat which is different.

In contemporary social theory the dominance of structuralist-functionalist thinking has largely been broken, first by theories (over)emphasizing action or interaction, and in more recent times by more sophisticated theories aiming at the integration of actor-oriented and structural analyses (such as Giddens 1976, 1979). Critical assessments of structuralist-functionalist theories have quite convincingly established that they are 'wrong' in the sense that they do not offer an empirically plausible or valid description, analysis or explanation of social action. But while theorists have aimed at substituting more adequate models in which action and structure are logically related, allowing for a better analysis of social action, they have ignored the fact that structural-functionalism is not only an (inadequate) scientific model but also an important folk model in the social groups which they study. Elimination of structuralist assumptions from theoretical models has obscured their continued empirical existence and social significance. If we want to get rid of them we must analyse the social processes in which they are maintained: we must analyse 'the structuration of structuralist rules', to paraphrase Giddens. We must not only examine them in terms of their theoretical validity but also as social practice. In social practice, these assumptions are found embodied in legal regulations and development plans, in the decisions of judges and administrators, and in processes of interaction between representatives of the state and local populations. This 'fact' seems to validate the assumptions held by development planners. This is why such assumptions can be maintained in the face of so much adverse literature. They may be 'wrong' scientifically, they may be misleading analysis, but they are not completely without a basis in experience.

The existence of such structuralist legal notions in legal regulations, decisions and development plans provides an empirical basis for the development planners' misconstrual of their social significance and for the maintenance of such misconstruals. Since the behaviour expected to follow from the legal notions regularly does not follow, new structuralist legal notions then have to be generated. In this circle, the interaction between villagers and those development agents who come into direct contact with them has an important, but largely neglected place.[6] I shall therefore be mainly concerned with the ways in which villagers through direct and personal experience are confronted with the normative structures of development policies and projects: through the statements and actions of administrative officers, extension officers, teachers, judges, agricultural officers, etc.; and vice versa, how bureaucrats are confronted with the villagers' law. This interaction setting is not the only one, and may not even be the most important one in which the normative elements of development policy and projects become involved in people's behaviour (see F. von Benda-Beckmann *et al.* 1989); nor is it the only one in which legalistic notions of law are generated and maintained. Collier (1976) and Quarles van Ufford (1987), for instance, have shown that local leaders play a central role as mediators between the bureaucracy of the state and villagers, and between state and village legal models. But for the purposes of my argument differentiating between a local population and its leaders is not crucial. It is not my aim to generalize comprehensively on such interactions. I shall focus selectively upon the more unpleasant encounters in which villagers do not comply with local bureaucrats' directives. It is in these situations that the role of traditional law becomes problematic, and the structuralistic interpretations and the scapegoating of traditional law are produced and maintained. One reason for this, and this is the main point I shall emphasize, is that in these interaction settings villagers themselves present a legalistic model of traditional law.

I shall first briefly sketch how law is involved in development policy and projects. Thereafter I shall turn to those normative models which do in fact confront each other in the interaction between development bureaucrats and villagers. On this basis I shall then show how the scapegoating of traditional law is generated and maintained. In conclusion I shall spell out some implications of my analysis for socio-legal research methodology.

THE NORMATIVE STRUCTURES OF DEVELOPMENT PROJECTS

In all contemporary societies salient elements of state policy have to be formulated in terms of law, be this the state budget in the Netherlands or in Indonesia, land reform in Latin American states, family reform in African or Asian states. Small-scale development projects are also framed in legal terms, although usually at the lower level of provincial, district or village regulations and other legal instructions. International or bilateral development projects are also based upon legal structures: inter-governmental agreements, administrative arrangements, plans of operations and the frameworks for implementation and management of projects are laid down in legal terms.

All development projects aim at some change, in other words, they ask of people to change their behaviour, in the hope that that changed behaviour will lead to desired social, economic or political consequences. People are asked to have their land registered, to marry monogamously, to apply for credit, to use fertilizer, to plant cash crops, to practise birth control, to praise the government and to pay taxes. These development activities are rationalized and justified in terms of models (see Allott 1980: 168). These models divide roughly into two components: (1) structures of institutional organization and action which provide options or directives for the activities of bureaucrats or villagers (the latter usually being the 'target group'), or for joint activities; and (2) rationalizations and justifications of these behavioural structures in terms of their supposed social consequences. The models are normative, in their behavioural programme, their goals and their underlying legitimation. In other words, development projects have the form of law.

The involvement of law in development planning and practice is no coincidence; neither is it a matter of conscious choice. It is largely a matter of political necessity and logic. Development, however way we define it, implies change. In as much as government agencies engage in development planning and implementation, they aim at changing behaviour. In other words, they try to exercise power. This exercise of power has to be justified and in contemporary secular and complex societies whose governments operate on the basis of democratic ideologies, state law is the primary source of legitimation for the exercise of power by or in the name of state agencies. This need to employ the legal form is particularly urgent, since the domains of social life in which behavioural changes are envisaged are already subject to normative rules and principles. Most development projects, whatever their scale, thus affect the existing normative framework in which people live in a double manner. They usually introduce new law, and, whether they do that or not, they affect the existing normative ordering in the domains of social action to which they are addressed.

The villagers are confronted with such normative development models through many channels of communication: through the mass media, through gossip and hearsay, and through their direct interaction with development bureaucrats. In general it can be said that in the course of transmission from the context in which the plans and projects were originally generated, to these local level bureau-

crats who are engaged in the implementation, the original models
of these projects undergo a series of reinterpretations, translations,
or transformations, by different actors and in different social settings
(see Collier 1976, Long 1989, Moore 1973, Quarles van Ufford
1987). The actual model which villagers meet is the one communicated to them at the point of contact, usually in the interactive
context in which development bureaucrats tell them what the plans
mean. This local version of state law or policy often has little if
anything to do with whatever plans, laws and policies have been
made on higher levels of political decision-making. Okoth-Ogendo
(1984: 80) gives the following summary account of how state agricultural policy in Kenya was transformed through the conduct of farm
level communication in general and of the substantive form in which
legal phenomena finally reached the farmer in particular.

> Firstly, most of them [bureaucrats] preferred to communicate to
> the farmer either by propaganda or through sanctions. In the
> former case they would simply exhort peasants to heed govern-
> ment policies, advice, and programmes and to obey the law of
> the land. In the latter case peasants were simply prosecuted for
> violations of legal rules to which they couldn't possibly have had
> any access. This was particularly evident in the area of agricul-
> tural marketing and land management. The principle was of
> course that knowledge of the law was presumed.

Also in Botswana (Werbner 1980) and Tanzania (Thoden van
Velzen 1977; Williams 1982) government policies in interaction with
villagers are regularly transformed into propaganda or into direct
demands for villagers' behaviour, both of which are different from
the original model of the policy or project. Writing about the Tribal
Land Boards in Botswana, Werbner states that state officials in their
implementation of the new land law 'work by rule of thumb; and
they have to make up the rules and procedures that they need,
somewhat at hoc, as they go along, in allocation of resources in the
name of a government policy' (1980: 133).

Villagers are thus confronted with local versions of state development law which often have nothing to do with the original version.
Their reaction to the local bureaucrats' demands or decisions
depends on how they interpret that local and not the original version. These interpretations, as well as the ensuing behaviour, are
related to and conditioned by the institutional context and the
system of relationships in which the villagers live, the other rules
and procedures which they consider to be relevant for their activi-

ties, and the consequences to be expected from the behavioural options they consider (see Moore 1973). Within this context, the villagers' interpretation of what the local versions of governmental law and policy mean for themselves is strongly coloured by their perception of local bureaucrats and their way of dealing with the law. Villagers tend to be 'legal realists' and strongly actor oriented. Of course, the local bureaucrats' version of state law and policy is not the same thing as the local bureaucrats' actions. Villagers can make that distinction and so should we. But in deciding what to do in response to the bureaucrats' demands, villagers concern themselves with what, according to their experience and expectation, the model – that is, what the bureaucrats say about it – will mean in practice.[7] They tend to identify the state's models with what the local bureaucrats do.

In those situations in which villagers do not want to follow the bureaucrats' instructions, the images villagers have of local-level bureaucrats are not very favourable.[8] At the risk of exaggerating slightly, it may be said that they regard local level bureaucrats as arrogant dummies – dummies, since local-level bureaucrats often do not seem to know what they are talking about. In village cultures where verbal skills are highly valued, the uneasy rhetoric or imperative jargon of bureaucrats is ridiculous and repulsive (see Thoden van Velzen 1977, Werbner 1980). Bureaucrats often do not know the local cultures of the people whom they are supposed to 'develop', and what they say about it, distorted as it will be to fit their bureaucratic rhetoric, is often felt to be offensive and stupid (see also Dove 1986). And when villagers listen to bureaucrats propagating development policy and state ideology, when they explain what they, the villagers, should do and why, and to what all this would lead, the villagers will easily find the bureaucrats cynical or stupid. Will joining a state regulated co-operative lead to the improvement of the economic position of the poor? Will social justice be achieved? Will registration of land rights increase legal security? Who, with a minimum of intelligence, could ever seriously believe such empty phrases? Also, villagers resent the arrogance of bureaucratic power, which is not based upon knowledge and skill but on the power of the state and what state officials consider to be state law. They resent the arrogance of people who will not work with their hands any more, who won't lift a finger when work is to be done, yet exhort them to work harder; who ride around on scooters or in cars and have villagers come on foot to their offices in vain (see Thoden van Velzen 1977).

At the point of contact, in sum, the versions of state law relevant in the interaction process are thus what local level bureaucrats state the model to be and the villagers' interpretations of these statements (cf. K. von Benda-Beckmann 1984, Lipsky 1980, Moore 1973, Thoden van Velzen 1977, Werbner 1980). The result often bears only a distant resemblance to what a development planner envisaged in a capital city far away from the local scene where policy is to be implemented.

THE VILLAGERS' LAW

If we look at the versions of local law which the villagers present in their interaction with local-level bureaucrats, we can observe that these also often differ from their local law in other interaction settings. Here, too, we have to do with reinterpretation and transformations of law. Let me try to illustrate this with an example from Minangkabau, based upon my own field experience (see F. von Benda-Beckmann 1979).

What do Minangkabau villagers think and say when they are confronted with government demands to have their rice land registered, their *adat* rights converted to state law rights, and to make and keep written genealogies of the persons entitled to land, all in the interest of modernization, legal certainty, and economic progress? They say that registration is contrary to *adat;* that their *adat* does not allow for individualized, ownership-like rights, and that *adat* prohibits the sale of land, certainly if this is lineage land, *harato pusako*.

This is, indeed, the version of Minangkabau *adat* as it has been reproduced in oral transmission and in literature, both by foreign observers and by Minangkabau writers themselves. But it is an over-idealized and 'old-fashioned' version of *adat*, different from current *adat* in the sense of the body of rules and principles which govern Minangkabau behaviour in land matters (inasmuch as behaviour is at all governed by rules). In daily village life one can observe forms of social practice which are regarded as valid and legitimate in terms of *adat:* individualized and ownership-like rights to *harato pusako* are regarded as legitimate under certain conditions. Land is pledged validly under conditions other than those laid down by classical *adat*. *Pusako* land is sold occasionally, and may be validly sold if all people concerned agree to the sale. Registration is certainly unknown in *adat*, but so are many other new developments which the Minangkabau gladly incorporate in village life and *adat*. Genealogies are orally transmitted, kept in many lineages, sometimes also written down, and are considered to be very important in land matters.

Villagers present their *adat* in legalistic terms. They argue that, since they are bound by *adat* prescriptions, they cannot act differently from the way they do. Their behaviour, their non-compliance with the bureaucrats' demands, can be shown to follow logically from the binding force of *adat* rules.

But this legalistic model of *adat* which villagers bring into the interaction with the bureaucrats is not their usual model. As has been noted by various scholars of *adat* law, their normative system is much more complex, flexible and negotiable than peasants make bureaucrats believe. It leaves room for a variety of behavioural alternatives (see F. von Benda-Beckmann 1979, K. von Benda-Beckmann 1982, 1984). That the application of *adat* rules and principles to a concrete situation depends on the circumstances of the actual case, or 'depends on situation and condition', *tergantung situasi dan condisi* as the Indonesians say, has become proverbial.

Why should the Minangkabau represent their *adat* in old-fashioned and legalistic terms? If they presented their own contemporary model of *adat* to the bureaucrats, it would be clear to everyone that Minangkabau *adat* does not provide strong reasons for not registering land. And this is what Minangkabau want to avoid, for they do not want to register land. They do not want to be ordered about. And in order to rationalize and justify their refusal to register land, they resuscitate an old-fashioned and legalistic version of *adat*.[9] This model is used in the interaction because it is the only way in which they can account for their behaviour in an acceptable way. They could scarcely say what they really feel about the matter of registration. What, for example, would the reaction of the district head or the governor be, if the villagers said what they thought in words such as these:

> Honourable sir, this land registration that you keep pressing us to do is something which we do not want to have anything to do with. So please stop nagging. Land affairs are none of your concern and we never asked for state laws concerning land. Besides, we are afraid that land registration is just another trick of the government to have us pay more taxes, with which you will finance the transmigration of Javanese to Sumatra. No thank you. And the registration process is quite different from what you have told us. It costs much more than you said and more

than the government promised in its cheap registration programme. The land registration officers will not come to our village
unless we pay them travel costs and other so-called administrative
fees. And talking about legal certainty: perhaps you were joking,
sir. The registrations which have been made so far were in secret.
They only served goals which could not be pursued in public, to
cheat people out of their inheritance rights.

I believe that most Minangkabau villagers react inwardly like this
when they think of registration; at least they did so when we were
doing research there fourteen years ago. But if they addressed local
bureaucrats like this they would be asking for trouble. It was much
safer to direct the bureaucrats' anger at their *adat* law. Then they
might be told that they were backward, that their law was not
recognized any more by the state, and that it was not conducive to
development . . . but the likelihood that they would be denounced
as a saboteur or a subversive element was small. And this made
quite a difference.

The local-level bureaucrats, like the villagers, interpret the villagers' law in the context of their own system of relationships and
expectations (cf. Lipsky 1980). In their case, too, perception of the
local law is coloured by their view of the villagers. Again at the
risk of some exaggeration, it may be said that they see villagers as
hypocritical opportunists. They see them as opportunistic because
they observe the villagers' efforts to take as much advantage as
possible of them (or of the state which they represent) without
seriously assuming the concomitant obligations. People want credit
but will avoid paying it back. People want new roads and bridges
but do not want to join a co-operative effort in building them.
People want schools but do not want to pay school fees. Etc., etc.
Villagers are regarded as hypocritical since they shield themselves
behind their own culture, their folk law, their world-view, when
they do not, or do not want to, follow the bureaucrats' advice or
instructions; yet they constantly deviate from it when it suits them.
They play the *adat* law purist, yet are the first to run to the police
to have a conflict settled. They will publicly reprimand fellow villagers for invoking the state court and go there the next day themselves. They nod in agreement when the district head or governor
elaborates on the necessities of land registration and conversion of
customary rights, and praise him and the head of state for their
wise development policy. But back in the village they decry the
government's efforts to change their land law, denounce its repug-

nance and inconsistencies with their local law and advise people to refrain from registering their land. Yet they may be the first ones to have their land registered, albeit secretly (for more illustration from Minangkabau, see F. von Benda-Beckmann 1979; K. von Benda-Beckmann 1984).

TRADITIONAL LAW AS SCAPEGOAT

We see how the idea that traditional law keeps villagers from acting in compliance with the development bureaucrats' demands and that it therefore can justly be blamed for failed development efforts is produced or maintained in local-level interaction. Local bureaucrats are confronted with a specific version of *adat* law and react to it. They see their attempts to implement policy frustrated by behaviour which is rationalized and justified in terms of *adat* law. They are therefore likely to regard folk law as an impediment to development. The reasons given by villagers thus are regarded as causes. The villagers' rationalizations and justifications of behaviour are seen as motivations, motivations of a strongly normative, even coercive character.

This view is often reinforced in other interaction settings. Research, and the communication of research results, can have such an effect, if description and analysis are informed by structuralist assumptions. Researchers analyse the state laws concerning land and the local legal system. They conclude that there are many differences between these, that some contradictions are really irreconcilable, that the state law does not fit into the patterns of the villagers' law. And they can produce relevant evidence for this. From there it is only a small step to explaining the villagers' non-compliance with state regulations in terms of these contradictions. If a researcher stays longer, he or she will discover that quite frequently people do not behave according to the – idealized – rules which have been stated in interviews or which have been pronounced in decisions of local authorities. He or she is then likely to construe any observations in terms of the discrepancy between ideal law and social practice and to conclude that *adat* law is not 'in force' any more.

Both these insights from research are gladly taken up by bureaucrats, for social science reinforces their own view and appears to tell them that local law can be abolished on two counts: first, it is inimical to development, and second, it is not even taken seriously by the people themselves, who are just . . . hypocritical opportunists. So both villagers and researchers provide the bureaucrats with a rationalization and justification for their, the bureaucrats', failure to implement the registration programme, and simultaneously for exerting more pressure on the peasants. Thus development bureaucrats, if called upon to explain their inability to implement development projects, can deflect any serious critique of their own shortcomings, or those of the policy they advocate, or of the procedures which they follow, and direct it at this transformed version of the villagers' model of *adat*.

These are, I think, the basic mechanisms through which the idea that local cultural and legal systems hinder development is maintained. And we can see that it is not just stupidity or simple ethnocentrism on the part of development planners which gives rise to this idea. The villagers themselves actively contribute to its maintenance.

METHODOLOGICAL IMPLICATIONS

The discussion so far and a few brief illustrations show us that in the interaction between local-level bureaucrats and villagers models of government and local traditional law are involved which differ in their content and structure from those produced and maintained in other interaction settings.

The basic message of my discussion for research directed at the involvement of law in social practice consequently is the need to contextualize, to look at different interaction settings in which normative conceptions are produced and maintained. This means that one must not generalize from observations in any single type of interaction setting (F. von Benda-Beckmann 1984, Schaareman 1986). Any social scientific research into law and its significance in social life which looks for 'the' law or 'the effective law or *adat*' is futile because it sets out from the incorrect assumption that law exists and can be described and analysed independently of context – or, what amounts to the same thing – that it is the same in all contexts. For this reason alone, reliance on key informants and questionnaire surveys is as unacceptable as a sole research method, as are the casuistic approaches which have dominated socio-legal studies for a long time (for earlier critiques see among other Gluckman 1973, Holleman 1973). Validity or effectiveness in one context, or in one respect, says in itself nothing about validity and effectiveness in other contexts. To refer to one of our findings from our research into Minangkabau village law in the 1970s: the *adat* of consensual decision-making (*musyawarah untuk mupakat*) may no longer be strong enough to ensure that valid decisions are actually achieved in villagers' problems. But it may still be strong enough to prevent any other form of decision-making to be accepted as valid and practicable by villagers (see in particular K. von Benda-Beckmann 1981, 1984). Conclusions based only on one or the other of these observations are distorting, and administrative measures based upon such conclusions will fail.

The importance of context helps to illuminate the fundamental difference in approach between social scientific research into law and the methodologies adopted by legal scholars, advocates and judges. The latter are concerned with a different enterprise: bound by legal rules which prescribe that they base their decisions upon 'the' correct law, they are required to make a choice of one correct law and to identify its source(s), that is, the interaction settings in which this true law is generated and maintained. Such an approach is incompatible with a socio-legal approach aimed at discovering the existence and social significance of legal rules 'in many contexts' (see F. von Benda-Beckmann 1983b, 1984, Galanter 1981, Griffiths 1986). Any attempt to fuse legal science and social science can only work to the detriment of both. This fundamental incompatibility was clearly recognized by Ter Haar (1937) who postulated a clear distinction between the science of *adat* (private) law on the one hand and anthropological approaches to *adat* law on the other.

The discussion also shows that we must distinguish more sharply the modes in which legal rules and procedures are involved in human action as a 'language of interaction' (Fuller 1978).

We have seen that the interaction partners use law, with more or less explicit reference to a particular legal model, in order to account for their behaviour, and in order to rationalize and justify their demands or their unwillingness to comply with the demands made by others. Law – a particular model of law – becomes 'a weapon in social conflict' (Turk 1976), a strategic resource employed in the interaction.[10] As such, it is important to both state bureaucrats and villagers. The one can use it to legitimate his demands, the other his refusal to comply with these demands. In the same sense it is, on a more general level, important to state governments or other development agents who have to frame their development policy in legal terms. In all these cases, the behaviour and objectives concerned must be represented as following logically from, or at least being in conformity with, the norms with which they are legitimated. In other words, the legal models involved imply a causative, deterministic character of law.

In such models of law, we can observe a transformation of the logical structure of legal propositions which is familiar from court procedures and judgements. In the interaction between local bureaucrats and villagers the conditional 'if-then' structure of general legal rules is transformed into what I have called 'concrete law' (F. von Benda-Beckmann 1979: 31, 32), into a reasoned, causal 'as-therefore' proposition in which concrete consequences are derived from general rules. If an observer generalizes on the basis of observed instances such concrete law, the prescriptive character of the 'as-therefore' rationalization is introduced into the 'if-then' structure of general rules (1979: 37). As a consequence, the flexibility and openness characteristic of much law, and local traditional law in particular, is lost, and the stereotype of prescriptive law is maintained. As I have pointed out earlier (1979: 37, 1986b: 100), this is one important reason why concepts or definitions of law based upon court decisions or, more generally, on sanctioning behaviour, have little value for a socio-legal methodology.

The mode of law involvement as resource in interaction is quite different from one in which legal rules are regarded as 'influences' or 'determinants' of behaviour, as sources of motivation or guidance for specific activities. As Moore (1978: 210) has pointed out with respect to dispute settlement decisions, and as I have here shown for quite different interaction settings, the reasons given for behaviour (decisions) must not be confused with its underlying causes.[11] In the situation I have discussed, people can be said to orient their behaviour toward a given model of law. But the model of law thus employed is not identical with the ones which they take as guidelines when they make up their minds how to act, in the same or in other interaction settings such as everyday land transactions. In such other contexts their considerations and strategies are usually motivated and directed by a multitude of quite different factors, which constrain the formation of goals pursued in their behavioural projects. Law usually is just one, and often not even the most important one, of these factors.

Failure to distinguish the different modes of law involvement can be especially misleading in situations of overt legal pluralism. In these situations actors are usually identified with the legal subsystem which they use in their argumentation. When causes for or influences on their behaviour are looked for in law, attention therefore tends to be directed toward the actors' 'own' law. But if people, villagers and bureaucrats alike, take account of law when making up their minds, they are usually influenced by the whole of their normative universe, out of which they select those aspects which they deem to be relevant points of orientation in a specific situation (see F. von Benda-Beckmann 1983b; K. von Benda-Beckmann 1984). They may consider not only non-legal factors but elements from their whole legal universe, including notions of *adat*, state law, and Islamic law, in arriving at their behavioural goals and strategies. For the villagers, the bureaucrats' model, as they interpret it (though not in the way that development bureaucrats want) is usually a quite important point of orientation. If and when people refuse to apply for credit, or to register their land, or to join a co-operative, they do take into consideration the bureaucrats' model. This model often does not appeal to them very much, but even so it may well be their primary source of (negative) motivation. Thus the villagers' behaviour may be influenced much more by the normative structures of state regulations or development projects than by their *adat* law, even where they use *adat* to rationalize and justify their behaviour. In those cases in which they do not wish to comply with development agents' directives it usually is not *adat* law which hinders development, and it is not modernity of development as such which villagers oppose: it is mainly development as propagated by arrogant dummies.

NOTES

1 This is a revised version of a paper presented at the International Seminar, 'Impacts of Development', held in Padang, Indonesia, in June 1988. I thank John Griffiths and Mark Hobart for their critical and constructive comments on the earlier version of this paper. In a slightly different form, this paper has been published in *Journal of Legal Pluralism* 28:129–48.
2 For a description and critical analysis of such ideas see F. von Benda-Beckmann 1983a, Fitzpatrick 1980, Greenberg 1980, Griffiths 1978, Merryman 1977, Moore 1973, Snyder 1980, Trubek and Galanter 1974.
3 See Abel 1980, Giddens 1976, Grace and Wilkinson 1978, Long 1989, Nelken 1985, and the authors mentioned in note 2.
4 See F. von Benda-Beckmann 1979, K. von Benda-Beckmann 1982, Gluckman 1972, Van Vollenhoven 1909.
5 See F. and K. von Benda-Beckmann 1984, K. von Benda-Beckmann 1982, 1984, Chanock 1978, Snyder 1981, Woodman 1985. See also the recent special issue of the *Journal of African Law* 28 (1984), on the transformation of African customary law.
6 These local-level bureaucrats are what Lipsky calls 'street level bureaucrats: public service workers who interact with citizens in the course of their jobs, and who have substantial discretion in the execution of their work' (1980: 3).

7 Villagers are socialized in their own normative system in which the dominant way of thought is that models, standards and prescriptions are given real meaning in the social processes in which these models are realized, and not so much through abstract formulations (see K. von Benda-Beckmann 1984). I have described this for villagers' reactions to the Indonesian government's land registration programme in F. von Benda-Beckmann 1986a.

8 For particularly vivid illustrations see Thoden van Velzen 1977. For further examples see also the essays collected in Quarles van Ufford 1987 and MacAndrews 1986.

9 Spiertz (1986) has given an interesting description of the strategic use of old legal notions in a dispute between villagers, administrative officials and the management of a hotel in Bali.

10 The 'use of law' is, of course, not confined to the rationalization and justification of action. It also covers the use of legally structured instrumentalities such as transaction forms or dispute settlement institutions; see F. von Benda-Beckmann 1983b.

11 Even Comaroff and Roberts (1981), who have presented us with perhaps the most sophisticated analysis of the problematic relationship between rules and outcomes in dispute settlement procedures, ultimately situate these two modes of law involvement – which they call the 'apparent dualism in Tswana Law' (p. 239) – along a one-dimensional continuum (pp. 238, 241), which only indicates variations in the degree to which the arguments of disputing parties and deciding judges are seen to be 'norm-governed' (see pp. 239, 241).

REFERENCES

Abel, R. (1980) 'Redirecting social studies of law', *Law and Society Review* 14: 805–29.

Allott, A. N. (1980) *The Limits of Law*, London: Butterworths.

Benda-Beckmann, F. von (1979) *Property in Social Continuity*, The Hague: M. Nijhoff.

—— (1983a) 'Op zoek naar het kleinere euvel in de jungle van het rechtspluralisme', inaugural lecture, Agricultural University, Wageningen.

—— (1983b) 'Why law does not behave: critical and constructive reflections on the social scientific perception of the social significance of law', in H. Finkler (comp.) *Proceedings of the XIth ICAES Congress, Vancouver*, Ottawa.

—— (1984) 'Law out of context: a comment on the creation of traditional law discussion', *Journal of African Law* 28: 28–33.

—— (1986a) 'Leegstaande luchtkastelen: Over da pathologie van grondenrechtshervorming in ontwikkelingslanden', in W. Brussaard *et al.*, *Recht in ontwikkeling: tien agrarisch-rechtelijke opstellen*, Deventer: Kluwer.

—— (1986b) 'Anthropology and comparative law', in K. von Benda-Beckmann and F. Strijbosch (eds) *Anthropology of Law in the Netherlands*, Dordrecht: Foris.

Benda-Beckmann, F. von, Eldijk, A. van, Spiertz, J. and Huber, F. (1989) 'Interfaces or janusfaces: a critical appraisal of the interface approach in development sociology from a socio-legal perspective', in N. Long (ed.) *Encounters at the Interface*, Wageningen: Pudoc.

Benda-Beckmann, K. von (1981) 'Forum shopping and shopping forums', *Journal of Legal Pluralism* 19: 117–59.

—— (1982) 'Traditional values in a non-traditional context', *Indonesia Circle* 28: 39–50.

—— (1984) *The Broken Stairways to Concensus: Village Justice and State Courts in Minangkabau*, Dordrecht: Foris.

Benda-Beckmann F. and K. von (1984) 'Transformation and change in Minangkabau adat', in K. von Benda-Beckmann, *The Broken Stairways to Concensus*, Dordrecht: Foris.

—— (1988) 'Adat and religion in Minangkabau and Ambon' in H. Claessen and D. Moyer (eds) *Time Past, Time Present, Time Future: Perspectives on Indonesian Culture*, Dordrecht: Foris.

Chanock, M. (1978) 'Neo-traditionalism and customary law in Malawi', *African Law Studies*, 16: 80–91.

Collier, J. (1976) 'Political leadership and legal change in Zinacantan', *Law and Society Review* 11: 131–63.

Comaroff, J. L. and Roberts, S. (1981) *Rules and Processes: the Cultural Logic of Dispute in an African Context*, Chicago and London: The University of Chicago Press.

Dove, M. R. (1986) 'The ideology of agricultural development in Indonesia', in C. MacAndrews (ed.) *Central Government and Local Development in Indonesia*, Singapore: Oxford University Press.

Fitzpatrick, P. (1980) 'Law, modernization and mystification', in S. Spitzer (ed.) *Research in Law and Sociology* 3: 161–78.

Fuller, L. L. (1978) 'Law and human interaction', in H. M. Johnson (ed.) *Social Systems and Legal Process*, San Francisco: Sage Publications.

Galanter, M. (1981) 'Justice in many rooms: courts, private ordering and indigenous law', *Journal of Legal Pluralism* 19: 1–47.

Giddens, A. (1976) *New Rules of Sociological Method: a Positive Critique of Interpretative Sociologies*, London: Hutchinson.

—— (1979) *Central Problems in Social Theory: Action, Structure and Contradiction in Social Analysis*, London: Macmillan.

Gluckman, M. (1972) *Ideas in Barotse Jurisprudence*, Manchester: Manchester University Press.

—— (1973) 'The limitations of the case method,' *Law and Society Review*, 7: 611–42.

Grace, C. and Wilkinson, P. (1978) *Negotiating the Law*, London: Routledge & Kegan Paul.

Greenberg, D. (1980) 'Law and development in the light of dependency theory,' in S. Spitzer (ed.) *Research in Law and Sociology* 3: 129–59.

Griffiths, J. (1978) 'Is law important?' inaugural lecture, University of Groningen, Groningen.

—— (1986) 'What is legal pluralism?' *Journal of Legal Pluralism* 24: 1–55.

Haar, B. Ter (1937) 'Het adat-privaatrecht van Nederlandsch-Indië in wetenschap, practijk en onderwijs', inaugural lecture, Rechtshogeschool, Batavia.

Hitchcock, R. K. (1980) 'Tradition, social justice and land reform in Central Botswana', *Journal of African Law* 24: 1–34.

Holleman, J. F. (1973) 'Trouble-cases and trouble-less cases in the study of customary law and legal reform', *Law and Society Review* 7: 585–610.

Lipsky, M. (1980) *Street Level Bureaucracy*, New York: Russell Sage Foundation.

Long, N. (ed.) (1989) *Encounters at the Interface: A Perspective on Structural Discontinuity in Rural Development*, Wageningen: Pudoc.

MacAndrews, C. (ed.) (1986) *Central Government and Local Development in Indonesia*, Singapore: Oxford University Press.

Macarov, D. (1980) *Work and Welfare: the Unholy Alliance*, London: Sage Publications.

Merryman, J. H. (1977) 'Comparative law and social change: on the origins, style, decline and revival of the law and development movement', *American Journal of Comparative Law* 25: 457–91.

Moore, S. F. (1973) 'Law and social change: the semi-autonomous social field as an appropriate field of study,' *Law and Society Review* 7: 719–46.

Moore, S. F. (1978) *Law as Process: an Anthropological Approach*, London: Routledge & Kegan Paul.

Nelken, D. (1985) 'Legislation and its constraints: a case study of the British Rent Act', in A. Podgorecki, C. Whelan and D. Khosla (eds) *Legal Systems and Social Systems*, London: Croom Helm.

Okoth-Ogendo, H. W. O. (1984) 'Development and the legal process in Kenya: an analysis of the role of law in rural development administration', *International Journal of the Sociology of Law* 12: 59–83.

Quarles van Ufford, P. (ed.) (1987) *Local Leadership and Programme Implementation in Indonesia*, Amsterdam: Free University Press.

Schaareman, D. (1986) 'Context and the interpretation of adat rules in a Balinese village', in K. von Benda-Beckmann and F. Strijbosch (eds) *Anthropology of Law in the Netherlands*, Dordrecht: Foris.

Snyder, F. (1980) 'Law and development in the light of dependency theory', *Law and Society Review* 14: 723–804.

—— (1981) 'Colonialism and legal form: the creation of "customary law" in Senegal', *Journal of Legal Pluralism* 19: 49–92.

Spiertz, J. (1986) 'Vreemde gasten: een casus uit Bali', in W. Brussaard *et al.* (eds) *Recht in ontwikkeling: tien agrarisch-rechtelijke opstellen*, Deventer: Kluwer.

Thoden van Velzen, H. U. E. (1977) 'Staff, kulaks and peasants: a study of political field', in L. Cliffe, J. S. Coleman and M. Doornbos (eds) *Government and Rural Development in East Africa*, The Hague: Institute of Social Studies.

Trubek, D. and Galanter, M. (1974) 'Scholars in self-estrangement: some reflections on the crisis in law and development studies in the United States', *Wisconsin Law Review* 1974: 1062–102.

Turk, A. T. (1976) 'Law as a weapon in social conflict', *Social Problems* 23: 276–91.

Vollenhoven, C. van (1909) *Miskenningen van het Adatrecht*, Leiden: Brill.

Werbner, R. P. (1980) 'The quasi-judicial and the experience of the absurd: making land law in North-Eastern Botswana', *Journal of African Law* 24: 131–50.

Williams, D. V. (1982) 'State coercion against peasant farmers: the Tanzanian case', *Journal of Legal Pluralism* 20: 95–127.

Woodman, G. R. (1985) 'Customary law, state courts, and the notion of institutionalization of norms in Ghana and Nigeria', in A. N. Allott and G. R. Woodman (eds), *People's Law and State Law: the Bellagio Papers*, Dordrecht: Foris.

7 Knowledge and ignorance in the practices of development policy

Philip Quarles van Ufford

THE PROBLEM POSED: AN EXAMPLE

The regional development project in one of the outer regions of Indonesia had been set up in the middle of the 1970s jointly by the Indonesian and Dutch governments.[1] After some years it was severely criticized by its western sponsoring agency for its apparent failure to create workable strategies which would benefit the poor. It was said to have invested too much energy in the constitution of a sizeable body of information concerning the region, analysing growing regional disparities, infrastructures, etc. This kind of work had been agreed upon at the inception of the project, as the whole idea of regional development in Indonesia was new and nobody really knew what it implied. Although the idea of collecting a body of information about the region to weigh up different policy options carefully had been regarded as sensible in the beginning, it could not be tolerated any more. And indeed the pile of reports seemed to grow uncontrollably, asking primarily for more research and refinement of data. The relationship between research and action proved to be more stubborn than envisaged. The sponsoring agency decided that the project director had failed to bring about definite action to benefit the poor. He was fired. What had been regarded as a careful planning exercise was now seen as mainly of academic, that is of very little, importance.

During the new negotiations which started the two governments agreed upon a number of concrete projects which would be selected for the continuation of bilateral co-operation in regional planning. So instead of the myth that better action results from careful analysis, a new policy was created: learning by doing. So, without much ado, the two governments started to spend money on actual projects, stating that their course could be changed when that seemed wise in the course of their implementation. The regional development effort thus continued and the earlier development myth was transformed through an inversion. Instead of 'planning from above', now a 'bottom-up approach' was propagated, one which involved the local participants in decision-making about the actual activities that would follow.

For the survival of the regional development scheme two things became of paramount importance: the allocated funds had to be spent and the new discourse of the participatory approach upheld. The two vital elements for the success and continuity of the scheme were of course quite contradictory as the need for spending rather sizeable funds almost precluded the views of people at the local level being taken into account in the planning exercise. So this tension had to be resolved.

The solution was found in the careful managing of the information and images of the local scene. One of the particular activities allocated to the peasantry involved the construction of pump irrigation. The pumps were designed in such a way that maintenance by local people would be relatively easy and inexpensive. Furthermore, the pumps would be fully owned by the peasants in a few years' time, through village organizations which had been set up some years before. So, by using appropriate technology and organizational provision for local participation, the project for pump irrigation clearly showed that a new era in development in the region had started, which was full in line with the official policy of poverty eradication and participation.

Two years after the new start the study department of the sponsoring agency sent a team into the field to make a thorough assessment of the various projects in the region. It was not one of the short-lived evaluation teams, which routinely pay visits to development projects but a longer-term exercise in 'institutional learning'. That meant that a close analysis of the projects was possible. The process of 'implementation' in some of the villages was studied extensively. The research report shattered the image of a 'bottom-up approach', as it became clear that the local organizations did not really represent the peasants, nor could they be expected to function effectively. The farmers' organizations had been set up throughout Indonesia by presidential decree some years before. As these units were the only legitimate channels through which the pump irrigation project could 'reach' the village, it also became clear that the projects' benefits would go to the friends and relations of the village head.

The scheme as a whole met with scepticism or outright opposition from most of the villagers.

Though the official report was meant to be a learning device for the western agency and would not be involved in the decision-making process of the regional planning project, the report was very badly received, not only by the expatriate project staff in the field, but also more surprisingly by the donor country's desk officers. It was never translated into the Indonesian language and was safely stored away. The project continued to be regarded officially as a success, not least because it clearly substantiated the importance of incorporating a participatory approach to the diffusion of technological innovations.

The politically important notion of a 'bottom-up approach' had been saved at the top level of the donor agency from the dangers of being confronted with too detailed information about what was happening locally. The official reaction had its specific administrative rationality: the report's analysis of the local farmers' organizations could not be used for a transformation of actual project activities. The project staff did not have the capacity to interfere in the villages in this politically sensitive area. If the staff admitted that the relations between the local officials and the peasants were indeed problematic, they would endanger the development project as a whole. The regional planning project depended very much on the goodwill of the Indonesian and Dutch authorities. The image of a 'traditional' and relatively homogeneous village community, represented by the 'peasants' organizations, thus became a precondition of survival of the project. These notions were central to the development discourse of the Indonesian government. Everyone involved in the project knew that these notions were false, yet there was no alternative to upholding the official development ideology.

THE PROBLEM POSED: SOME THEORETICAL CONSIDERATIONS

The short history of this development programme illustrates that there are at least two social fields in which problems of constituting knowledge and ignorance must be discussed: (1) the relations between the project officers and the local population, and (2) the relations of the project staff with the sponsoring agencies who have authority over funding and the continuation of the programme. In this chapter I shall argue that the two social fields are antagonistically interrelated. That means that the kind of knowledge which is produced by the project as a whole results from a balancing of conflicting exigencies which the project staff face in the course of their work.

The introductory case indicates that there is a discrepancy between the language of the development agency, i.e. a stress upon the 'bottom-up approach' and 'local homogeneity', which creates an image of the active involvement of peasants in the project's activities, and the virtual absence of any such involvement as observed by the anthropologists in the study team. Yet project staff were required to substantiate the notion of 'active involvement' in their reporting to the Indonesian officials and the western sponsoring agency. The concept of 'local organization' served this important purpose. The concept suggested that the peasants had done their homework, that links had been established with the staff members, in short that the goals of the project were taken seriously. The project's survival depended on this as the official documents required a participatory approach.

A contradiction emerged. For the need to know what was going on locally and the need to remain ignorant of what was happening were inextricably connected. This became clear when the project staff fairly aggressively opposed the findings of the research report. The project's survival depended upon maintaining – or creating – sufficient ignorance about what was happening locally. There was no viable alternative. It was quite impossible for the staff members to discuss the requirements of official views, which were probably unmanageable anyway.

In order to understand the rationality of this delicate balancing of knowledge and ignorance, we must place development projects in a proper theoretical perspective. For this purpose it is useful to distinguish between two (sets of) models which represent the relationship between the production of knowledge and development activities differently: (1) an idealistic, or systems, model,[2] and (2) an arena, or survival, model.[3]

The first model is idealistic because it takes the desirability and manageability of social change as a point of departure. For this purpose the emphasis is on the question of which kind of change is desirable. The distinction between goals, means and results is based on the idea that the relationship between the different groups of participants in various social fields are relatively unproblematic. Once the goals are formulated by the officials, these are to be implemented locally. That presupposes that these goals are not changed once the activities resulting from budget decisions start.

From this perspective evaluation and feedback are equally seen to be unproblematic. Such evaluation and feedback are supposed to help officials understand how far the goals have been achieved during implementation, and so lead to 'institutional learning'. Then the project cycle starts all over again, with new budgetary allocations and goals to be implemented again. The concept of 'system' suggests that the different groups of participants are mutually dependent and integrated. Their relationships do not pose a problem which must be studied in order to grasp the dynamics of policies and programmes.

This systems model in a sense reflects the interests of those who are responsible for the initial formulation of the project. It provides an image of efficiency and manageability, of internal coherence and argumentation, as well as of integration between the different organizational levels, and so of effectiveness. So the model helps to create trust among a wider public, on which the development organization is dependent for its funding. If things go wrong, the model also suggests that the causes of failure are to be found outside the coherent and integrated administrative 'machinery'.

While the systems model is a 'minister's model', which analyses the processes of development policy from the point of view of those who are responsible and set such policies in motion, the arena model is different. It has therefore been called a 'sceptical model' (cf. Lammers 1983). Yet this is true only in relationship to 'the minister', as his need to present an image of effectiveness is not taken as a point of departure for analysis. The arena model does not conceptualize the policy process as an integrated whole, but as a series of multiple negotiations between different groups of participants. These may be found within one specific agency as well as between different levels of organization, namely the western donor agency, Third World counterparts, local project staff and the local population. These various groups, while related, also possess and defend different views and interests, or try to in various ways.

While the idealistic model assumes 'sufficient' control at the 'top', the arena model assumes that the linkages between the different groups of participants are problematic. The relations between these different groups constitute an arena, a space in which the problems of differential interests and interpretations of what should be done must be settled. While the first model assumes that these struggles have been settled at the beginning, the arena model does not (Quarles van Ufford 1988; Rondinelli 1983). Initial goals and strategies may be accepted by members of different groups. Yet these same participants may articulate different views and interests later on when money starts to flow in. There is no clear-cut distinction between support and resistance, between implementation and the transformation of original intentions, indeed between power and vulnerability, as my introductory case suggests. So we have carefully to study the relations between the various groups of participants who are involved in policy processes. We cannot take for granted the notions of order which underpin the first model. We have to study how and why the policy process is transformed, blocked, neutralized or even 'implemented' over time, how and when different views of development shape and reshape policy, and how the participants make use of different bases of power at different levels.

The definition of a particular problem of development is closely related to, and constrained by, the nature of the specific capabilities of the various development agencies involved. Definitions of development are vital 'symbolic capital', which is carefully tended by the agencies. These 'analyses' should not be seen as equivalent to a disinterested, scientific analysis. On the contrary, the capacity to control definitions of what is supposed to be happening locally is of the utmost importance to the agencies as, in a way, they constitute their organizational identity and their 'logo' in the development market. Such representations provide the means for the agencies to gain political support and access to funding in their own constituencies. The need to construct notions of manageability is also related to this. The problems of development must not only be construed in a way which appeals to wider audiences, but they must also help to make the role of the agencies appear of vital importance. In other words, the images of the local scene must be made to fit organizational needs, and lead to an integrated discourse in which the capabilities of the administrative 'machine' and the definitions of development constitute a single whole.

All this implies that the official 'knowledge' of local situations and what is at stake in development is bound in a way to be 'wrong' from the point of view of a 'disinterested' anthropological analysis. The question then arises of how much people are actually constrained by the official myths of development and administrative rationality and how much their actions are affected by other kinds of knowledge. How far do they have room for manœuvre, or remain bound by (inevitably biased) official views? From my initial example we could see that the local project staff actively opposed the study report which questioned the peasants' active 'bottom-up' involvement in the pump irrigation project. It was very dangerous publicly to endorse a study which questioned the manageability of the project's aims and legitimacy. Yet the people concerned were privately aware of what was involved and this knowledge may have affected what happened later.

My view of the matter differs from those of some anthropologists who have critically studied the representation of local processes propounded by colonial and post-colonial governments in their policies. Breman (1987), Tjondronegoro (1984) and Kemp (1988), for instance, have carefully analysed governmental representations of local peasant society as relatively homogeneous and stable in Java and Thailand. Their own historical and anthropological research shows that these representations cannot be accepted. It is my contention, however, that they have missed one aspect of the problem: they treat the statements of the colonial and post-colonial governments as equivalent to scientific knowledge. Their criticisms do not take into account the fact that official images of local society and its changes are first and foremost political statements. The question of whether these statements are true or false may well be of secondary importance for the authorities. The official statements are part and parcel of a power struggle, with the government trying to impose a standardized representation of what is happening in local society on to the people in question. As political statements, the images of the local scene also serve to legitimize the role of government itself.

Ten Broeke (1990) has shown, for instance, in her analysis of community health care programmes in East Java that, that while Indonesian officials speak of a relatively stable and homogenous village life, that does not imply that they necessarily believe this to be true. In just the same way as the project staff in the opening example tried to marginalize knowledge about the 'real' situation, the reporting of policy progress at the local level was 'managed'. The intermediate levels made sure that the continuity of their existence was secured. And indeed, for the same good reasons, their superiors did not wish officially to 'know better' themselves.

This means that we have to study how knowledge and ignorance are constituted in the processes of policy formulation and implementation as a whole. It does not suffice to confront the policy-makers' 'wrong' images of the local scene with 'true' scientific observations. Such a distinction misses an important point. We must try to understand the part played by knowledge and ignorance in the struggle for power between the various interdependent, yet relatively autonomous groups of participants. The various representations of the local scene are instruments to be used in the political arena. F. and

K. von Benda-Beckmann (1987) have shown, for instance, how peasants in various parts of Indonesia invented new images of 'age-old indigenous legal practices' in their dealings with government. When confronted by the inroads of modern law, the peasants realized that appeal to 'tradition' would be a formidable political weapon for them as well. They knew just how much the government was attached to promulgating such ideas of tradition; and they played their hand rather effectively.

In development policy-making the goals cannot be regarded primarily as operational, in the sense that they steer the actions which follow. The goals and analyses as initially formulated are primarily instrumental for those top levels of management at which decisions about funding are made. This means that there is an inherent ambiguity, an inescapable contradiction, in development policy, which cannot be solved. The development effort must fit the interests and views of those who set it in motion and at the same time appeal to the various publics which are at the receiving end. As achieving both at once is usually quite impossible, knowledge and ignorance are implicated in complicated ways in the attempt to reconcile the irreconcilable.

In the case-study that follows, I shall analyse some of the ways in which this ambiguity is coped with by different groups of participants who are interrelated in one overall administrative framework, which links the local sphere ultimately with a western donor agency. My argument will be that in the short run the ambiguities can be overcome by segmenting the different levels of organization. This compartmentalization consists of a careful balancing of knowledge as well as ignorance by the various parties involved; and it is this which makes the coexistence of multiple, and often contradictory, bodies of knowledge possible. Such segmentation also helps to sustain the overall framework of relations between the various groups of participants. The survival of development policy and its administration are dependent on sufficient ignorance. Further, it greatly encourages willingness to ignore facts about the local level. This construction of both knowledge and ignorance provides some sort of stability. The following case-study is based on my field-work on a Church community in Central Java. The dynamics of policy processes can be traced over a longer time-span than is possible in comparable, but often much more short-lived, development projects.

COPING WITH CONFLICTS AT THE LOCAL LEVEL

The Gereja Kristen Jawa (GKJ), the Javanese Church of Central Java, has a long history of 'developmental' policies. That means that it has always perceived the transformation of Javanese society as concomitant with processes of religious transformation. Even before the early 'ethical policy', that of assimilation, which was adopted by the colonial government at the beginning of the twentieth century, the modernization of Javanese society was regarded by the Church as an integral part of its religious vocation. Long before the concept of development was coined, a model of modernization was provided by the Dutch mission, leading to a great number of institutions intimately linked to it: schools, hospitals, clinics, primary health care, co-operatives, agricultural extension, credit facility schemes and so on. All these modern 'secular' institutions were intimately related to 'religious' bodies of the Church, together constituting one Christianized world, or *umat*.

This powerfully integrated model for secular and religious modernization required Javanese Christians to make a rather drastic break with their past. The multitude of organizations which were set up not only symbolized the vigour and vitality of this appeal, but also provided the Javanese with the means of entering into a new way of life. Better educational facilities, access to modern medical care, to credit, the waiving of medical and school fees, and the provision of scholarships from primary school to university, political protection through access to the authorities, all accompanied the extension of the Church's activities in a large part of rural Java.

It is quite understandable therefore that the GKJ quickly grew in numbers from the middle of the 1960s, after a period of political turmoil, massacres and economic crisis. The fact that Christians, though mostly firmly anti-Communist, had not taken part in the mass killings of the Communists greatly increased the Church's standing. In many rural areas this led to a great influx of converts and new local congregations were set up. As a matter of fact this was facilitated by large infusions of money from abroad. The Dutch mission, closely co-operating with the Church of Central Java, had already covered the costs of running the local congregations for a long time, and continued to do so, contributing almost 95 per cent of local budgets at the end of the 1960s.

For the first time in its history, the GKJ entered the rural scene in a substantial way. Tens of thousands of people became Christian, mostly in the villages. This stretched almost to the limit the Church's capacity to absorb and integrate these people into the institutional framework. The religious model of modernizing orthodoxy had evolved so far mostly in an urban setting. The *hukum adat kristen* (Christian *adat* law), which required a radical break with Javanese religious practices, for the first time in the twentieth century directly impinged on the way of life of a great number of people outside the cities.

The Church leadership dealt with this development in its customary manner. It set up local structures through which trusted people would represent not only the world-view of the centre, but also as 'local leaders' would start to transform the way of life of their rural flocks. Much had to be done, as the 'modern' world-view and life-styles differed greatly from those in the countryside.

Official orthodoxy rejected most rural *abangan* religious practices. (*Abangan* is the term often used of localized religious ideas and practices in Java, which often owes more to Hinduism and Buddhism than to Islam.) The Church singled out various kinds of activity as *abangan*. These included the participation of villagers in communal meals, *slametan*, with their kin and neighbours; *ruwatan* ceremonies which dealt with various forms of evil; the ministrations of traditional healers, *dukun*; and the provision of advice by less specialized wise men and women, *sesepuh*. The activities also extended to ceremonies to strengthen the solidarity of the village, *dukuh*, such as the annual cleaning of the village, *bersih desa*, and village graves, as well as offerings made during the agricultural cycle and so forth.

The incompatibilities between official views and *abangan* religious practices became entrenched in the local situation. According to the formal administrative arrangements, the regional Church leaders, the *pendeta utusan*, were in sole charge of their assistants, the *guru injil*, and were responsible for supervising the various activities of the latter in all matters to do with the growth of the Church. The regional leaders also had exclusive access to Dutch missionary organizations and funding. These bodies had committed themselves to sharing the responsibility for these missionary tasks with the Javanese Church. This support had enabled the *pendeta utusan* to establish a network of assistants in the region who, after some initial theological training, were each provided with a job as their agent in one of the villages. This system of personal networks and dependencies was firmly entrenched in the Church's history and was a continuation of the approach adopted by the Dutch mission before the Second World War. As a trusted person, and formally even the representative of the Dutch, a *pendeta utusan* exercised extensive control over his assistants in the villages. They received their means of livelihood from him, and reported to him on a monthly basis. In a way, their lives were ones of unending personal indebtedness, *hutang budi*, which made it effectively impossible for them to question his views publicly, should they care ever to disagree with him. The *guru injil* could therefore be relied upon to be faithful assistants to their superiors who would conform in their religious views and orthodoxies. When assistants complained about the difficulties which this entailed they did so in private, except in rare cases.

These *guru injil* were, however, also considered officially to be representatives of the local 'communities'. They became chairmen of various bodies in the local congregation. Being invested with the personal 'trust' of their superiors, the *guru injil* were seen as being able to take on the arduous task of transforming and developing the local situation. As official ideology had it, the local communities could now be trusted to 'handle their own affairs'. And the substantial flow of money which came from abroad could only help the local leaders in this task.

The establishment of 'local' institutions and leaders, officially perceived as representing both the Church's views and the local population, did not bridge the gap. Describing the position of the local leadership as 'dual', as some have done, while correct, is inadequate. The leaders of the local congregations were much more dependent on their superiors in the cities than on their local constituencies. Being tied to their superiors in manifold ways, they faced the delicate task of gaining the trust mostly of peasants, whose lives they set out to change! This was the more delicate in that, were the official approach implemented, it would entail disruption in the fabric of peasants' economic, social and cultural relationships.

The administrative bridges built to overcome the gaps between an urban-based form of religion and the actualities of the countryside proved to be extremely fragile, in most cases even becoming formidable buffers. The two different worlds could easily become antagonistic camps, which would destroy any hope of building a bridge between them. Indeed the very efforts of introducing a new Christian way of life through 'local participation' in fact increasingly isolated the local officials from their own constituencies. At the local level, village factions became even more divided as a result of strategies that had been devised to cope with the difficulties, official policies had brought about.

In response to what was happening local leaders and newly-converted peasants set up various strategies. A first set of strategies was designed by some of the new converts. It was one of defence. It aimed to keep local religious practices beyond the purview of Church officials. This enabled them to avoid open conflicts. On the one hand, they could acknowledge and honour the value of official views in their dealings with the Church leadership, on the other they could remain relatively autonomous in deciding how far they wished the Church to affect their daily lives in practice. At the same time local Church leaders initiated an increasing number of development projects. In so doing they hoped to increase their local power base and to become more successful in changing their flocks' way of life.

ESTABLISHING DIFFERENT DOMAINS WITHIN THE VILLAGE

The following short case-studies outline the first strategy for overcoming the difficulties brought about by the conflict of official views with the exigencies of the peasants' own situations. It involves reinterpreting existing religious practices and separating them off from officially approved Christian ones. The first case is about a household's conduct of life-cycle ceremonies; the second is about the problems of maintaining the unity of the *dukuh* (hamlet), under the increasing pressures brought about by religious differentiation of the community.

In the village of Salur various *slametan* (communal meals) take place around birth. On the day a child is born a *Slametan Brokohan* is held, attended only by members of the household. The family convenes to eat rice porridge, part of which is red (*jenang abang*) and part white (*jenang putih*), symbolizing male and female 'wells of life' respectively. After the meal the placenta is placed in a pot, together with a needle to frighten off bad spirits, and also a pen and paper which indicate the family's hopes of having a clever child. The pot is buried next to the front door of the house. Following *Brokohan*, a number of further ceremonies are held, to which other people are invited: neighbours, village officials and kin. The post of the door is chalked white, a wooden *kris* (sword) is hung on the portal, a white thread is spun around the house, a comb, paper, mirror and knife are placed in the baby's bed, as offerings (*sesajen*), designed to ward off bad spirits. These practices involve not only the family, but also the neighbours and others, as does *jagong bayi*, when all convene at the parents' house for the first five nights to sit and watch over the baby. Together with the rite of *puputan* on the fifth day, which celebrates the detachment of the umbilical cord, these acts and ceremonies constitute a five-day whole: *sepasaran*. The end of these five days is marked by a *kenduren* ceremony to which the whole neighbourhood is invited. The baby then enters village life.

How do Christian families in Salur deal with the fact that they are supposed to report the birth to their pastor at once? They know that he requires them not to engage in these ceremonies any more. But what would that mean? If they complied, they would isolate themselves from their neighbours. What if they are invited to a neighbour's house on the birth of a child? They cannot go if they do not also invite these people into their own house. While it would be possible to stop practising parts of the *sepasaran* ceremonies, such as the *Slametan Brokohan* which is for the family only, they cannot dispense with the other parts, except at great cost.

In Salur the conflict between the different demands was solved in a delicate way. The parents would report the birth of their child to a *sesepuh*, a man or woman of great local respectability. In some instances, the latter had been nominated as 'advisers' to local Church organizations, without possessing any official responsibility. The *sesepuh* would take part in the *jagong bayi*, infusing it with his interpretation of a prayer meeting (*kempalan pandongo*) by reading from the Bible and praying for the baby, thereby symbolizing the Christian loyalties of the parents to their kin and neighbours. Only some days later would she or he report the birth of the child to the pastor, and arrange for baptism in church. In this way the parents were spared a great deal of trouble, as indeed were the officials as well.

On one occasion, however, the pastor tried to integrate the *sepasaran* ceremony into the official baptism service on a Sunday and to replace the *slametan* in the parents' house. This disrupted the carefully balanced reciprocal obligations of all concerned, and led to serious trouble in the neighbourhood for the young parents. As their neighbours were not invited to celebrate the end of the first five days, it signified that the parents had failed in their social duties. Thereafter the pastor was kept in ignorance for a number of days about births taking place in his own congregation, by the *sesepuh* as well as by his own Christian flock. The result was that he was allowed to pursue his orthodox views with all the more vigour, because he was never contradicted nor was he faced with what was actually being done.

The policies of secrecy and segmentation within the village could only be successful when non-compliance with official views could be hidden from official scrutiny, or when – as occurred sometimes – the official leaders could legitimately protest that they had not known what was going on. Some of these local *abangan* practices, which the Church officials tried to transform, were not private or informal affairs, but belonged to the public realm, where no claims to ignorance were possible.

One of the major issues where the official views of the Church unavoidably clashed with village practices was the *Slametan Bersih Desa*, the annual ritual cleaning of the village, which included the *Slametan Mbaureksa Desa*, the cleaning of the graves and the worship of the village founders.

In the *dukuh* Teluk Putih, almost five hundred inhabitants had converted to the Christian faith in the early 1960s. They made up an unusually high proportion of the village population as a whole, approximately 40 per cent, and included some members of the village administration. This set the case of Teluk Putih apart because, owing to political pressure, government village officials rarely converted. It was standard policy for Church officials to forbid its members to participate in the cleaning and embellishing of houses and roads in the village, or to convene at the village graveyard to tend the graves and worship the ancestors.

This policy placed the *bekel*, the hamlet administrator, in a most awkward position. He was caught between his loyalties as a village official and as a member of the Church. He was one of the *sesepuh*, one of the local dignitaries, who advised local Church leaders. For the · *bekel* it was unconceivable not to participate in the *Slametan Bersih Desa*. He even had to play a leading role in it. Yet to do so would bring him into open conflict with the pastor, who had arranged harvest ceremonies for the Christian peasants as an alternative.

As this case involved the public realms of both the village administration and the Church, it was now the pastor who avoided a confrontation with the local government. While upholding official Church views, he started negotiations with the *bekel* about the meaning of the *Slametan Bersih Desa*. They agreed that an interpretation of its social function as symbolizing and strengthening village unity was a better reflection of its significance than a religious analysis of its contents would be. This common ground enabled them to find a way out of their difficulties. The *bekel* made it possible for the pastor to participate in the *kenduren*, the ritual meal, which marks the end of the village ceremonies, and offer his views and prayers next to the *modin*, the nearest Islam has to a 'village priest'.

These cases provide us with some insight into how recently converted Christian peasants dealt with the constraints of their new faith's dogmas by compartmentalizing their lives and creating areas of opacity, in which a carefully constructed ignorance was allowed to prevail. What these two examples suggest is the subtle flexibility of the relationship between the Church's official views and representatives on the one hand, and the need for accommodation with the peasantry on the other.

Problems over the appropriate action on the birth of a child, which affected the local constituents personally and as members of the *dukuh*, was resolved by a *sesepuh*, a respected man widely sought for his advice. One might say that a new layer of intermediaries was emerging which could keep the local faithful at a distance from their own leaders. It was this man who reconciled the religious practices of the hamlet with the demands of dogma by reinterpreting the relationship between the two – and left the *guru injil* in his blissful ignorant orthodoxy.

The way in which potential conflict over the *Slametan Bersih Desa* was handled shows similar sensitivities at work, although this threatened to bring more senior figures into confrontation. Although the pastor had reached an accommodation with the *bekel*, the compromise between the two was never formally acknowledged to the central officials of the Church. Official repudiation of *abangan* religious practices remained unambiguous and intact. The compromise remained a local matter. In this way the rejection of *abangan* practice time and again by the central authorities of the Church as well as the continuation of these same practices was made possible. And in some cases, the high officials of the Church had no wish to scale the fences of their ignorance either. In other arenas in which they were engaged, the semblance of untarnished orthodoxy was an important asset for them, for instance in their dealings with the Indonesian civil service over the issue of freedom of religious expression in Indonesia or in their negotiations with western missionary agencies.

THE FLIGHT INTO DEVELOPMENT PROJECTS

Local development projects became increasingly important for *guru injil*, the local Church leaders. They needed new sources of power, as their position within the village was steadily weakened. In dealing with an elusive peasantry and uncooperative village elders, outside support was very welcome. One means of coping with the situation was by trying to exploit their external relationships as far as they could. Through their superiors they might be able to attract funds for all sorts of activities to benefit their flock socially and economically. Applying for money for development projects became an important way of coping with the delicacies of their position.

For their part, the *pendeta utusan*, who were mainly responsible for the rapid growth of the Church, used this very growth of demand to justify to their Dutch sponsors their request for funding for all sorts of projects. It was clear, they argued, that the Javanese Church leaders were facing an extremely difficult job. Reports from the local congregations showed that there was a need for all sorts of new activities. These included the training of local cadres and consciousness-raising programmes; the establishment of new education facilities and medical posts; rotating credit associations and even such small schemes, suitable for a rural setting, as the introduction of better hens and cocks, new breeds of rabbits and goats. In one instance, a scheme for the working of communal land owned by the Church was set up, which enabled new Church members to make their contributions to their local congregation in the form of time or labour rather than money. Applications for all these sorts of development activities were submitted to the western development sponsors and they were often successful.

These funds reached the local communities through the *guru injil*, the assistants of the regional co-ordinator. In most instances, however, the introduction of the projects met with opposition, as they were seen as a device on the part of the leaders to create new forms of dependency upon themselves. Moreover, in those villages where schools and clinics had been set up, a new elite of petty traders, shopkeepers, primary schoolteachers and so forth emerged, for whom the development projects provided a means to enhanced status, as well as power. Many of them played an increasingly important role in local politics, for instance by acting as buffers to mute the authoritarian demands of the orthodox *guru injil* upon the villagers.

At the same time, for the members of the newly-emerging village elite, the array of local development activities constituted a danger. It was clear to them that, by controlling the money which flowed in for the various projects, the local pastor was trying to improve his local power base, whereas they saw the projects as a means to increasing their own power. As they had often attained official positions on local Church boards, they had the right to ask questions and to demand some say in the planning and execution of these projects. While they kept silent on theological matters where the pastor's authority was difficult to question, about the more worldly issues of economic and social affairs they were far less inhibited. On the contrary, here they could claim some influence and expertise.

So, instead of strengthening the powers of the local Church leadership, the development schemes turned into arenas for fights and power struggles which were often bitter. The new projects brought about distrust and conflict. Accusations of fraud and mis-management became the order of the day. The result was a stand-still; and activity evaporated in most of the projects. Many of the peasants withdrew still further from local Church life.

The outcome, then, was an unexpected deadlock, which led to much bitterness among the *guru injil*, who grew increasingly isolated in the villages. They clung to their patrons, the *pendeta utusan*, the sole basis of their power and the sole source of help. His loyalty and support was more than ever the only hope they had of coping with their ineluctable difficulties. And they depended on him not only as the source of authority for their teachings, but also as their means of livelihood. But what could he do? Neither his continued support, nor its withholding offered an acceptable solution to these conflicts. Yet even more was at stake than the bitter lot of his local friends. If the kind of trouble he was facing became known to his counterparts in the Netherlands, what conclusions would these old and trusted friends draw? Might the consequence not be that they would cut off development aid?

BALANCING KNOWLEDGE AND IGNORANCE IN THE HIGHER REACHES OF THE CHURCH

These difficulties posed as serious a threat to the *pendeta utusan* as they did to their village clients, the *guru injil*. The whole administrat-ive structure through which the money flowed could fall asunder, were the conflicts to become known to their friends and sponsors in the Netherlands.

In the region where I had been doing field-work, the *pendeta utusan* wrote a letter to an old Dutch friend, who had worked in the area as a missionary. The pastor invited his friend to travel with him to some of the villages where they both had worked some ten years before, when they shared overall responsibility for the rural groups of Christians, who later grew so fast. The Dutchman now had a different job in one of the main cities in Java. He was well liked everywhere. He spoke Javanese fluently and it was known that after he had left he had continued to devote his energy to maintaining the support from his home base for the region.

The invitation was accepted. A few weeks later, the Dutchman took off for a few days and went to visit his old friend. Privately he had heard of the difficulties which his former colleague and many of his assistants faced, of accusations of fraud and mismanagement. Some of the local people had even written a letter directly to the Dutch missionary organization asking for a new and much more open procedure in planning and handling new undertakings of the Church. The Dutch had refused, however, to deviate from their existing formal agreements. None the less, the accusations and the letter had done a great deal of harm and more might follow.

The two friends set out on a journey lasting several days and visited many of the local parishes which the Dutchman had known before. The journey had been announced in advance. They were well received, as most people knew him personally, or had heard of his reputation as an open and honest man. Yet, in some of the villages, there were people who openly informed him of the difficulties they were facing, making it apparent that conflicts were frequent. He listened carefully. Though he emphasized that his primary interest was in learning about how local officials coped with the problems of the rapid growth of their congregations, he did not miss the finer points of discord behind the layers of etiquette and the protestations of great hopes for the future. Throughout the journey, the *pendeta utusan* gave his friend the front seat in the discussions and kept rather quiet, although he remained present the whole time.

Later, I discussed the visit with the Dutchman. I asked him whether he had been aware of the important political implications of his visit. I put forward my own analysis of what was going on, namely that both the *pendeta utusan* and members of the new emerging local elite were competing for his support. He was quite open in his views on the matter. Yes, he had been fully aware that discord was rife behind the scenes, that suspicion flourished and accusations were flying about. But what could he do? He did not intend to write to the officials in the Netherlands about it. Difficulties which arose at the local level had to be solved there. These were not his, nor anybody else's, responsibility. Such issues had to be resolved by the Javanese themselves. It would be utterly impossible for him to make an honest judgement about the intricacies of each of these affairs.

Similar views were shared by most other Church officials. In another part of Java, where similar difficulties arose, the Dutch formally stated that the administrative arrangements and procedures were clear, and they would not countenance deviation from them. It signalled the reaffirmation of their trust in those who had formal responsibility, the *pendeta utusan* and the *guru injil*. Increasing awareness of the difficulties which were arising locally, in part the results of official policies, was pushed aside. Ignorance had to envelop the highest levels of administration. It was the only way in which the development effort, the orderly flow of money, the whole discourse of economic and social improvement and the image of local self-reliance could legitimately continue. At least that was the position for some years.

CONCLUDING REMARKS

My opening example of the pump irrigation scheme was part of a bilateral government project geared towards 'developing' the social and economic life of a peasantry which was facing growing inequalities in the region. My later case materials were drawn from the 'developmental' expansion of a middle-class, urban-based Javanese Church into rural society. Although the conventional study of development rarely looks into issues of religious transformation, religiously and secularly inspired efforts to change local society have much in common (Quarles van Ufford and Schoffeleers 1988). A comparison is instructive.

By way of conclusion I shall discuss three related aspects of development policies in practice. It is important to note that practices in one social field (for instance at a local, or project, level) cannot be studied without reference to other social fields. Development policies extend down from urban and cosmopolitan centres, where the primary ideas, projects and strategies are conceived, to the different regions and the implementation of actual projects in villages. Each sphere affects the others. The question is, how? I suggest that three aspects of development policy in practice deserve attention. These are:

1 the ways in which processes of integration and compartmentalization are interrelated,

2 the images of success which obscure an incompatibility between administrative rationality and effectiveness,
3 the differences between a systems and an arena approach.

1 The decisions made initially about the nature of the programmes to be carried out signals not only the start of policy, but also, in a way, the end of a particular process of decision-making. The negotiations which take place at this stage may tell us more about the groups in question and their world-views than they do about the recipients of development of whom policy is geared. So the goals and strategies agreed upon are designed above all to convince a broader public which knows nothing about the social situation destined to be transformed. In a sense, ignorance and bias are not just important, but inevitable, at this stage, although no one involved would admit it.

Further, a strategy must be devised; that is, a network of relations, through which the plans will be implemented, must be agreed upon. At that stage 'counterparts' (e.g. the authorities at a lower level of organization, project staff, etc.) become relevant to the policy process. In order to create the image of 'feasibility' or 'manageability', the latters' consent to the original plans becomes vital, because they are supposed to know 'the local scene' and to carry out the designated tasks. The impression of manageability is primarily important at the 'highest levels' of the bureaucracy, which remains relatively ignorant of what is going on. The counterparts – be these representatives of religious bodies, non-governmental organizations (NGOs) or engineering firms, as in the first case – complete the mental and organizational closure of the donors or political centres. The counterparts should feel satisfied: their opinions have been taken into account.

For the counterparts the problem now arises as to how far they can actually operate on the basis of the agreement which has been made. Yet more figures enter the scene: other participants and interests have to be taken into account. And these have often not been envisaged in the original plans. All sorts of different exigencies have to be contended with.

At this point the administrators of a project have to face a dilemma: whether to comply faithfully with the original aims of the project or to reformulate the policy to make it more workable in practice. This is not a simply a new, or later, phase in the policy process; it may in fact turn into an entirely new policy.

The case materials outlined above suggest that efforts to execute policy and to remain faithful to the original plan and goals are bound to fail. Attempts to integrate the various social fields in practice lead to (often defensive) reactions. The more faithful the implementation, the more intense the counter-reaction. We saw, for instance, how local Church leaders gradually became isolated in their own constituencies. A new layer of intermediaries, the *sesepuh*, landed up helping to keep different local social fields within the Church separate from one another. The continued efforts to put official policy into practice only served to increase the compartmentalization.

What is striking is that this process of compartmentalization did not lead to a kind of truce, which the local participants had intended, but brought about open conflict. The official leaders did not accept the terms of the local compromise and tried to gain the upper hand by establishing new bases of power by setting up yet more development projects. The effect was only to make conflicts within the village more intense and attempts at compromise less successful. However, even those opposed to the leadership did not question the usefulness of each development initiative in itself.

My opening example of the pump irrigation scheme, however, presents a different picture. The staff members on the project accepted a kind of truce in their dealings with the village authorities. They took the view that the establishment of local organizations was indeed a clear indication of local 'participation', as decreed by bureaucratic ideology. They were quite violent in their response to the researchers who had demonstrated that these organizations were no more than façades. This information – accurate as it may have been – was unacceptable. The staff members chose to ignore, and not to act upon, a reliable 'scientific' analysis of local social dynamics and instead to stick to the official discourse. Images of local participation could only be upheld by the project staff by keeping their distance from the villages.

2   In the long chain of social fields, which together make up the development policy process, all the participants are engaged in at least two different sets of activities and roles: they have to face differing and often conflicting views and demands. Within these social fields the participants all try to establish and maintain some sort of autonomy, either by making use of the sources of power which development may make available to them or by compliantly building castles in the air, behind which they may hide or withdraw entirely. They are all engaged in managing their own survival as

well as trying to carry out the tasks assigned to them. The two responses do not articulate well: they remain potentially incompatible and in conflict. So how are the tensions managed?

One possibility emerged from the case material outlined above. The *pendeta utusan* had his assistants under tight control and so built up an executive loyal to the policies which had been agreed with his sponsors in the Netherlands. The more effective he showed himself to be to them, the more he isolated himself from his own local constituency. The case-study also suggests that the more faithful, or even forceful, the attempt to engineer desired changes locally, the more it runs into trouble. Paradoxically the more meticulously the assigned tasks are executed, the more this may undermine the policy effort as a whole.

This may well be one of the reasons why so many development projects are short-lived. They may well be declared a success by the sponsor and project staff before the processes of renegotiation have had a chance to get under way. Different views often become visible only after the project's completion. The debates about problems of 'sustainability' (a current diplomatic concept in development discourse), about the problems of decline and disintegration after development projects have been completed indicate as much. The reactions to development projects are often suspended or suppressed until after completion. Early success and later collapse are intimately intertwined. In the much longer-term development endeavours, for instance of western missions and Churches, these successive stages, or moves and counter-moves, become part and parcel of the policy process itself and lead to regular crises.

The incompatibility between the requirements of survival and of effectiveness comes to the fore in these cases. The participants in the policy process 'manage' this tension in how they make use of knowledge and ignorance. We saw this in the battle waged by project officers against an independent report on the shortcomings of their 'bottom-up approach'; in the ways in which the *sesepuh* kept their endorsement of 'unorthodox' local religious practices hidden from their own superiors; in the Dutch missionary's defensive handling of the information about local conflicts; in the negative response of the Dutch agency to letters from the field, informing them of the administrators' mismanagement. Tensions manifest themselves and must be managed at all levels of organization.

3 A systems approach is clearly very appealing to policy-makers. It presents development as manageable, intellectually simple and

explicable to an ignorant audience: it is a 'minister's model'. It assumes that the 'output' is dependent upon 'input', that adequate analyses of relevant factors, carefully designed goals and strategies, sufficient means and the helping hand of 'feedback mechanisms' will ensure that everything runs smoothly. The model's appeal is, however, more political than analytical. It exists primarily to serve the former purpose.

The model does not, however, enable us to understand how the participants within the administration actually operate and why. That remains a 'black box', unknowable. The assumptions of coherence and manageability, rational as these may seem in the specific context of planning, do not apply to the complex networks of relationships and to the infinite varieties of the actual situation in which development activities are carried out. Ignorance therefore becomes an important asset for those who are engaged in policy processes. Lack of insight into what is actually going on in the 'implementation' process in fact becomes of paramount importance. Ignorance is a defensive construct against the false assumptions which, for cultural and political reasons, underpin development policy-making. Ironically these false assumptions have kept going much longer in the field of development than they have in 'the modern world' itself.

What is needed therefore is a much better balance between normative (or ideological) and analytical models. Critical research is no goal in itself. It may contribute to the open search for alternatives. While notions of intervention and the role of the state are increasingly debated by development institutions, dispassionate academic analyses of policy practices and their consequences become important. The assignments of consultancy, monitoring and evaluation, which anthropologists may be given by policy institutions, are no substitute for this.

NOTES

1 I would like to thank Mark Hobart for suggesting amendments to the draft of this chapter, and for his attempts to wrestle my somewhat serpentine Dutch English into a more manageable form.
2 There are various ways of distinguishing approaches to the study of development policy practices. The concept of a 'systems approach' stands for a range of analyses in which political points of view have helped shape the conceptualization of policy processes (on this point, see for instance Bailey 1980, Grindle 1980, Long 1988). Political views and scientific analyses are interrelated. Conventional Marxist and modernization

approaches in the field of development studies have shared a basic lack of interest in analysing policy processes as such (cf. Grillo and Rew 1985, Long 1988). Though the rules of developmental change are construed differently, the dynamics of policy are taken for granted (cf. Bourdon 1986, ch. 5). Thus development policy is seen to be primarily dependent on macro-sociological processes of political and economic change. The role of the state – as arbiter, exploitative, etc. – of (international) development organizations and NGOs are defined from that context. Studying the dynamics of policy processes in between the macro- and micro-levels of society thus becomes of secondary importance. 'Agency' is attributed a priori to one set of actors, the state, the people (e.g. Chambers 1983), NGOs (e.g. Fowler 1989) etc., with the others becoming constraining factors (e.g. Erler 1990, Tjondronegoro 1984, Hoebink 1988, ch. 1). Policy processes remain ignored in these studies, yet another aspect of ignorance.

3 The concept of an 'arena approach' – I apologize for the narrow trans-actionalist connotations – is identified with quite different kinds of studies of development policies. Norman Long has formulated an 'actor approach' (1989, 1992). While Long's research is geared to examining the 'interface' between local institutions and various local groups, others have paid more attention to the dynamics of policy processes at higher levels of organization in development projects (e.g. Elwert and Biersch-enk 1988, Ferguson 1990, Quarles van Ufford 1988). Postmodern approaches to organization theory (e.g. Mintzberg 1989; Morgan 1986) have contributed much to a better understanding of conflicting tendencies within institutions and organizations as well as the complementarity of different lines of analysis of organizational phenomena. These newer approaches to organization theory may be of great value when applied to development policy processes. Two recent doctoral dissertations in the Netherlands (Sciortino 1992 and de Vries 1992) have paid explicit attention to the complex and contradictory interactions between the various levels of organization in development policy processes.

These resemble, as well as differ, from a recent post-structuralist (and in my view too coherent and 'systemic') analysis of the World Bank's development discourse about Lesotho (Ferguson 1990).

REFERENCES

Bailey, J. (1980) *Ideas and Interventions: Social Theory and Practice*, London: Routledge & Kegan Paul.

von Benda-Beckmann, F. and K. (1987), 'Adat and religion in Minangka-bau and Ambon', in H. J. Claessen and D. S. Moyer (eds) *Time Past, Time Present, Time Future: Essays on Indonesian Culture*, Dordrecht: Foris Publications.

Bourdon, R. (1986) *Theories of Social Change: a Critical Appraisal*, Berke-ley, Calif.: University of California Press.

Breman, J. (1987). *The Shattered Image: Construction and Deconstruction of the Village in Colonial Asia*, Amsterdam: Centre for Asian Studies Amsterdam.

ten Broeke, Y. (1990) *Het Ontwikkelingslabyrinth; de Locaal-Context van Primary Health Care Programma's in Indonesie: een Case Study uit Oost-Java*, Amsterdam: Centre for Asian Studies Amsterdam.

Chambers, R. (1983). *Rural Development: Putting the Last First*, London: Longman.

van Doorn, J. A. A. (1982) 'A divided society: segmentation and mediation in late colonial Indonesia', in *Papers of the Dutch-Indonesian Historical Conference* Leiden: Bureau of Indonesian Studies.

Elwert, G. and Bierschenk, T. (1988) 'Aid and development', *Sociologia Ruralis* 28 (2, 3).

Erler, B. (1990) *Todliche Hilfe: Bericht von meiner letzten Dienreise in Sachen Entwicklungshilfe*, Cologne: Dreisam Verlag.

Ferguson, J. (1990) *The Anti-Politics Machine: 'Development', Depoliticization and Bureacratic Power in Lesotho*, Cambridge: Cambridge University Press.

Fowler, A. (1989) 'The role of NGO's in changing state-society relations', *Policy Development Review* 9 (1).

Grindle, M. (ed.) (1980) *Policy and Policy Implementation in the Third World*, Princeton, N.J.: Princton University Press.

Grillo, R. and Rew, A. (1985) *Social Anthropology and Development Policy*, London: Tavistock Publications.

Hoebink, P. (1988) *Geven is Nemen: de Nederlandse Ontwikkelinghulp aan Tanzania en Sri Lanka*, Nijmegen: Stichting Derde Wereld Publikaties.

Kemp, J. (1988) *Seductive Mirage: the Search for the Village Community in Southeast Asia*, Amsterdam: Centre for Asian Studies Amsterdam.

Lammers, C. (1982) *Organizaties Vergelijkerderwijs: Ontwikkeling en Relevantie van het Sociologisch Denken over Organizaties*, Utrecht: Het Spectrum.

Long, N. (1988) 'Sociological perspectives on agrarian development and state intervention', in A. Hall and J. Midgley (eds) *Development Policies: Sociological Perspectives*, Manchester: Manchester University Press.

—— (1989) *Encounters at the Interface: a Perspective on Social Discontinuities in Rural Development*, Wageningen: Agricultural University.

Long, N. and Long, A. (1992) *Battlefields of Knowledge*, London: Routledge.

Mintzberg, H. (1989) *Mintzberg on Management: Inside our Strange World of Organizations*, New York: The Free Press.

Morgan, G. (1986) *Images of Organization*, London: Sage.

Quarles van Ufford, P. (1988) 'The hidden crisis in development: development bureaucracies between intentions and outcomes', in P. Quarles van Ufford, D. Kruyt and Th. Downing (eds) *The Hidden Crisis in Development: Development Bureaucracies*, Amsterdam: Free University Press and Tokyo: United Nations University Press.

Quarles van Ufford, P. and Schoffeleers, M. (1988) 'Towards a rapprochement of anthropology and development studies', in Quarles van Ufford, P. and Schoffeleers M. (eds) *Religion and Development: Towards an Integrated Approach*, Amsterdam: Free University Press.

Rondinelli, D. (1983) *Development Projects as Policy Experiments*, London: Methuen.

Sciortini, R. (1992) *Caretakers of Cure: a Study of Health Centres in Rural Java*, Amsterdam: Centre for Asian Studies Amsterdam.

Tjondronegoro, S. M. P. (1984) *Social Organization and Planned Development in Rural Java*, Oxford: Oxford University Press.

de Vries, P. (1992) ' "Unruly clients": a study of how bureaucrats try and fail to transform "gatekeepers", Communists and preachers into ideal beneficiaries', unpublished Ph.D. thesis, Agricultural University of Wageningen.

8 The negotiation of knowledge and ignorance in China's development strategy

Elisabeth Croll

In recent years there have been several attempts to redefine development in order that it incorporate more equal forms of exchange between the agencies of development or change and local populations with the explicit aim of reducing divisions between variously termed 'superior' ideologies of development and 'inferior' systems of local knowledge. One of the strategies frequently suggested to mediate the two is that development policies and projects take greater cognizance of indigenous and local systems of knowledge. In this respect, one development strategy which has frequently been identified in the literature as combining to an unusual degree both a new national ideology of development and local systems of knowledge is the strategy formulated and implemented in the People's Republic of China after 1949 and before 1976 (see Aziz 1978). One of the distinguishing features of China's new development policies was the degree to which national policies, agencies and mechanisms of development formally acknowledged the potential contribution of local populations and local systems of knowledge.

Respect for the traditions and knowledge of local populations, together with explicit recognition of their qualities and 'innate goodness', underlined the premiss that any development strategy undertaken without their participation and co-operation was bound to fail.

The wisdom of the masses is limitless. The greatest creativity exists only with the masses, the greatest wisdom exists only with the concentration of the wisdom of the masses. In fact, any difficult problem, any matter which we [the government] cannot think out for ourselves, can be easily managed and quickly illuminated as soon as it is discussed with the masses.

(Ch' en Po-ta 1949 and Townsend 1969: 73)

On this basis, a new pattern for policy formulation was evolved which allowed for and encouraged consultation with and the participation of local populations. This new formula was generally referred to as the 'mass line'.[1] In practice, what this formula demanded was that the scattered and unsystematic views of the masses be collected by the state, carefully studied, co-ordinated, and translated into policy.

> In all practical work of our Party, correct leadership can only be developed on the principle of 'from the masses, to the masses'. This means summing up (i.e. co-ordinating and systematising after careful study) the views of the masses (i.e. views scattered and unsystematic), then taking the resulting ideas back to the masses, explaining and popularising them until the masses embrace the ideas of their own, stand up for them and translate them into action by way of testing their correctness. Then it is necessary once more to sum up the views of the masses, and once again take the resulting ideas back to the masses so that the masses give them their wholehearted support. . . . And so on, over and over again, so that each time these ideas emerge with greater correctness and become more vital and meaningful.
>
> (Mao Zedong 1952: 113)

By this means the state not only claimed to 'learn from the masses', but on this premiss, knowledge itself was seen to derive from social practice. In his philosophical essay, *On Practice*, Mao Zedong wrote,

> Practice, knowledge, again practice, and again knowledge, this form repeats itself in endless cycles and with each cycle the content of knowledge and practice rises to a higher level. Such is the whole of the dialectical materialist theory of knowledge and such is the dialectical materialist theory of the unity of knowledge and doing.
>
> (Mao Zedong 1966: 19)

Despite some glaring exceptions, local knowledge and traditions in many fields, including food production, processing and storage, local technologies, famine fare and medicinal and healing arts, were incorporated into the new development policies and programmes designed to meet the basic needs of local populations. What additionally distinguished China's development policies was not only that they were formulated to take account of local knowledge, but that the process of their implementation also allowed for local adaptation and interpretation.

A second major characteristic of China's new development strategy was the number of and extension of policies and programmes to embrace China's villages and the greater degree of state intervention within local populations.[2] In China there was a singular, identifiable and centralized agency of development – the state. Within the state structure, the flow of information and command operated vertically, and the entire bureaucratic structure of the state could be divided into three levels; the centre (state council and ministries), regional (province and city), and local (commune and village production units).[3] Each administrative level followed the organizational pattern of the one above but with fewer subdivisions and sections, and the bureaucratic structures of the state directed by the Communist Party constituted a single line of all-inclusive authority and extensive controls embracing the village. However the state also explicitly permitted and encouraged the local agents to take account of local environments and adapt national policies and programmes accordingly.

It was a characteristic of central development directives that, rather than specifying any detailed plans for policy implementation, they were mainly goal-oriented and only very generally outlined programmes for implementation. They were frequently accompanied by examples of policy regulations for model insitutions or programmes and by advice that these could and should be varied in their implementation to suit the diverse conditions of a country as large as China (Barnett 1967). Moreover, instead of announcing the development directives of all administrative levels simultaneously, development policies were gradually transmitted or filtered downwards from one administrative level to another in a procedure which was designed to allow for some flexibility or negotiations between the various levels and the continuous translation of policies to suit the local environment. Although each administrative level had full policy and operational control over the units within its jurisdiction, each administration above the local level was largely responsible for translating the policy directives received from above for those directly below. The planning process and implementation procedures were thus designed to combine both general state goals and aims incorporated into the national development policies and the specific needs and wishes of the local environment and population. However, although national policies and programmes of development were formulated, transmitted and translated at each level of the state administrative hierarchy, at the local level and within the village they were communicated directly to the local population by members of those same local populations who had sole responsibility for their implementation.

In rural China before 1976, those considered best fitted to act as local-level agents of change were local leaders or basic-level cadres[4] of the village or production team who were themselves members of the local population. They were not salaried officials or members of the state administration or even 'outsiders', but they were both resident and working members of local production units who were usually 'recommended' by both local state cadres and villagers to manage the internal affairs of the village and represent it in its negotiations with the state.[5] Hence in the implementation of new development policies among local populations, basic-level cadres were both representatives of the state and therefore in receipt of 'outside knowledge' and, at the same time, senior village residents and members of primary neighbourhood and friendship groups who had themselves also inherited and transmitted local systems of knowledge. As 'insiders' in receipt of 'outside' knowledge, they were therefore considered to be placed in the unique position of 'facing both ways' and in a favourable position to assist in the formulation of new development policies to take account of local village custom and practice and to persuade and influence local populations to adopt these development policies.

In persuading local populations in China to adopt the new policies, a distinguishing feature of China's development strategy was the function assigned to ideology and the emphasis placed on its communication and popularization in introducing and maintaining social change. The primacy assigned to persuasion and education in policy implementation reflected the quite central premiss in China that under certain conditions or under certain circumstances, ideology had its own power or effectivity to determine the economic base. In implementing development policies, the mass campaign in support of a few clearly defined and immediate goals became one of the main vehicles by which the state and its local agents intervened and attempted to articulate major changes among local populations. Mass campaigns aimed at swiftly, singularly and dramatically involving local populations in their own consciousness-raising processes by educating them in the history and the meanings underlying customs and outmoded patterns of social behaviour and by this means to persuade and convince them to implement voluntarily the new policies (see Barnett 1967: 32–5, 437). In these mass campaigns,

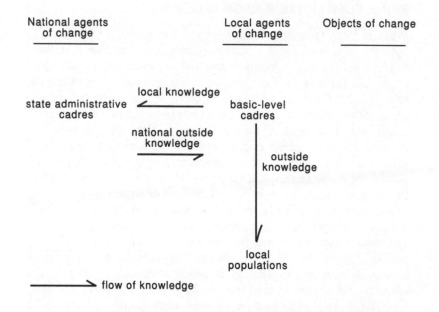

National agents
of change

Local agents
of change

Objects of change

state administrative
cadres

← local knowledge

basic-level
cadres

national outside
knowledge →

outside
knowledge

local
populations

→ flow of knowledge

Figure 8.1 The mass line in policy formulation and implementation

the state set great store on the oral abilities of basic-level cadres who as insiders and inheritors of local knowledge were considered to be particularly well placed to cultivate close face-to-face ties with local populations and to incorporate them as participants or as agents of change in their own local processes of development. In diagrammatic form, the all-inclusive notions of agency and the relations between national and local agents of change in the formulation and implementation of development policies could be presented as in Figure 8.1.

In sum it was the importance assigned to local knowledge and the active involvement of local populations in the formulation and implementation of China's development policies which attracted the attention of development theorists and practitioners alike outside of China. However, although in theory a certain degree of respect was accorded to local knowledge and the agency role of local populations, in practice 'outside' knowledge became increasingly privileged. Local populations, including local leaders, were increasingly redefined as objects of change and negotiation of knowledge and ignorance manipulated in favour of constantly changing interest groups.

PRIVILEGED OUTSIDE KNOWLEDGE

What is interesting about many of the theoretical and policy discussions of development is that they frequently assume that there are certain common elements to national and local systems of knowledge, that there is little conflict, potential or realized, between the two and that there are no vested interests in the supremacy of one or the other. In rural China, conflict between the two was inherent within the very terms of their definitions. Although the mass line allowed for and indeed encouraged the transmission upwards of local knowledge and its incorporation into national ideologies and policies of development, the very process of incorporation modified the local system of knowledge as inherited or experienced by local populations and radically defined its socio-economic and political context. For what also distinguished the Chinese development strategy from many others was the conscious, continuous and planned nature of social change; it was directed towards the achievement of certain defined and explicit goals which were unique both in the breadth and depth of their scope. In China, the state not only formulated and implemented reforms continuously as part of a broad process of planned social change which embraced both the economic base and socio-economic and political institutions, but it also introduced a new ideology radically redefining the attitudes, beliefs and norms previously governing all forms of social behaviour. For example, conventional village notions of privilege, hierarchy, kinship, family, property and privacy were all challenged by the new development policies and the conflict between the two systems of knowledge was increasingly played out within the village where it showed no signs of being easily or rapidly resolved.

In rural China, local knowledge systems and local populations may have remained unusually intact. There had been no large-scale rearrangement or territorial redistribution of rural persons, and the countryside continued to be categorized by discreetly bounded villages which varied in size from a few dozen to a few hundred households. These villages had a new definition and a new function once they were incorporated into communes, production brigades and production teams, but however the village had been organizationally redefined, its spatial continuity remained. Moreover, apart from the exchange of women in marriage, there was very little permanent or even temporary movement between production brigades, teams or villages, and this very important demographic factor encouraged almost exclusive identification with and involvement in the dominant primary groups of the village, be they based on kinship, common neighbourhood or friendship.[6] However, although the solidarity of local populations might derive from and develop kinship and neighbourhood ties, they were almost entirely encapsulated by a single government structure combining administrative, productive and propaganda functions, which was represented in the village and directed by basic-level cadres who in much of rural China constituted the only link with systems outside the village. In these circumstances not only were local populations likely to have remained unusually intact, but the villagers both continued to inherit and remained in continuing contact with local traditions, customs and technologies so that local knowledge systems may also have remained unusually intact. In the emerging conflict between new national, 'outside' and traditional, local 'inside' systems of knowledge, the perceptions and definitions of agency originally incorporated within the mass line were gradually modified by all the participants.

From the point of view of the higher state administrative cadres, the local populations, because of their ignorance of outside knowledge, their backwardness in adopting new ideologies and their resistance to the new development policies, were increasingly re-categorized from agents to the main objects of change. From the point of view of the state cadres, basic-level cadres became and were assigned an increasingly important role as the sole agents of change within the village. From the point of view of the local populations, it was the basic-level cadres who were identified as the chief purveyors of new and outside systems of knowledge and the primary agency for radical change within the village. By virtue of their association with national agencies of development and as representatives of the higher state cadres (often referred to collectively by villagers as the 'higher ups') with a new monopoly of the lines of communication and controls over the local population, basic-level cadres were increasingly privileged persons and their outside knowledge increasingly privileged. Simultaneously in both state and local languages of agency, it was the basic-level cadre who was commonly recognized as the main agent of local development and change and local populations as the main objects of change.

Although in theory, basic-level cadres were placed in a unique position to combine both outside and indigenous knowledge systems, in practice they found themselves simultaneously 'wearing two hats' and in an increasingly difficult position representing both outside and local interests. To mediate the two, they commonly evolved local strategies whereby they adapted and interpreted new development policies in order that local socio-economic and political institutions and relations might be modified to combine elements of both old, 'inside' and new, 'outside' systems of knowledge. For instance new structures might coincide with the old, long-established village hierarchies, customs might be only partially transformed or basic-level cadres might tacitly redefine the 'class labels' of ex-landlords and rich peasants. Elders of lineage or sub-lineages might be permitted by basic-level cadres unduly to influence village affairs but via new and permitted mechanisms. Studies of policy implementation at the local level have frequently concluded that new political, social and economic practices have been evolved which represent both a significant departure from previous customs and practices, a concession to the new ideology and, very importantly, an adjustment to the local physical and economic environment.[7] Local modifications to national policies might be omitted from or only partially reported in basic-level cadre reports on village affairs; or frequently new ideological terms might simply be redefined by basic-level cadres to fit local practices (Croll 1981). The practical mechanisms of mediation and policy implementation by basic-level cadres could thus be represented in the diagrammatic form of Figure 8.2.

What was common to these new local development strategies combining outside and local systems of knowledge was that they fell short of the all-inclusive goals of the state for radical and total social change, which had been incorporated into the national ideology of development. In periodic assessments of rural development policies what increasingly dismayed the state was the slow pace of development and change in the villages, which was increasingly attributed to basic-level cadres and their failure correctly to communicate and implement national development policies at local levels (Baum and Teiwes 1968: 13, Croll 1981: 165–76) As a result, basic-level cadres were in their turn re-categorized as *objects* of change. This re-categorization was achieved by introducing new rituals of rectification and purification, which not only substituted for the mass campaign but involved the continuous redefinition and negotiation of knowledge and ignorance. In the new rituals of rectification and purification, local populations were subdivided into objects and agents of change by the privileging of new forms of knowledge within the village, and ignorance of these new forms of knowledge was generated among basic-level cadres.

National agents of change   Local agents of change   Objects of change

Figure 8.2 Patterns of policy implementation

THE GENERATION OF IGNORANCE

As basic-level cadres were increasingly chastised for their failure correctly to define, communicate and implement the new policies and were themselves increasingly defined as objects for periodic criticism, rituals of rectification and purification became an institutionalized part of development policies and programmes in rural China. In these campaigns of rectification and purification initiated by the state, cadres of the state administrative hierarchy communicated new forms of knowledge and new policies, not to basic-level cadres as hitherto, but to other individuals or groups within the local population who were selected out as appropriate recipients of such knowledge and information. Prior to the campaigns, representatives of state cadres, usually organized into work teams, had

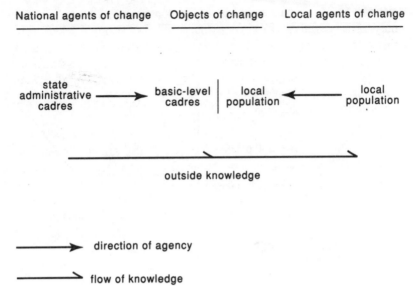

Figure 8.3 Mechanisms of purification and rectification

already visited the village for just such a secret purpose. Depending on local circumstances, they might either select persons of local knowledge or status or persons who were for some reason dissatisfied with the status quo and had poor interpersonal relations with village leaders or neighbours. The privileged information communicated to them might take the form of details of imminent policy changes, types of social behaviour and social practices which would be the objects of future criticism campaigns or it might take the form of new ritual skills. The primary objective of the state in transmitting this new knowledge was to place the recipient individual or group in a privileged position *vis-à-vis* the basic-level cadres and the rest of the local population. As Figure 8.3 illustrates, exclusive and limited transmission of outside knowledge had the effect of generating new spaces of ignorance within the village and redefining the local agents and objects of development and change.

Unfortunately, at the present time the identification of local mechanisms of rectification and purification can only be tentative for the relevant ethnographic data are largely elicited from indirect, informal and literary sources. However a novel recently published in China, focusing on village structures and relations and based on the first-hand experience of the author, provides some very clear insights into the ways in which mechanisms of rectification and purification may have operated (Gu Hua 1983). In the first example taken from this prize-winning novel, very popular precisely because it was seen to represent so closely the experiences of its readers, the construction of a new and large house, the first to be erected in the village for some years, caused something of a stir among the local population and leadership alike. In 1964,

> Li Guigui and Yuyin were building their new brick, tiled house with whitewashed walls. It had an impressive archway overlooking the flagstone street, and two French windows upstairs which opened on to a pretty balcony. Downstairs, stone steps led up to its red-lacquered gate. So this building combining Chinese and western features towered over its ramshackle neighbours, outshining even the department store, the grocery and the eating house. It was the fourth biggest building in Hibiscus – and private property! Even before the scaffolding was dismantled, the townsfolk gathered there every day to admire it!
>
> (Gu Hua 1983: 68)

The reaction of neighbours was mixed. The house might be much admired, even envied, but nobody could quite believe that within the village a young couple could legitimately have made such savings and afforded such grandeur:

> 'Fancy making enough from bean curd to build a mansion like this!'
> 'It's grander than the Salt Guild before Liberation.'
> 'It's profiteers who get rich. This must have cost two or three thousand [yuan].'
>
> (1983: 68)

Even among the local leaders there was also some uncertainty as to how this new phenomenon should be viewed. In terms of new national development policies it could be interpreted as either a conspicuous advertisement of ill-gotten individual riches from free market enterprises and in direct opposition to collective enterprise and rewards, or it could be admired and emulated as an example of socialist gain deservedly earned as a result of hard work, thrift and diligence. To forestall criticism and legitimate the new house, Yuyin, with the tacit consent of local cadres, invited them and neighbours to feasting and celebrations:

> On the first of March, at the crack of dawn firecrackers exploded

in front of the new house, waking up the whole of Hibiscus. The big red-lacquered gate stood open, and on it was pasted a couplet with gold characters on red paper:

'A hard-working couple have made a socialist fortune;
Our townsfolk add lustre to the people's commune.'

(p. 69)

All the cadres of the village sat in seats of honour, and the most senior of their number made a speech which officially validated the occasion as one for celebration.

'Comrades! Today we're all as pleased as our hosts, coming here to celebrate the completion of their new house. An ordinary working couple, relying on their own hands, they saved enough money to build it. What does that mean? Hard work can lead to riches, a better life. We want to live well, not badly. That shows the superiority of our socialist system, the brilliance of our Party's leadership. So that's the first thing to remember as we tuck in. Secondly, as fellow townsfolk, what attitude should we take to the owners of this new house? Envy them? Try to imitate them? Or make snide remarks on the sly? I think we should imitate them and learn from them. Of course not everyone can keep a bean-curd stall. But there are plenty of other ways to develop collective production and family side-lines. Thirdly, don't we talk a lot about building socialism and advancing to communism? Communism isn't something we can sit and wait for. A few years ago, we tried eating in the communal canteen, but it didn't work out. I think we'll know that communism is coming to Hibiscus when, apart from good food and clothes, every family builds a new house like this, even bigger and better than this! Instead of thatched roofs and adobe, instead of rickety wooden stilt-houses, we must have rows of neat storeyed buildings, a street as smart as in a city.'

(pp. 70–1)

However during the feasting, at which there was a good deal of eating and drinking, certain of the more astute villagers observed that one of their members who was usually at the centre of such festivities was for the first time in his life unusually quiet and subdued. Although he was a somewhat disaffected, idle and still-poor peasant who had marginalized himself from the political affairs of the village in the past, he had usually joined in any free feasting with alacrity. On this occasion, the villagers wondered if he was envious, very busy and preoccupied, or unusually worried about something. Another disquieting possibility that occurred to the canny was that 'he had some inside information, and knowing what was brewing, was on his guard' (p. 72). After the event it did indeed emerge that he had already been selected out for privileged communication by visiting representatives of the state cadres and he had therefore been placed in a superior and advantaged position compared to his leaders and neighbours. They had in contrast remained ignorant of the coming campaign, which was to be directed against new riches and conspicuous consumption, of which celebrations, feastings and new houses were obvious examples.

In the second example taken from the novel, a young man who had recently risen to a leadership position in the local community as a result of a previous campaign, was selected by the 'higher ups', the state administrative officials of the county, to travel northwards to visit a far-off model commune. On his return from such an unusual journey, he was visited by local cadres and villagers alike, who were all eager to learn of his outside experiences:

> 'Secretary Wang! Seems you travelled thousands of li (miles) by special car and train, and ate special grub for a whole month. . . . Now that you've been all that way, seen so much of the world and brought back valuable experience, you must tell us all about it!'
>
> (p. 143)

He had indeed observed and learned of much that was new:

> 'Rich experience. Enough to last us for several lifetimes. Including something we'd never even heard of. If I hadn't seen it with my own eyes I'd never have dreamed of it.'
>
> (p. 146)

He couldn't wait to show off his new knowledge and new ritual skills to the villagers, and in his haste he bypassed the usual procedures of first making a report to local state cadres and party members. Within a few hours of his return he had called the villagers to a meeting on the old stage of the market-place where, brilliantly lit by a paraffin lamp, he reported on his new experiences:

> 'I've just had the honour of going north to gain experience with the delegation from our county and district. We travelled thousands of li [miles], spent over a month. Dazhai [production brigade] is a red banner for the whole country, a model in agriculture.

People from all over China and abroad are learning from it. Dazhai has lots of valuable experiences. For instance they award work-points for politics and run political night schools. Their poor and lower-middle peasants are in charge of the schools, of supply and marketing, sanitation, culture and sport. They've done away with private plots and markets. But, above all, they lay stress on politics! Class struggle is what counts, they read the Chairman's works every day and are loyal to our leader. So the gist of their experience is "three loyalties and four infinites". Up here in the mountains we don't know about that. But now I've brought you word of it and I'll show you what it means, so that every morning you can "ask for instructions" and every evening make your "report".'

(pp. 148–9)

The villagers were intrigued and mystified by his demonstration of the morning and evening rituals, which involved various physical gestures, special handling of the little red book and accompanying recitations. Local cadres were also amazed, relayed the details of these rituals to higher state cadres who in turn recognized that the distant origins of these rituals made them an important innovation in the region, the neglect of which might lead them into trouble. They therefore invited the young man to demonstrate his new rituals, declared him a 'model' and sent him to pass on his experiences to other communes. In receipt of privileged knowledge, the young man became a privileged person; he was received and sent off in a jeep and in style, with firecrackers, drumming and gonging and 'treated to more chicken, duck, fish and meat than he'd ever seen before in his life' (pp. 159–60). During this period of privilege, he was again selected out by the higher ups to lead a rectification campaign against local cadres who were thought to have muted lines of class demarcation, relaxed class struggle in the villages and allowed their own class standpoints to become confused. However within a short period of time, the young man's new and outside knowledge was no longer so new and having been routinized or institutionalized was soon in its turn upstaged by new forms of knowledge. In turn also, the young man himself, no longer in possession of privileged knowledge or so privileged in person, became the object of a new criticism campaign.

What is common to these and other examples is the continuous redefinition of objects and agents of change within the local populations and leadership by simultaneously communicating and privileging outside knowledge and generating ignorance. It can be argued that it was the constant redefinition of agency within local populations which occurred during the successive cycles of rectification and purification incorporated into China's development strategy that eventually jeopardized the development policies themselves.

CYCLES OF PURIFICATION AND DEVELOPMENT

In the new national ideology of development, development policies were presented as 'pure', and cycles of 'rectification' and 'purification' the major means of achieving such purity. At the local level, however, the process of rectification and purification was utilized not so much in the search for purity as in the manipulation of interpersonal and inter-group relations. What was not originally reckoned on at the national level was the extent to which national and local knowledge systems might conflict and generate their own competing interest groups or that the negotiation of knowledge might be used in the periodic campaigns of rectification and purification to manipulate and settle disputes between individuals and interest groups in a similar manner to other phenomena such as witchcraft or sorcery. In these circumstances, rectification campaigns could come to take the form of cycles of score settlement and factionalism quite outside their official and public terms of reference and quite disrupt the implementation of the very development policies and programmes they were designed to purify.

All the evidence so far available suggests that the constant intervention of outside agencies of development and the negotiations of knowledge and ignorance had the effect of fragmenting the local population and undermining the very solidarity of collective structures upon which development policies rested. By constantly generating new patron-client relations within the village and by introducing and privileging new outside knowledge, the definition of agency and the spatial boundaries between knowledge and ignorance in the village were in a constant state of flux. Such a process of intervention by the higher ups generated much gossip, rumour and suspicion and therefore a degree of tension and insecurity and divisions in interpersonal and inter-group relations within local populations. In anticipation of or in the presence of such intervention, villagers turned their backs, closed their doors and withdrew into negatively sanctioned family domestic and private affairs. This may well have been responsible for reducing the village solidarity on which collective structure and productivity largely rested.

Theoretical studies of collective organizational structures and their productivity have suggested that the evolution of a structure and a system of incentives which enabled collective action to extend the domain of individual action and yield organizationally optimal outcomes was ultimately dependent upon 'personal relationships between members of the group' (Marshall 1985: 9). However this behavioural approach to productivity usually centred on examining and defining appropriate work relationships of production and did not extend to and include other aspects of political and inter-personal relations. So while most attempts to explain the recent rapid and radical disaggregation of collective structures in rural China concentrate on examining short-falls in economic performance, resource allocation, economic incentives and pricing policies, a more important factor may be their association with constant and unpredictable forms of political intervention. That is, the constant redefinition of agents and objects of change within the village disrupted inter-personal and inter-group relations to such a degree that they deflected energies from production and threatened the very existence of the structures themselves. It is interesting to conjecture that after 1976 it was initially not the new ideology of development itself that was rejected in the villages. But divisiveness and intra-village struggles generated by this process of development affected inter-personal and inter-group relations to such a degree that there was a constant state of tension and insecurity generated within the village.

If it can be argued that despite the incorporation of local knowledge and local populations into China's development strategy, the development policies were themselves jeopardized by the process of their implementation, it can also be argued that the new rituals of rectification and purification are unlikely to be generated in the future. They are unlikely to occur in the future, not only because of their proven unpopularity, but also because the negotiation of knowledge and ignorance on which such rituals depended can no longer be monopolized by the state. The rituals depended on the single control and authority of the state to intervene in village affairs and the maintenance of a more or less exclusive patron-client relationship between state cadres and village agents. These in turn required the encapsulation of the village by single and vertical lines of authority and channels of communications with few alternative sources of or access to 'outside' knowledge. Once new reforms introduced after 1976 had separated political and economic authority, redefined responsibility for agricultural production to the individual household and altered the balance of production for the plan and for the market and of public and private forms of resource allocation, then new political and economic structures, new channels of communication and new sources of information and plural systems of status and authority incorporated local populations into broader political and economic networks.[8] Since 1976 villagers have thus had direct access to multiple channels of communication and information, to new forms of economic and political association other than state-sponsored ones, and restrictions on mobility and movement of persons have been reduced. As a result, the negotiation of knowledge and ignorance in China today cannot be subject to the same state control and manipulation; outside knowledge can no longer be so singularly privileged or knowledge and ignorance so singularly defined.

NOTES

1 For a discussion of the mass line in English, see Barnett 1967, Schurmann 1968, Townsend 1969.
2 For a discussion on the relation of policy to villages prior to 1949 see Hsiao Kung-chuan 1960.
3 For a discussion of bureaucratic structure in the People's Republic of China see Barnett 1967, Lewis 1970, Schurmann 1968.
4 In China a cadre is any person who holds a formal leadership post in any organization. See Saich 1981: 132–4.
5 For a discussion of leadership at the local level see Oksenberg 1969: 155–215.
6 For a discussion of primary groups within collectives see Croll 1981: 165–83.
7 For examples, see Chen 1973, Croll 1981.
8 For a discussion of these changes see Croll 1987a, 1987b.

REFERENCES

Aziz, Sartaj (1978) *Rural Development: Learning from China* London: Macmillan.
Barnett, A. D. (1967) *Cadres, Bureaucracy and Political Power in Communist China*, New York: Columbia University Press.
Baum, R. and Teiwes, F. C. Ssu-Ching (1968) *The Socialist Education Movement of 1962–1966*, China Research Monographs, Berkeley, Calif.: University of California Press.
Ch' en Po-ta (1949) 'Yu Shih ho Ch' un-chung Shang-liang' ('Discuss everything with the masses'), in Liu Shao-ch' i *et al.*, *Lun Ch' un-chung Lu-hsien (On the Mass Line)*, Hong Kong, p. 24.
Chen, Jack (1973) *A Year in Upper Felicity*, London: Harrap.
Croll, Elisabeth (1981) *The Politics of Marriage in Contemporary China*, Cambridge: Cambridge University Press.

—— (1987a) 'New family forms in rural China', *Journal of Peasant Studies*, July.

—— (1987b) 'Reform, local political institutions and the village economy in China', *Journal of Communist Studies*, December.

Gu Hua (1983) *A Small Town Called Hibiscus* Beijing: Panda Books.

Hsiao Kung-chuan (1960) *Rural China: Imperial Control in the Nineteenth Century*, Seattle, Wash.: University of Washington Press.

Lewis, J. (ed.) (1970) *Party Leadership and Revolutionary Power in China*, Cambridge: Cambridge University Press.

Mao Zedong (1952) 'Rectify the Party's style in work', in *Selected Works of Mao Zedong*, vol. IV, Beijing: Foreign Languages Press.

—— (1966) *On Practice*, Beijing: Foreign Languages Press.

Marshall, Marsh (1985) *Organisations and Growth in Rural China*, London: Macmillan.

Oksenberg, Michael (1969) 'Local leaders in rural China 1962–1965: individual attributes, bureaucratic positions, and political recruitment', in A. D. Barnett (ed.) *Chinese Communist Politics in Action*, Seattle, Wash.: University of Washington Press.

Saich, Tony (1981) *China: Politics and Government*, London: Macmillan.

Schurmann, F. (1968) *Ideology and Organisation in Communist China*, Berkeley, Calif.: University of California Press.

Townsend, J. R. (1969) *Political Participation in Communist China*, Berkeley, Calif.: University of California Press.

9 Bridging two worlds: an ethnography of bureaucrat–peasant relations in western Mexico

Alberto Arce and Norman Long

The extended case which forms the core of this chapter represents a journey into the everyday lives of bureaucrats and peasants in Jalisco, Mexico. The ethnography provided the means by which the researchers could begin to explore the different bodies of knowledge operative in the lives of these actors.[1] The presentation of the case follows the chronology in which we slowly acquired a picture of the dilemmas and expectations of the peasants and bureaucrats involved. The central figure in the events that follow is Engineer Roberto, a *técnico* (technical agronomist) working for the Ministry of Agriculture and Hydraulic Resources (SARH) who was assigned to a remote area of the rain-fed district in which he worked. We concentrate upon the perceptions and interpretations of the actors concerned, rather than on a detailed mapping out of the social and political alliances involved.

SETTING THE SCENE FOR BUREAUCRAT–PEASANT INTERACTIONS IN RURAL JALISCO

The context for the incident analysed is the Mexican Food Programme, the SAM (Sistema Alimentario Mexicano), which was one of the most comprehensive attempts by any Mexican government to create a rural development programme oriented to the needs of rain-fed agriculture rather than irrigated export-oriented production. It was also seen as an assault on rural poverty through increasing the production of basic staples such as maize and beans grown by small-scale peasant producers. As Carlos has commented, 'SAM is Mexico's version of a rural "War on Poverty" ' (1981: 11). It set out to recover Mexico's self-sufficiency in grain (mainly maize), reduce the risks of rain-fed production through technological innovation, improve peasant income and diet, and to organize peasants in what were called 'superior forms of organization' designed to increase producer participation and negotiation *vis-à-vis* outside interests (see SAM 1980).

The programme was launched in March 1980 during the presidential period of López Portillo.[2] A central tenet of the policy was the linking of the peasant producer to a new government-promoted structure concerned with the development and management of a basic food chain (*cadena alimentaria*), concentrating primarily on maize. This notion of a food chain emphasized the necessity of a closer interaction between peasant production, marketing, food processing and consumption.

In order to carry out the new programme, it was necessary to transform the existing administrative system and to establish a more technocratic approach to rain-fed agricultural development. A core element in this was the establishment of a new type of administrative unit called the 'rain-fed district'. These rain-fed districts were to be organized and co-ordinated under the Ministry of Agriculture (SARH, Secretaria de Agricultura y Recurses Hidraulicos). Each region of the country was divided into districts, coinciding with existing politico-administrative divisions of the individual states. At state level a body (La Representación Regional) was set up to oversee and control the personnel and operations of the districts. It also organized the planning and allocation of funds for the different agricultural, livestock, forestry and irrigation activities, which were to be implemented by the lower-level district staff. The latter consisted of a Head of District, his deputy, the heads of specific sub-programmes dealing, for example, with mechanization, fertilization, or the organization of producers, and various supporting administrative and secretarial staff. Below this level were the operational units (Unidades de Temporal) that dealt directly with the farming population. Each unit was made up of a unit head, his deputy, a secretary, and several *técnicos* (technicians trained in agronomy, animal husbandry, irrigation, etc.) who were themselves heads of operational zones (Zonas de Operación), which were on average about 2,000 hectares in size. The original idea was to provide the head of the zone with a team made up of several *promotores* (organizational promoters and extensionists), but this never materialized. The *técnico* was, then, the 'front-line' implementer of SAM in direct and regular interaction with his client population. He was accountable to his superiors in the unit and district and was expected to follow certain administrative procedures in the implementation of the programme. At the same time, however, he accumulated experience in dealing both with the demands of the administrative system and its routines, and with those of his peasant clients.

A *técnico*'s involvement with these two contrasting, and often conflicting, social worlds produces a body of knowledge based upon individual experience which leads him to devise his own strategies of intervention in both the village and official administrative arenas. Although it might seem that such strategies are highly idiosyncratic, being based upon the chronologies of experience of particular individuals, in fact they are shaped by the possibilities for manœuvre and discourse that already exist within the two arenas and by the dynamics of the structural contexts within which the different parties interact. The different social actors (e.g. government officials of various kinds, rich and poor peasants, and others such as traders or even researchers) develop their own everyday shared understandings or models for action that originate from and acquire their potency and legitimation through social interaction and confrontation with opposing views and forms of organization. As we shall show in the case that follows, a *técnico* cannot simply escape these influences and constraints by attempting to ignore their existence; and if he does do so, he is then likely to lose legitimacy as a *técnico* in the eyes of both peasants and bureaucrats.

This is a complex process which we intend to elucidate through the analysis of an extended case-study which focuses upon the dilemmas of Roberto, a *técnico* who tries to bridge the gap between the interests of peasant producers and the programme administration and its priorities. He criticizes the shortcomings of the SAM programme and openly acknowledges the existence of administrative malpractice. As a result he tries to introduce new initiatives to assist producers, which he sees as both enhancing his prestige and social position as a *técnico* and also facilitating a more positive involvement by the producers themselves. However, this leads to his being labelled a troublemaker (*un grilloso*)[3] and to his being sent to a special 'troublemakers unit' for remedial treatment. His failure to persuade his administrative boss to accept his solution for bridging the gap between peasant and government interests has the further repercussion that the peasants can use his case to confirm and reinforce their existing model of government practice and personnel. Their experience with this particular *técnico* reinforces their beliefs in how the dominant system works, although this same set of events may later also be used to justify further attempts to restructure relations between them and the intervening agencies and interests. The situation also becomes an important factor in the reproduction of their particular livelihood strategies, which they effectively conceal from government, and in the reproduction of their own local forms of knowledge. The combined effect of these various processes is to keep the social worlds of peasants and bureaucrats in opposition, through the linking of contrasting types of everyday knowledge and through the mutual generation of socially constructed systems of ignorance.

THE FIRST ENCOUNTER WITH THE LIFE-WORLD OF THE TÉCNICO

We first met Engineer Roberto, the *técnico* of the *ejido* or peasant community of La Lobera, in San Cristobal de la Barranca, at a Sunday lunch at the Municipal Centre. San Cristóbal is located about 100 kilometres to the north-west of the city of Guadalajara, close to the border with the state of Zacatecas. San Cristóbal is one of the least developed areas of Rain-fed District No. 1 of Zapopan which, until the beginnings of the 1980s, was cut off from the main communication routes. Access was improved by the construction of the Guadalajara-Balafios highway, which made it possible to travel from San Cristóbal to Guadalajara in one hour. Before this the trip took between five and six hours by donkey.

This area of the Guadalajara region is mainly devoted to livestock production, supplemented by agriculture and independent, small-scale opal mining carried out by local exploiters. The municipality, made up of a population of about 3,700 inhabitants, has a romantic tradition of *gavillas* (bandits) who robbed gold from the Zacatecas mines and who hid it in the deep gulleys of the municipality. Today the municipality still retains an image of being associated with illegal activities, such as the production of *agave* (a cactus plant from which tequila and other products are manufactured) and marijuana.

Our meeting with Roberto was by chance. The Municipal President had invited to lunch the head of Zapopan Rain-fed District, the head of the unit, the agricultural *técnicos* from San Cristóbal and Lobera, several 'sons of the municipality' working in Guadalajara, such as a lecturer from Guadalajara University and *compadre* ('co-parent') of the Municipal President, and other local dignitaries resident in the area. The ostensible purpose of the occasion was to press them to provide more government development assistance for the municipality.

During the lunch the head of the district said that, in his opinion, the only future for San Cristóbal was to develop tourism. This was, he explained, 'the first restaurant I have seen in this area and this can be the beginning of the "take-off" of the municipality'. He went on to say 'as you can see, this is a place of hot springs' and that therefore it was good for this type of trade. He also added that San Cristóbal, like Cuquío to the north-east, was one of two extreme cases of low maize productivity in his district. Then, referring to the theme of out-migration, he said, 'this is an historical tendency of several munici-palities around Guadalajara which will not be stopped by agricultural development because it is in the blood of the producers. It is natural for them to go to the USA instead of going to Zapopan or Guadala-jara'. At this point, several local residents objected strongly to this view; so he rephrased it more sharply by underlining 'the laziness of the Mexican people', and by re-emphasizing his point about the prob-lem of poor communications. He went on to say, 'if I just had enough steamrollers and excavators then I would send them here to build roads, but I don't have them'.

After lunch we talked with the *técnico*, Engineer Roberto, from La Lobera. At this time of the year, during the rainy season, the *ejido* of La Lobera is cut off and the only way to get there is on foot, a journey that takes about six hours. Roberto described the place as comprising about 70 producers who, owing to their iso-lation, were not receiving fertilizers regularly. A government pro-gramme of credit had been officially operating in the *ejido* for some years but, according to him, these producers had still not received last year's subsidies for agricultural inputs. He also said that people were friendly but suspicious of outsiders. They feared that outsiders would come to steal the few possessions they had. He added,

> These feelings of mistrust were the reasons why they did not wish to obtain credit from Banrural (the state agricultural bank), because they run away from situations where they have to sign or put their names to paper. I have been working for a year with them. La Lobera is a rough place, but I like it because I am not one of those *técnicos* who likes to be a *chupa barba* [a 'yes man' or someone who sucks up to his boss][4] and these are the qualities needed to work in Zapopan. In La Lobera I am direct and honest with producers and as a result have persuaded about fifty of them to join the fertilizer programme.

He went on further to explain:

> The *ejido* is poor in terms of cash, maize is grown principally for self-consumption; they keep cattle but do not eat meat unless

one of the animals falls [in the ravine], and the main diet is beans, tortillas, milk and eggs. . . . The *ejido* has no electricity but they have some televisions operated by car batteries. . . . Concerning customs, the people are very traditional. We young lads [*muchachos*] had to peer through small holes in the billiard hall at the girls [*chavas*] passing by. To wander around with them, chatting and so on, implies that the man is a *cabrón* [a rogue]. . . . Before I went to work in La Lobera, no *técnicos* had been there for a long time. They do not like working there. I managed to survey the *ejido* but I believe that much of the information given was untrue. The producers tend to exaggerate the inputs they invest in production and underestimate the number of cattle they possess. I am supervising 750 hectares when a *técnico* is required to be in charge of 2,000. It is impossible to know the profits made from cattle because producers market them [illegally] in Zacatecas [rather than in Guadalajara]. My first contacts in the *ejido* were with the young men [*chavos*], after that the older women, and only much later the *productores* [producers, here implying 'heads of household' who are usually male]. Some young producers were very suspicious because they cultivate marijuana: they thought that since I worked for *el gobierno* [government] I was going to grass on them [*zorrearlos*[5]]'.

After this, Roberto shifted the subject of the conversation to ask us whether we thought SAM was a failure. Our reply was 'Yes, but we have to study why it failed'. He answered us directly:

I know why it failed; many of us pocketed the money that was meant for the producer. And we acted irresponsibly. During this period they gave between 2,000 pesos (about US $40) weekly for petrol, even when they knew that it was impossible to spend that amount of money. When I had to handle the tin containers of insecticide (for the *ejido*), sometimes they overturned in the truck. I just used to dump it, and I did the same when it went bad, and reported to the office that it was lost. No questions were asked, and things that were not accidents, but due to one's own negligence, were simply written off as lost, and no more. A colleague from my unit was actively involved in collecting the bills for buying fertilizers, insecticides and seeds from the producers. He took charge of handling producers' claims for subsidies. This person took more than 20 per cent of each subsidy which was paid directly to him in cash. For the producer, who never knew the details of the programme or the amount he should receive, this was a gift [*una ganancia extra*]. Therefore here comes the contradiciton: these same people who received 20 per cent less than they should, organized in his honour fiestas, barbecues, and invited him to eat gratis in their homes, because they saw this *técnico* as the person who got them money they never expected to receive. In this respect, *un functionario corrupto* [a corrupt civil servant] from the point of view of the government institution is seen as *un functionario excelente* (an excellent civil servant) from the side of the producer. When you are a *técnico* it is often difficult to understand exactly when you are acting in a good or bad manner. It is strictly prohibited to take money from the producer, but last year on visiting this particular plot [here he pointed to a field owned by one of the leaders of the *ejido*], which we do so regularly because it is close to the road, we were always offered water-melons, courgettes and tomatoes to take with us.

At this point, we intervened to suggest that surely it was quite different to receive products other than cash, to which Roberto answered,

No that is not relevant [*no le hace*]. It's the same thing. What was I going to do with four or five boxes of water-melons and courgettes? After I had given some kilos to my family and friends, I still had some boxes left – which I could not just give away as gifts in the neighbourhood – so I took them to sell on a stall in the Guadalajara market. Whatever I get for them is simply profit for me. In the end then [to receive cash or products] it is the same thing. The producer sees technical assistance from a totally different point of view. . . . Nowadays it is prohibited to receive anything from producers but things continue as always. Take for example when the producer needs certain administrative papers. If there is no incentive then we do not process the papers. I can give a thousand and one reasons for not doing so. So the producer, despite the regulations, will bring gifts for the *técnico* to speed things up. In these things regulations do not serve. The failure of SAM was due to the fact that they wasted resources madly, *a manos llenas* [handfuls]; and we were guilty. This is the cause of the present-day economic crisis: a crisis which means that they cannot even finance the travel expenses of *técnicos* to go to communities like La Lobera.

THE *TÉCNICO'S* VISION OF THE LIFE-WORLDS OF PEASANTS AND BUREAUCRATS

A spatial image underlies Roberto's view of the peasants of La Lobera, namely that the community is isolated geographically. Geographical isolation is associated with being a 'rough place', poor in services and resources, and being culturally 'traditional' and therefore outside the mainstream of 'modern' life. A further implication is that they are outside the area of major influence or priority as far as government development schemes are concerned.

Being isolated, the people are suspicious and do not trust outsiders, whom they suspect of threatening or stealing their few possessions: their material resources as well as their girls. This reference to the need to protect daughters must be interpreted in the context of the local custom of 'wife abduction' whereby the man 'steals' the bride-to-be before negotiating with the father of the girl. The *técnico* was ignorant of the full significance of this attitude towards the protection of daughters. In later discussions with peasants from La Lobera it emerged that heads of households do in fact allow marriage to take place with outside men from San Cristóbal de Barrancas, providing these marriages give them benefits in the form of political leverage or contacts. This is balanced by trying to press the young men to find women from the community of Cuyutlán where they could obtain, through marriage, easy access to credit, since this community specializes in the production of marijuana. Thus, far from being simply 'backward' or 'traditional', this prescription and control of women was central to La Lobera's political and economic survival and relative autonomy from the wider system.

A second image that relates to the first is Roberto's view that the peasants consider the *técnico* as part of a system of intervention based upon trickery, since some peasants engage in illegal activities, such as marijuana and poppy cultivation, and the marketing of livestock in Zacatecas in clandestine slaughterhouses, which it is the business of *técnicos* and others representing central government to report. *Técnicos* therefore represent a threat which it is best to avoid by engaging in counter-trickery. Roberto emphasized this by describing how he surveyed the community but got inaccurate information. His comments thus reveal a degree of awareness of the lack of fit between the reality of peasant life and the assumptions made by government development programmes.

This element of mistrust (by both bureaucrats and peasants) creates the basis of the development of systems of ignorance that systematically exclude information that contradicts the assumptions of their models. This was later illustrated for us by an account given by elders (*viejos*) of the community who told of an incident when a bank official arrived in the community to check on the results of the harvest with an interest in determining how many producers could repay the credit. The official credit system of SAM operated to protect those who suffered a complete loss by exempting them from the need to repay their debts. This meant they could reapply the following season. In these circumstances, the peasants of La Lobera, many of whom had suffered some but not a complete loss, declared to the official that more than half of the *ejido* had suffered a complete loss, and when he doubted this statement, they said, 'Are you questioning our word? Shall we go to the fields?' At which point they stood up and hoisted their trousers, adjusting their belts. This, it appeared, was interpreted by the official as a sign that they were moving their hands towards their revolvers. So at that moment, the official said he did not wish to see the gardens, and simply signed the claim application. From that day on they have not seen another bank official!

This incident shows not only that the official failed to read or respond to the peasant cue to negotiate a settlement, but that, in the eyes of the peasants, his reactions merely confirmed their general suspicions of government personnel. The combined effect of these types of encounters is that government services to the area remain inadequate and ineffective, thus underlining the 'isolation' and 'marginality' of La Lobera.

This type of mutual mistrust is part of the everyday reality of the people of La Lobera when they have to deal with outside intervening parties. Although officials such as the bank representative or the *técnico* command control over resources and have the support of outside authorities, according to the *técnico* they are clearly vulnerable when they operate outside their own social space. In the same way, the peasants of La Lobera were 'ignorant' of the newly-enforced laws of *depistolización* (i.e. the disarming policy enforced in the 1980s) when, one day, they set off for Guadalajara, only to be disarmed by the municipal police in San Cristóbal. In order to recover their arms they had to bribe the authorities, since the law said arms should be confiscated.

Roberto's comments on the nature of the peasants of La Lobera coincided partly with those of his superior, the head of the unit. The latter stressed that the area was exotic and could therefore be a centre of tourism (on another occasion he suggested that a funicular railway could be constructed from Guadalajara to La Lobera to promote tourism). This implied that the area was not considered to be within the main area designated for the implementation of agricultural development programmes, even though the *técnicos* were expected to promote the production of basic staples.[6] The mention of migration and the 'laziness of the Mexican' simply confirms this view and draws upon a well-established stereotype, current in popular and sometimes also in academic circles, that peasants lack commitment to local development and therefore migrate away. There is in this model no understanding of the cyclical nature of labour migration, nor of other alternatives to agriculturally-based development.

Another dominant theme that emerges from the first encounter is the notion that, as a government official, self-criticism is fine, although at the same time the administrative system tends to neutralize this by providing these same people with flexible and ambiguous concepts, such as notions of 'corruption', and 'negotiation' that justify a degree of criticism of the system as well as some space in which to develop their own strategies. In this way 'deviations' can be legitimized by the fact that peasants may gain better returns: that is, they may give gifts to the *técnico* in order to obtain support for credit or other services. The element of deception reappears, however, in the fact that the peasants may not be told precisely what their rights are. Hence the *modus operandi*, which may bring mutual benefits to the *técnico* and peasant farmer, is one that creates areas of ambiguity and ignorance in both bodies of knowledge. In this way, both sets of beliefs are kept basically intact.

A VIEW FROM BELOW: A SKETCH OF LA LOBERA AND ITS AGRICULTURAL PROBLEMS

This first encounter with Roberto and with the other agricultural staff present at the lunch in San Cristóbal motivated us to learn more about the *ejido* of La Lobera. We decided to collect basic background information, drawn mainly from the agrarian archives in Guadalajara, and to plan a trip to the community.

According to the agrarian archives, La Lobera was originally part of a hacienda of that name. However, in 1970, under the agrarian reform law, it was granted land, although it was not legally recognized as an official peasant community, an *ejido*, until 1976. The reform affected 150 hectares of rain-fed and 1,100 hectares of pasture land, benefiting some 47 households. This area was extended in 1981 to benefit a further 25 households, although at the time of the research this land had not yet been allocated.

The track to La Lobera starts on the western side of San Cristóbal de la Barranca and the journey can take up to five hours by jeep. The track crosses the river Cuixtla which, during the dry season, does not carry much water. During the rainy season, however, the river increases its height to 5 or 6 metres, leaving the *ejido* isolated. The track is very narrow with many slopes and precipices. On the way to La Lobera there is a remarkable change in vegetation. Papaya, mango and banana trees grow in San Cristóbal, because of the humidity and hot climate, but as one journeys towards La Lobera, this tropical vegetation is replaced by *nopales* and *pitayos* (prickly pears and their fruit) and by the *huizaches* (lizards) that are better adapted to the dry heat of the Sierra. At an altitude of 2,000 metres, the landscape around the *ejido* is composed of a forest of dwarf oaks and pines.

The *ejido* has a school which has operated since the mid-1970s, although the building was only finished in 1982. There are two small shops and also a billiard hall where producers meet to talk in the evenings. The community has no electricity, no adequate drainage system and no telephone. The *ejidatarios* have built a small water tank, which is supplied by spring water from the Sierra. The tank serves as the most important meeting place for the women of the community, who come together during the mornings and in the evenings. La Lobera's only form of rapid communication from outside is the messages transmitted over a commercial radio based in Guadalajara. There are three tractors in the *ejido*, two of which had just been bought at the time of research. The oldest arrived during the SAM project and was owned collectively by the *ejido*, but owing to mechanical breakdown it had lain idle for a year. There is one lorry in the community and a few pick-up trucks. The present-day structure of production consists of *ejido* agricultural land, which is allocated to households each year in small plots, *ejido* pasture land, which is used collectively by those who own livestock, and some individually-owned plots. Our sample of 23 households showed that 87 per cent possessed 1–5 hectares, one household possessed 10 hectares, and two owned more than 11 hectares.

According to *técnicos* at the SARH district office, agricultural production in La Lobera is classified as falling under a model of production for self-consumption (*producción para el autoconsumo*). Yet according to our research the situation is more complex. Producers declared that approximately 70 per cent of their maize production was for self-consumption, while 30 per cent was for the market. The latter was marketed outside official state-controlled channels in small quantities in response to the immediate demands for cash to meet household needs. Also, producers preferred to feed their cattle on maize and to sell the livestock later. According to producers, this was the only way for them to make a profit from agriculture. In other words, La Lobera is a commercially-oriented agricultural community where, in spite of its isolation, money is highly valued. This commercial character has encouraged some producers to develop their means of production, although the majority still operate with relatively low levels of technological input. Thus they use tractors only for opening up land, while the rest of the agricultural tasks are organized using animal traction and with the help of family and seasonal wage labour. The majority of households, however, use fertilizers and insecticides, which were introduced in 1980. Family labour remains the main factor in this system of production, although during peak agricultural periods, some 44 per cent of households hire temporary labour. Farmers must rent tractors from one of the three persons owning them. The use of tractors reduces the risk of not having the land prepared in time for the first rains.

There is constant pressure to produce maize and a high commitment to agricultural work. With an average of 2 tonnes of maize per hectare, La Lobera in fact manifests the highest productivity level in the municipality of San Cristóbal. Producers use a fallow system called *año y vez*, which consists of dividing the *ejido* land into two areas, one of which is cultivated, while the other is left for livestock. Every year producers rotate the area of cultivation. They explained that this system had proved itself to be the best way of avoiding soil disease; as they put it, 'the soil knows the seed' and therefore will reject seeds used in the previous year.[7] This view contrasted sharply with that of Roberto, the *técnico*, who regarded this form of cultivation as 'traditional and uneconomic'. In his opinion all land should be ploughed, and the amount of insecticides and pesticides increased to promote a more intensive system of production. Producers argue against this, emphasizing that crop disease has increased since insecticides and pesticides have been introduced.

These two different perceptions of agriculture and agricultural development reveal a conflict of interests, objectives and beliefs between development agency personnel and producers. This is also seen in attitudes towards the use of the tractor. While some producers regarded the tractor as necessary to save time, many argued against its use, because the soil did not receive proper preparation, making it necessary to plough with animals afterwards. The use of animal traction, it was maintained, achieved a better soil consistency for sowing. And another factor shaping attitudes towards the tractor was that the tractor owned by the *ejido* and introduced under the SAM credit programme had broken down quickly and this created conflict among producers over what to do with it. It took a year and a half for the community to resolve this. Finally, they sold the tractor complete with all its agricultural attachments, to two *ejidatarios*, one of whom was a shopkeeper. The latter paid each *ejidatario* 5,000 pesos (US $50) and invested 200,000 pesos (US $2,000) in repairs. *Ejidatarios* recognized that it was sold cheaply, but they pointed out that the important thing was to have it repaired and solve the community's problems. It was this experience that made some producers oppose the use of the tractor and blame the government for giving them something that was unprofitable and which finally ended up favouring only two producers in the community.

As we pointed out earlier, the increase of maize production was the central aim of the SAM programme offered to communities such as La Lobera. The apparent resistance to such modernization, seen for instance in their unwillingness to adopt what was regarded as a more intensive system of maize production, presented major obstacles to the 'mission' of *técnicos* in the community. *Técnicos* were not in a position to ask for more government assistance if they were unable to improve maize production in their areas of responsibility.

An additional problem in the SAM model was its failure to recognize the fundamentally diversified nature of local rural economies. In a public meeting with *ejidatarios* in La Lobera, one them exclaimed forcefully,

> The potential of the *ejido* is in livestock and in opal mining. If you ask us, you will find that we have more experience as miners than as agricultural producers. In the dry season, the people who don't go to the USA, go to work in the mines as labourers or as *pepenadores* [i.e. those who scavenge among the discarded deposits around the mines]. We cultivate maize and the introduction of improved seeds is good for us, because we can feed it to the livestock. Simply to produce maize is not good business for us, because our costs are greater than those producers in Zapo-

pan. We have to pay for the transport of the agricultural inputs and after that the cost of moving the harvest down again. So we try to sell the least possible maize because our profit lies in feeding our cattle and selling three or four cows during the year.

PEASANTS' VISIONS OF THEIR LIFE-WORLD AND THAT OF THE GOVERNMENT

The foregoing account shows that the peasants of La Lobera do not regard themselves as being outside the market, as assumed in the bureaucratic model which classifies their agriculture as directed primarily towards self-consumption. In fact, their everyday experiences are geared to maximizing, where possible, economic return through the market. This was the reason why they did not market much maize, finding it more profitable to feed it to their cattle which they later sold in other markets. Moreover much of the maize marketed was traded through unofficial channels and therefore not included in government figures.

These two elements – their commitment to the market and the use of alternative channels for marketing – are crucial for understanding the peasant economy of La Lobera. The model perpetuated by the administration fails to grasp these critical dimensions, providing the *técnico* with a frame of reference which systematically ignores the actual situation of the *ejido* and the need to understand its problems. This serves the administration well because it allows them to classify the *ejido* as not worthy of much attention, or of programmes of major investment. This aspect is further highlighted in the section which follows when Engineer Roberto suggests that La Lobera is institutionally classified 'as a punishment area for troublesome *técnicos*'.

However, the peasant situation is more complex than simply their relation with the market. It consists, in addition, of relations within the community between the richer and poorer households, as expressed in the hiring of temporary wage labour for agricultural production. It also includes the ways in which ideas about technological 'improvements' have been processed through a body of local knowledge, thereby creating certain incompatibilities with the model of development promoted by *técnicos*. This is illustrated by peasant views about tractors. The majority of peasants agreed that tractors save time by allowing them to delay ploughing until the last moment before the rains come. But they also know that this does not allow enough time for the night frost and the sun to kill the bacteria (*plagas*) that attack the plants. Most people therefore maintained that tractors do not provide proper care for the soil. This is linked to the belief that the land is a living entity that requires careful nurturing. A further point about tractors is that people stressed that tractors generate conflicts between households within the *ejido* over their use (note the difficulties that arose with the collectively-owned tractor).

These views should not be interpreted to imply that there is a reluctance to use technology to increase production or productivity; rather they point to a different conception of soil conservation and management of agricultural production. Newly-introduced inputs must find a place and be given social meaning within local bodies of agricultural knowledge and practice, although at the same time we must recognize that this is a dynamic process which transforms these new elements as they are incorporated. New instruments and methods acquire meanings and uses not anticipated or intended by the agricultural planners. This process is clearly shown in the example of Don Jorge, a poor peasant, who breaks up the technological maize package in order to use the herbicides to reduce weeding with the *coamil* (slash and burn hill cultivation) system of production.[8]

The successful reworking of both new and existing elements of knowledge in order to devise viable household strategies leading to 'a better life' (*una mejor vida*) is further illustrated by the case of Don Pedro, a rich peasant. Don Pedro's view of how to achieve a better life includes three crucial elements: sound enterprise, education and technological innovation. These elements, however, cannot be realized without some strategy for obtaining them. This entails organization and resources. He accomplishes this by drawing upon the labour resources of the household and consolidating his ties with his sons. For him, limiting his family size makes no sense, since, as he puts it, 'my sons have never been an obstacle. On the contrary, they have helped me to overcome difficulties' – one example of this being the way they have jointly co-ordinated trips to the USA to obtain money for a tractor, which they later rented out to their neighbours at a profit.

Don Pedro is acknowledged in La Lobera as someone who has made it, as a kind of reference model for others wishing to achieve a better life. In fact one can trace similar elements in the strategies of Don Jorge, who is still struggling to accumulate enough cash to buy his first cow. Don Jorge points out that once one has acquired the first animal, then it is just a matter of time before the improvement of one's economic situation. Although he lacks sufficient resources to make the trip to the USA, he participates with a group of poor producers in organizing the marketing of maize to Zapopan. Being much younger than Don Pedro, he lacks family labour and other resources. This leads him to set up a network of close bonds with three good friends who collaborate in agriculture and small-scale trade. Thus both Don Pedro and Don Jorge, though placed at opposite ends of the status spectrum, manifest a strong commitment to organizing their own affairs, outside government control. They also place premiums on co-operating with family or long-standing friends who are status equals.

Despite evidence of increasing social differentiation in La Lobera, these two contrasting cases share, more or less, the same perceptions and opposition towards the 'world outside', and especially towards government agencies. Don Pedro declared, 'They dislike our system of production'; and Don Jorge said, 'They won't give us more money because they saw we cultivate too few hectares of maize'. These expressions capture in a nutshell the common assumption made by peasants, whether rich or poor, that government works against them and has little interest in understanding their own systems of production and their problems. And this functions as an ideological barrier to developing relationships of *confianza* (trust) with government personnel. This view of course is legitimized by the 'bad' experiences they have had, either individually or as a community, with visiting government officials, and which now constitute a kind of collective memory. We shall return to this point later when we discuss the confrontation of peasant and bureaucratic models in the final section of the chapter.

This discussion of peasant views and ideology leads to the conclusion that producers are basically oriented towards keeping control over the organization of their households and local enterprises, whilst at the same time attempting, where possible, to profit from whatever outside resources may come their way. In this way they operate within what Moore (1973) has called 'semi-autonomous social fields' wherein, in the face of both internal and external pressure, individuals or groups possess the capacity for preserving some normative consensus and control over their own social arrangements. Thus, despite their geographical and institutional 'marginality' and their poverty *vis-à-vis* other social strata or sectors, they nevertheless know how to live with their 'isolation' and extract some benefits from it.

BRIDGING THE GAP BETWEEN DIFFERENT LIFE-WORLDS AND KNOWLEDGE SYSTEMS

Engineer Roberto had been working in La Lobera for a year and a half at the time of our research. He was 23 years old, and his father worked in the central offices of the Ministry of Agriculture and Hydraulic Resources (SARH) in Mexico. He recognized that it was through his father's influence that he had obtained his post as *técnico*. According to Roberto, he did not know much about agriculture, since he had studied electrical and mechanical engineering, but, he said, 'I have learned by experience'. He was working in La Lobera as a result of an institutional sanction: according to him, 'In the District, La Lobera is considered *un área de castigo* (a punishment area) for troublesome *técnicos*, who are sent there as a way of making them resign from the Ministry'.

Roberto went on to tell the circumstances of his placement in La Lobera:

I was working in Cuquío and, as in this unit, I didn't appear very often at the office; but that didn't mean I was not working. One day after I came back from a field visit and reported my findings to the unit, I had a shock. There were three memos accusing me of having been absent from work for a month, so the district had decided to deduct those days from my salary. I got furious and went to sort out the problem at the district [office].

When I found the senior staff member who had sent me the memos, I said to him, *'Oye cumpa . . . porque me has puesto los memorandums?'* [Hey, mate, why have you sent me memos?]. He then became aggressive, saying, 'Hey what?' That was enough, and I said, *'Oye hijo de la chingada, porque me pusistes éstos memorandums que no son ciertos?'* [Hey, son of a bitch, why did you send me these memos which are not true?]. Then things exploded and he said that my attitude was going to cost me the post. I laughed at him and, in front of the staff, I challenged him saying, 'I bet you won't be able to throw me out'. He replied, quite sure of himself, 'OK, be ready then, because tomorrow we are going to carry out an inspection of your area'.

The next day I picked them up from the office. They were dressed as if they were going on a safari. I laughed and said that Cuquío was not the other end of the world. When they arrived and asked the producers they didn't find anything wrong with my work, but they still recommended a change of unit. So, I was sent to Unit No. 3 because the head of the unit had a reputation for being an organizer and a *chambeador* [hard worker]. The head of the unit received instructions to make me work hard and that was how I finally ended up in La Lobera.

The *técnico* was proud of his attitude and considered himself different from the rest of the *técnicos*. He disliked their behaviour as a group, because they were obedient to the head of the unit, spent their money in *convivencias* (office fiestas)[9] with him and did not give a damn about the producers' situation. Roberto said he was hated by other *técnicos* in the unit, to the extent that several times they had stolen his field notebook and stopped him from doing his reports. Roberto claimed he did not conform to the expected norms of behaviour in the ministry and the reason he could get away with it was that he was protected by his father.

Roberto did not value organization or professional training as important qualities for a *técnico*. Thus part of this hostility was directed against the professional agronomists because according to him, 'all that was needed was *cojones* [balls] to gain the *confianza* [trust] of producers and the rest depended upon how influential your contacts were at the agency'. Roberto constantly emphasized that while he had to walk six or seven hours to arrive in La Lobera, the others had their *ejidos* near the unit.

THE *TÉCNICO* AND THE PRODUCERS

On our first visit to La Lobera we went with Engineer Roberto, because he offered to be our guide and to introduce us to some producers in the community. This first stay in La Lobera gave us the opportunity to observe him at work for a period of a week.

The first problem Roberto was confronted with was the death of several cattle. Producers said that they had sent for the veterinarian, but that the medicine he had prescribed had not solved the problem and that the animals were still dying. So Roberto went to see one of the more severe cases. He asked the producer about the symptoms of the disease, and the producer explained, 'Before dying, the cows became mad and rejected food and water'. Roberto replied,

This looks like rabies but to be sure you have to take the head of a dead cow to Zapopan, because the laboratory has to confirm the diagnosis. Rabies is carried by the vampire bat that lives in the caves of the Sierra, and I am afraid the only solution for this disease is to bring the fumigation brigade here. For that to happen we have to persuade the head of the district that this is a serious problem. To get his interest I need to show him that producers are interested in participating in the Ministry pro- grammes.

Roberto had the idea that a baling machine was necessary in this area for cutting and baling the fodder for livestock. He was sure that, with a petition signed by the majority of the producers, the district head would accept the petition. So he asked the producer if he was interested in the use of this type of machine and asked him to sign the petition. Because of his concern for his livestock, the producer signed the petition. He then tried to get something concrete from the *técnico*, saying, 'So what about the cattle then?' Roberto, having obtained the signature of the producer, had lost interest in his problem. It appeared that if he showed too much sympathy he could end up with extra problems to solve. So he suggested, 'What I would like to do is take you to talk with the *mero jefe* [the real boss] in the district, so you can explain the problem directly to him'.

The producer, realizing that the *técnico* was not considering his case important enough, demanded, 'Why do I have to go to the district? Is it because you don't report what is going on here?' Roberto replied,

Of course I do, but it's the staff. They always take time to decide what to do. So, in my experience, the best thing is to go directly to the person who can solve the problem. Let's go together next Monday, and I will introduce you to the boss.

The producer was doubting:

Well, I have to go to Guadalajara this Friday, so I will try to stay there until Monday, but if I can't go to the district would you please report the disease to your superior?'

All that evening the *técnico* worked hard convincing producers of the importance of the baling machine and collected some signatures for his petition. Producers listened to him, but without much enthusiasm.

During the second night in the community, after we had lit the firewood and warmed ourselves with *tequila de la Sierra*, producers started to come to have a drink and to chat with us. Don Martin, an influential person in the community, told us about his life: the hard experiences of raising a family and of how his sons had migrated to the USA in search of a better situation. Roberto sympathized, saying that those who suffered should be compensated. Then he changed the topic of conversation to much more practical matters, telling Don Martin that the community did not yet know his (Roberto's) worth because they had shown no *confianza* in him.

> If you had *confianza* [he said] I could bring things to the community, projects from the ministry to benefit all of you, but I can't do it alone. I need producers' support. You have to sign the petition. We have to put pressure on the ministry so that resources are allocated to La Lobera.

To this, Don Martin replied,

> Look *técnico*, the government has promised a lot of things and nothing has happened yet. This is the reason why the producers listen to you politely, and why they don't believe in your promises too much.

At this point, Roberto became annoyed and said,

> I recognize that *el pinche* [bloody] government is only concerned with one thing – to *chingar* [cheat] the producer, and that is why the producers don't support our work. But if you organized yourselves I could get things done. I have good contacts in the ministry. My father is *el mero jefe* [the real boss] in Mexico, and if I ask him to do something I know he will support it. Even my boss in the unit can't touch me. He wants me to live here, but I don't take any notice of his orders. I come every one or two months.

Roberto was beside himself. So we explained that things could not change overnight, but nevertheless he began to cry, saying to Don Martin,

> I have discovered that after a year producers don't even know my name and that means no *confianza* in me and, without *confianza*, I can't work. I need your support to put pressure on the unit. I am not interested if the producer is an *ejidatario* or a small private producer. I want to help, through my actions, to increase production.

Then he turned to one of us and said,

> Listen *licenciado*, don't tell me things can't change overnight. I am 23 years old and want my idealism to be realized.

He then went into the school and shouted,

I am fed up with people telling me that things can't change. Sometimes I feel like taking a weapon. The first *cabrón* [bastard] I would shoot is the President, because he is at the centre of the web and I am caught in it. I can't take it any longer.

With this comment, general criticism against government policies started. The *técnico*, in an excellent performance, separated his position from that of the institution and presented his sentiments as proof of his honesty and idealism. It was late, and Don Martin had been impressed by the *técnico*'s performance. He said,

Técnico, tomorrow you will get all the signatures you need for your petition, [and added] our problem is how to use the resources of the *ejido* more profitably. My opinion is that what we need to do is to plant fruit trees. I got the idea after a visit to the USA. A cherry orchard could be very profitable.

At this, Roberto realizing what Don Martin's support would cost, began to make promises again:

OK, if that is what you want, I can get the trees for you. As a matter of fact, I just bought some for San Cristóbal. We have to do this through petitions, and people here have to give me the money immediately after the trees arrive here.

Don Martin replied, 'If it is just a matter of money, tomorrow I can collect it for the trees', to which Roberto responded, 'Well then, I think we can work together, because I have contacts in . . .'

It was late. The group was now small, as producers had withdrawn to rest. Only Roberto and Don Martin remained talking, reassuring themselves of the importance of their deal and how profitable cherry trees could be in the Sierra.

AFTER THE PROMISES, THE AFTERMATH

Next day Roberto radiated optimism. And, as Don Martin had promised, producers signed Roberto's petition. At last he had aroused interest about the baling machine, and producers came to us in a much more relaxed state than in the previous days. They told us about the needs of the *ejido*. We were able to work with them, and we were invited to play billiards and to visit their homes. The producers showed us what *confianza* was – that variable which it was difficult for the field-workers of the ministry to establish. We left the community with our survey completed, the petition for the machine signed and a briefcase full of promises that the *técnico* was expected to fulfil.

Roberto reported his work to the head of his unit and suggested that producers were interested in obtaining access to a baling machine, and that he had collected signatures. The head of the unit pointed out, however, that the policy of the ministry was not to support livestock activities, but the production of maize. So he suggested that Roberto should explain to them the ministry's policies and make clear that the unit could not provide them with such a machine.

Roberto said that he could not do that because this petition was the first he had managed to get from them. It was the first sign that producers wanted ministry asistance. Therefore, like it or not, he could not fail the producers. He would take the case to the district. According to Roberto, the head of the unit tried to get hold of Roberto's petitions. But, 'he was too late; the petitions were already in the district. These were signatures for the trees'. The head then became angry because his authority had been challenged by a subordinate. He said that Roberto had taken on responsibilities that had not been approved, that this was insubordination which would cost Roberto dearly.

Roberto bitterly remembers that the head of the unit then went to the district, withdrew the petition, and made the papers 'disappear'. According to Roberto, 'The head of the unit knew that he was creating a problem for me by this action, because I then had to explain to the producers why the petition did not receive attention'.

Roberto's interpretation was that the head had acted in this way so as to assert his authority and show the unit who was in control. He had failed to see the importance of the machine in terms of the work of the *técnico* in the field. Roberto explained that this was the traditional way in which bureaucrats in the ministry killed off the initiatives of *técnicos*.

Some weeks later, Roberto was once again transferred to another unit. The promises of the *técnico* had clashed with the interests of the administrative hierarchy.

EPILOGUE

We returned to La Lobera during the rainy season to stay another week with the producers. After we had exchanged greetings and were brought up to date with the latest community events – a new *ejidal* president, the arrival of a new tractor, how the old one was repaired, etc. – producers started to enquire of Roberto.

One peasant said, 'What has happened to Roberto? He hasn't appeared again since the last time he came with you'. We informed them that he had been moved to another *ejido*. A producer, with a resigned attitude, shrugged: 'You see, the government doesn't help us. We pay taxes, but for what, do we ever receive any service?' Another producer said, 'That's the problem, just when we were starting to get to know the *técnico* and *tenerle la confianza* [have trust in him], the government withdraws him and now we have to start all over again'.

Producers recalled that they had had three *técnicos*. The first one only came to introduce himself to the community and never returned. The next was the best, because he came often and was always present for the meetings. The last one (Roberto) they did not know well. He had promised a baling machine and trees, but he had never come back to tell them what had happened. Producers were convinced that the government had deceived them once again. Their irritation led them to tell us of a recent incident involving the Agrarian Reform Agency, with whom they were trying to legalize the *ejido*'s land area:

> Last week we were called by radio to San Cristóbal, because personnel of the Agrarian Reform wanted to have a meeting with us. We went there, but we arrived in the *pueblo* one hour late. Well, the official had already gone, leaving the message that he was not there to accept the irresponsibilities of the producers. This is *el gobierno* [the government]. Why doesn't the official come here if he wants punctuality! They know where we live, but they don't like to get their shoes dirty. These are all tricks because we are not important to the government. They don't give a damn about us.

Don Jesus added,

> Yes, the government only comes here when they are suspicious about us because we plant *mota* [marijuana]. The last time the army was here in January, they broke into our homes [*allanaron*] and ransacked our possessions. The officer assembled us and said that in Cuyutlan he had found 70 plants of *mota* and that he knew that it was planted in La Lobera too. He asked us to name the people who were cultivating *mota*, otherwise he could use

other methods to make us talk. The government likes to humiliate us, but not to help us.

Don Tomas recognized that the producers had only two ways to make cash quickly:

One is to migrate to the United States to work there, and with some luck, to come back after three or four years with some money. The other way is to cultivate *mota*. Its cultivation is easy, the only thing necessary is fertilizer. It is worth the risks because a kilo of *mota* is bought for 60 or 70 thousand pesos in Guadalajara. With maize you can't make money, but with *mota* it is different.

Last year, the family of Donoso bought a new tractor, complete with all its implements. They could do that because they cultivated *mota*. From where else do you think they got 3 million pesos [US $3,000] overnight?

The producers did not expect to receive help from the government. Migration and the cultivation of marijuana provided cash which could then be invested in livestock. Livestock was perceived by them as their only way of improving local production. A recent economic assessment of the *ejido* shows that they possess more than 700 head, valued over 25 million pesos (US $25,000). Maize is a less important factor in their economy and the *ejido* falls largely outside the area of agency control.

As we emphasized earlier, producers' lack of interest in cultivating maize for marketing through CONASUPO is not because they have no market orientation, or because they are not eager to receive the benefits of the programmes in the form of credit, fertilizer and insecticides. Indeed, where possible they use these inputs to further their own economic interests rather than the targets set by SARH. This is why implementers, such as the head of the unit, are opposed to distributing extra agency resources to an area that is outside their control. The isolation of La Lobera then is perceived institutionally as acting in favour of producers, since they can easily divert programme resources to finance their own economic ventures.

On the other hand, technical assistance in the production of maize is perceived by producers as marginal to the way households organize their production and livelihood strategies. Hence the influence of a strategy such as SAM was resisted by a production system much more complex than that portrayed in the rain-fed policy plans. The assumed isolation of the community is relative, since 57 per cent of the producers claimed to have heard about SAM, even if only 31 per cent of them knew its aims, and only one person had received information about it from the ministry. In other words, resistance to SAM must be understood in terms of the programme's emphasis on the specialization of maize cultivation; and, on the other hand, in terms of the low agency diffusion of its aims among producers. The area, in spite of its potential and its need for agricultural development, was not considered a priority region for the implementation of ministry programmes.

ROBERTO'S DOUBLE DILEMMA: ADMINISTRATION AND THE PEASANTS

Our central actor in the case-study, Engineer Roberto, apparently obtained his position in SARH through the influence of his father. Surprisingly, he had no proper agricultural training. He was also special in the way he perceived the careers and motivation of his colleagues (he called them *chupas barbas*), and in terms of his negative assessment of the administrative system which did not, in his view, deliver the promised services to the farmers. Finally, he was very disparaging of the value of an agricultural training for working in the countryside, maintaining that all one needed was drive and common sense. These characteristics and attitudes meant that people perceived him as an odd man out, and that he was the target of ridicule and of pranks within his field unit, and institutionally seen as a troublemaker. In his account of how he came to La Lobera one can identify some of the reasons why he was continually in conflict with administrative authority. He showed arrogance and a lack of respect towards his superiors. He did not conform to the expected patterns of administrative behaviour, and he hid behind the presumed support of his father. However, he did show some commitment to bridging the gap between peasant and bureaucrat or *técnico*. This he saw largely as a matter of establishing the right personal style, understanding and *confianza*, rather than as a structural problem involving the differential power positions of public authorities and their clients. In practice of course, as we see from the case, he did not hesitate to present himself, whenever he considered it strategic to do so, as an authority with access to centres of power, as a well-doer actively trying to improve the lot of the peasantry, or as a government official fulfilling his administrative tasks.

In all these respects he was a bit of a madcap. Even so, in several of the social situations described, he managed to manipulate the negotiations to his advantage and to create a further basis for communication. When he first arrived in La Lobera he quickly established his authority through diagnosing the illness suffered by the cattle as rabies. This diagnosis confirmed his status as an expert and placed the other parties (both the farmer and the researchers) in an inferior position. After this he went on to provide a solution, namely the fumigation of the cave of bats.

This opened the way to establishing a defined context for the interface between the peasant and the *técnico*, both carrying with them, or somehow 'representing', their own social worlds. This relationship was unequal not only in terms of their perceived levels of knowledge or expertise but also in terms of their assumed ability to command resources. Roberto suggested that outside authorities (i.e. the head of district) should be involved and that the farmer should take the head of a dead cow to Zapopan for analysis. He offered to assist by making the necessary contacts, provided the farmer signed the petition for the baling machine. This baling machine had become his latest obsession (not surprising, really, given the fact that Roberto was trained in mechanical engineering and that livestock was crucial in the economy of La Lobera, which was something he, at least, if not the ministry, had come to realize).

Once the farmer has signed the petition, Roberto's next move was to invite the farmer to accompany him to Zapopan to present the issue to the boss, knowing full well that this was likely to present a problem since peasants did not like to leave their sick livestock and the distance was large and transport difficult. There was also no surety that the meeting with the boss would solve the problem. The farmer procrastinated, saying that he might be able to be in Guadalajara on the Monday morning when they would meet the boss. The outcome was that Roberto had managed to shift the centre of attention away from the immediate problem of the cows dying to fulfil his own obsession for getting signatures for his petition for the baling machine. This incident shows the facility with which he could defuse the situation, having securely established his position as the *técnico*. This demonstrates the extent to which power enters the scene in favour of the knowledge of the *técnico*, irrespective of the scientific validity of his advice – the power of the 'guru' in situations of emergency! Roberto weaves his way through all this with considerable skill, displaying good understanding of different types of knowledge, but in the end achieving nothing effective for the peasant in question. In this respect Roberto is probably not exceptional since Mexican government field-workers have to acquire the techniques of managing these different, and potentially conflicting, bodies of knowledge and cultural frameworks if they are to survive in the field.

The second incident illustrates a different interface situation. It was during the evening when we, the researchers, were sitting round the fire with some of the peasants that he suddenly erupted. He confronted the peasant leader with an accusation that there was no *confianza* in him even after all this time. The peasant leader intervened, exclaiming that it was not so much due to his person but to the fact that the government made many promises that it did not keep.

This occasioned a redefinition of the terms of interaction whereby the notion of *no confianza* (lack of trust) came to characterize the link between the peasant and bureaucratic worlds. Having established this, Roberto then proceeded to try to win the *confianza* of Don Martin, the peasant leader. This he achieved through his heart-rending drama, which included tears and an outright verbal attack on the principal researchers and the President of the nation. He viciously accused the government of 'cheating' the producer, and took our research contribution as a questioning of his idealism. Although somewhat inebriated, he managed to seize the initiative to argue that, despite the shortcomings of the bureaucracy, some *técnicos* were able to do something for the peasantry, a remark countered by Don Martin who used it to put forward his own slightly crazy cherry tree project, which he justified through his own experience in the USA. In return, he promised the *técnico* that people would sign his petition. This was accomplished in the morning very smoothly, after which Roberto and the research team left.

Roberto was, however, much less successful in manipulating cultural attitudes and administrative priorities within his own administrative domain. Hence Roberto's plans for 'helping' the peasants and for bridging the gap between the two worlds were shattered. His boss's opinion was that he had stepped beyond the competence of a *técnico* responsible for implementing the rain-fed policy and had not strictly followed administrative rules and priorities. So his fate was sealed: he would be resocialized in a new, even more isolated, field unit made up of 'troublemakers' or 'hard cases'.

In the end, therefore, the critical factor affecting Roberto's attempts to link the two worlds was, not so much the resistance of the peasantry, but more the constraints, development priorities and ideology of the administrative system under which he had to perform and was evaluated. At the time, he was one of the few *técnicos* who tried to bend the rules a little in the direction of certain perceived mutual interests of himself and the peasants. If he had succeeded he might have helped create an organized interface between the two parties and have integrated them into a long-term and mutually beneficial working relationship. As it was, however, Roberto's case simply revealed to us the enormous gaps in communication and the power differentials in Mexico between peasants and state development agencies. On the other hand, from the peasant point of view, his case showed the possibilities for establishing *confianza* with individual *técnicos*, who could bring some benefits, but also the impossibility of having close and trusting ties with central government agencies, which peasants continued to see as merely coming to La Lobera to enforce 'the law' and to destroy the basis of their economic survival and autonomy. This view was shared by both rich and poor peasants alike.

There is, of course, always some room for manœuvre and some space for *técnicos* to devise ways of accommodating the different and often conflicting interests; and they may be rewarded or penalized by administration or peasantry, or by both. But the struggle goes on. The set of relations is never in equilibrium. The struggle is, as we have tried to show, as much a struggle over types of knowledge and devices for creating ignorance, as it is a struggle over material resources or political power.

NOTES

1 The case data for this paper were collected during 1983–4. The research was supported by the Economic and Social Research Council of Great Britain and affiliated to El Colegio de Jalisco, Guadalajara. Assistance was given by students of ITESCO and the University of Guadalajara. Special thanks are due to the main participants in this case for letting the researchers into their lives with such *confianza*. A fuller version of this paper, which elaborates more fully the theoretical issues only touched upon here, is to be found in Arce and Long 1992.
2 Lopez Portillo had, some years earlier (1965–70) as *Secretaria de la Presidencia* (Minister of the President), initiated a study aimed at reforming the bureaucracy. It appears then that he wished to use the SAM programme as a test case for developing a more efficient and rational public administration.
3 This word comes from *la grilla*, meaning the process of politicking and manipulating people for personal or small-group gain. It is likened to the monotonous and strident noise that a cricket makes when rubbing its legs. Here Roberto is perceived by his superiors as an expert in this

activity. The term *grilloso*, instead of *grillo*, implies that one has this expertise.

4 In Mexico there is a well-known saying that runs, '*Con tal de barbear el jefe va quedar bien con el, son capaces de empenar el alina al diablo*' (Those that crawl to the boss to keep in well with him are capable of selling their soul to the devil) (Mejia 1985: 23). This saying and the use of *chupa barba* in this administrative context highlights the fact that this behaviour is institutionalized around a set of cultural notions concerning the relations between juniors and seniors in Mexican social life.

5 The verb *zorrear* comes from the word *zorro* (fox), an animal known for its cunning. Here the implication is that the Mexican government is always devising ways of tricking people.

6 This assessment is sustained by an analysis of the number of *técnicos* and other personnel allocated to different municipalities in Rain-fed District No. 1. The distribution is highly skewed with the majority of field-workers concentrated in more developed areas of the district. For details see Arce 1986: 53–8.

7 Producers exchange maize seed amongst themselves, even if the seed is exactly the same type. They maintain that this 'tricks' the soil into thinking that the seed is different from that of last year.

8 The same strategy has been noted for peasant producers in the highlands of Peru by Figueroa (1978: 33–5), who argues that herbicides are the first items of modern technology to be absorbed into existing farming systems.

9 *Convivencias* are important social gatherings, usually organized by the head of the unit or his deputy and financed by contributions from the office staff. They take place every one or two weeks in the different *ejidos* that fall under the jurisdiction of the unit. The invitations are extended to all personnel of the unit and sometimes staff from the district office are also invited. The secretaries and other female employees are responsible for the preparation of food and are often chivvied by the males to hurry up with the meal! At these gatherings the gender divide is very sharp: the women sit preparing the salads (with their eyes running from the onions) and the other dishes, whilst the men stand on the veranda of the *ejido* 'country house', drinking tequila with ice and lemon, gossiping at length about events in the district. These gatherings are crucial for consolidating links and loyalty among and between the different status groups and for the development of networks of political support. As the men become more inebriated, they engage in 'rituals of rebellion' whereby they challenge their superiors by criticizing administrative procedures etc.

REFERENCES

Arce, A. (1986) 'Agricultural policy administration in a less developed country: the case of SAM in Mexico,' Ph.D. thesis, Manchester University.

Arce, A. and Long, N. (1992) 'The dynamics of knowledge: interfaces between bureaucrats and peasants,' in N. Long and A. Long (eds) *Battle-*

fields of Knowledge: The Interlocking of Theory and Practice in Social Research and Developement*, London: Routledge.

Carlos, M. (1981) *State Policies, State Penetration and Ecology: A Comparative Analysis of Uneven Development and Underdevelopment in Mexico's Micro-agrarian Regions*, La Jolla; Calif.: University of California.

Figueroa, A. (1978) 'La Economia de las Comunidades Campesinas: El Caso de la Sierra Sur del Peru,' Publicaciones CISEPA, No. 36, Lima: Universidad Catolica del Peru.

Mejia, J. P. (1985) *Asi Habla El Mexicano: Diccionario Basico de Mexicanismos*, Mexico City: Panorama Editorial.

Moore, S. F. (1973) 'Law and social change: the semi-autonomous social field as an appropriate subject of study,' *Law Society Review*, Summer: 719–46.

SAM (1980) *Sistema Alimentario Mexicano*, Mexico City: Federal Government of Mexico.

10 Potatoes and knowledge

Jan Douwe van der Ploeg

One of the indispensable links in the reproduction of potato farming over time, is the continuous selection and multiplication of potato seed.[1] In the Andean highlands these tasks still are, to a certain degree, integral parts of farm labour as praxis. They imply a specific structuring of time and space, as well as the management of a specific knowledge system, which can be described as *art de la localité* (Mendras 1970). In this paper I will first briefly discuss some general features of *art de la localité* as it manifests itself in agriculture. Then I will highlight several aspects of a particular local knowledge system, which is to be found among potato growers in the Andean highlands. Special attention will be given to those aspects related to the management of potato breeding. Finally, the now rapidly spreading scientific knowledge system, which entails new methods of potato selection and which tends towards a rapid marginalization of local knowledge, will be discussed.

ART DE LA LOCALITÉ

A crucial feature of local knowledge in craft-based agriculture is the way it is interwoven with the labour process. It is knowledge generated in and through labour as dynamic process. Knowledge, the labour process and those involved in it compose a unity hard to unravel into separate elements. The labour process is essentially a craft. In the first place it entails a permanent interaction between 'mental' and 'manual' labour, and in the second it presupposes a continuous interpretation and evaluation of the ongoing process of production so as to enable intervention at any required moment and in any desired way. Through such interventions (which, for evident reasons are hard to predict exactly) the magnitude of the harvest and the quality of the final products are to a great extent determined. Thus the labour process does not lend itself easily to any standardization or exact planning. Diversity both permeates and is created by the process itself. Thus, the decisions taken during the labour process indeed determine the results and, when evaluated in connection with the results, this decision-making also leads to the generation of new or more detailed knowledge.

Art de la localité then, is potentially a dynamic knowledge system, and highly complicated and detailed as well. This last characteristic predominates when the labour process involves a broad and complex range of ecological, economic, social and cultural conditions. Then a very detailed and multi-dimensional knowledge is generated, a *savoir-faire paysan* as Lacroix (1981: 95) puts it: ' "Savoir-faire paysan" is understood as the management of the labour process, within the context of the local ecosystem, in order to improve the valorization of elements provided by this local ecosystem' (my translation). On the other hand it could be argued that this same focus on local conditions and on the localized interaction between labour and local ecosystem acts temporarily as a boundary and as a potential limit to these particular knowledge systems.

Art de la localité has been characterized as a kind of knowledge that goes directly 'from practice to practice' (Bourdieu 1980). It does not pass through a theoretical stage in which 'discourse' is developed; there are, so the argument goes, 'no theoretical expressions'. 'Experience is not expressed in a univocal, clear language' (Koningsveld 1986), so the space for any further elaboration of this kind of practical knowledge is seen as being minimal. There are just a father and his son working on a lonely field, the former every now and then transmitting a rule of thumb to the latter, or just punishing him, as a 'padre padrone', when the work is not done properly. This image (presented in a fair number of rural sociological studies as well) is, in my opinion, fundamentally wrong.

There is, of course, 'theory' in *art de la localité*, but this theory is organized in a way that markedly differs from scientific discourse. The syntax for instance is not the nomological one of science; the scope is not a presupposed universe but one specific to the localized labour process itself. Legitimation is not sought in the construction of laws, but in the coincidence with perspectives and interest, which again are perceived as part of the locality. As Darré, who did a beautiful study on the notions and concepts used by French dairy farmers in the conscious and goal-oriented practice of cattle-feeding, concludes, 'Elle (i.e. l'art de la localité) n'est pas non plus mesurée à la verité du discours scientifique: nous chercherons sa pertinence en la rapportant au group pour lequel elle est associée à un ensemble d'activités techniques' (1985: 43). Perceived through the matrix of scientific criteria *art de la localité* becomes indeed nearly invisible, ignorance of the people involved being one of the most common assessments.

Apart from this, Darré makes it clear that if the need arises, even the typical theoretical expressions of *art de la localité* (often of a metaphorical kind, as I will demonstrate further on) can be transformed. Such a transformation occurs when, for instance, farmers have to confront newly emerging technical elites as agronomists, technicians, etc.

LOCAL KNOWLEDGE CONCERNING THE SOIL THAT IS TILLED: THE IMPORTANCE OF METAPHOR

Andean farmers are faced with a huge variety of different ecological conditions. Moreover, they consciously aim at increasing this variety by (1) trying to have their plots on different ecological 'floors' (Mayer 1981) and (2) by trying to improve each plot, not along standardized lines, but by following the specific set of conditions each plot presents to them. The plots are observed, interpreted, evaluated, cultivated and improved by means of an impressive cluster of bipolar and rather metaphorical concepts. The concepts *fria/caliente* (cold/hot), for instance, are used to characterize certain aspects of what we would call soil fertility. It is related – but not in an exact or unilinear way – to the amount of nutrients and humus in the subsoil. *Dura/suavecita* (hard/soft) is another conceptual pair: it refers to the degree in which the soil has been tilled in previous years. It communicates simultaneously another important meaning, that is, the degree to which the particular plot has been cared for and so, the degree to which the plot may be considered as 'grateful'. The soil is not simply equal to 'land' in its physical or geographical sense. It is *pacha mamma* (mother earth), and when she is *suavecita*, then 'mother earth is generous'. She is 'grateful for the respect paid earlier to her'. *Pacha mama* and associated categories such as 'hard' or 'soft' refer to the specific localized interaction between man and nature. *Alta/bajita* (high/low) again express notions that at first sight seem quite imprecise, especially if one walks with farmers through their fields, and one hears them describe lower-lying fields as 'higher'. But then, it is not only altitude (taken as a mathematical notion) which causes a certain plot to be described as *alta* or *baja*, but also the winds, the way topography shelters it from the cold, and even the degree of *calor*, of being *fria* or *caliente*, are taken into account. So in certain respects the different concepts are inter-related; the concepts overlap, not in accidental but in strategic ways. Taken together they form a 'network of meaning' as Hesse (1983: 27) would argue. These and other concepts are not unequivocal, nor do they lend themselves to precise qualifications. They cannot be built into a nomological model (of the kind used in applied science and in technology development, as will be discussed further on). When one separates these concepts from the people who use them or from their context they indeed become 'inaccurate'. Of course this inaccurate character does not prevent farmers from establishing quite exactly the overall condition of specific plots. They are also quite able to communicate with each other on this topic. The inaccurate nature of the concepts used even seems favourable for such an exact interpretation of a plot's condition and the ensuing dialogue. For interpretation and communication can only be active processes: concepts must be weighed against each other every time a specific plot is being considered. Hence the conceptual overlap becomes strategic. In synthesis: it is precisely the vagueness or 'imprecise' character that allows for this active process of interpre-tation and change. 'The farmer', to quote Mendras (1970: 47), 'felt as if he had "made" his field and *knew it as the creator knows his creation*, since the soil was the product of his constant care: plowing, fertilizing, rotating crops, maintenance of fallow ground, and so on.'

LOCAL KNOWLEDGE CONCERNING CROPS AND VARIETIES: A FOLK-TAXONOMY

Most farmers cultivate 12 to 15 plots continuously and in addition a number of plots in turns. Farmers also interchange plots, sometimes following quite complex schemes that embrace whole communities. Each plot is thoroughly known by its cultivator. A specific combi-nation of concepts, which are each in themselves rather vague, allows him to establish the best way to cultivate it (and in the long run, to improve it). 'This personal knowledge of the field' (Mendras) is one of the basic elements of the *art de la localité*. It is local knowledge, which is hard or even impossible to generalize. It is local knowledge because it presupposes an active, knowledgable actor, who actually is the 'agent' of the unity and constant inter-action of mental and manual work. It can also be defined as local knowledge because it allows these actors to obtain a high degree of control and mastership over the highly diversified local situation. In this *art de la localité* the knowledge of the fields is permanently co-ordinated with the knowledge of the genetic stock each farmer has at his disposal. Most farmers maintain up to 30 or 40 different cultivars in their fields as well as in their *chacrita*.[2] And through socially regulated exchange they can easily obtain up to a hundred different cultivars, each of which is known to them, their neighbours, and friends in other villages.

The distribution of cultivars over the plots makes for an extreme heterogenity. Some fields contain only one cultivar, others between 2 and 10, sometimes interplanted in the same row, or with each cultivar in its own row. Mostly one finds a *chacrita* as well: small plots of 20 or 25 square metres, which contain up to 30 or 40 cultivars. This heterogenity not only leads to continuous experimentation (which genotype fits best with the specific phenotypical conditions of each plot)[3] and risk aversion, but it also results in the production of new genotypes:[4] 'The crop evolution of the cultivated potato is closely linked to the mixture of species and genotypes which promotes hybridization and crossing between ploidy levels and among clones' (Brush *et al.* 1981: 80). On a more global level Brush *et al.* consequently state that this consciously produced heterogenity has three consequences: 'a) the maintenance of numerous genotypes over space and time, b) the wide distribution of particular genotypes, and c) the generation or amplification of new genotypes' (ibid.).

Crucial in the maintenance and correct handling of this genetic diversity is the availability of an 'folk taxonomy', another interrelated set of concepts used for the identification and naming of varieties, for the selection and definition of planting patterns as well as for the exchange of cultivars between farmers (an exchange that sometimes covers distances of up to 30 or 40 kilometres). In several ethno-botanical studies the impressive range as well as the taxonomic structure of this nomenclature has been highlighted. What is important here is that this taxonomy is to be seen as an integral part of the *art de la localité*. Not only does it follow some of the features already noted (such as the 'vagueness', the 'overlap' of criteria, the need for an active interpretation), but in some respects it is even directly linked with the typical knowledge of the different phenotypical conditions represented by the variety of plots. I often noted farmers stating for instance that such and such a tuber could not be a *calhuay* (the name for a type of tuber) since it could not be grown under specific conditions considered to be ideal for the *calhuay* cultivar. Or they state bluntly that a *ccompi* is a *calhuay*, even though they know quite well that the particular cultivar is indeed a *ccompi* and not a *calhuay*. But that is exactly what metaphor is: 'an attempt to understand one element of experience in terms of another' (Morgan 1986: 13). Thus the well-known *ccompi* (interpreted here as a cultivar) is related to and temporarily interpreted in terms of the soil conditions required by *calhuay*. Andean farmers are often labelled as being ignorant. It was indeed the first conclusion that passed through my mind when hearing the expression that a *ccompi* was equal to a *calhuay*. But then, such an argument differs in no way from our everyday patterns of speech in which we say such things as 'god is a shepherd', or 'the man is a lion' (or, as sometimes occurs, 'a mouse'). Metaphor is strategic. It is the theoretical expression through which the communication of multiple meaning is organized, being its rather 'loose' framework (including the overlaps), an essential prerequisite as well as an important vehicle for the very dynamism entailed in these particular knowledge systems. Through metaphor co-ordination of different domains of knowledge is realized; through metaphor the proper dynamics, created by this co-ordination can be understood and oriented. I will try to illustrate this by means of the practice of selection as elaborated by Andean farmers.

SELECTION: THE CO-ORDINATION OF KNOWLEDGE-SEGMENTS

Now, how is selection organized? At first sight it seems quite simple: the 'best' tubers (these are normally the smaller ones) from the 'best plants' are laid apart and will be next year's seed potatoes. In reality the process is far more complex; it can be, at least partly, illustrated in Figure 10.1.

Each plot is known as a typical set of phenotype conditions. Then the most suitable genotype is selected for each plot. It should be noted that this selection is in no way to be considered as trial and error. It is a clearly goal-directed process, which takes shape within (and can only take shape within) the global framework of the *art de la localité*, the internally co-ordinated, and finely tuned knowledge on plots, cultivars, labour processes and earlier experiences (one's own and others'). To complicate matters even further, it should be underlined that the above-mentioned expression 'the most suitable genotype', does not refer to a static state of affairs. The problem is that 'the most suitable' genotype changes every time, sometimes slowly, sometimes abruptly. This is because its definition is dependent on different criteria, such as yields, prices, response

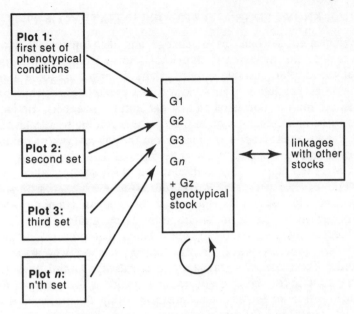

Figure 10.1 The structure of peasant-managed potato selection

to changed plot conditions, and so on, criteria which in their turn are variable as well. Through the process indicated, in which the plots (and the labour invested in it) form the starting point, a finely tuned adaptation is reached. But this is not the point where the dynamics of local selection stop. The process always goes beyond the limits reached in previous cycles. The dynamics of the selection process are based on two things. The first one has already been indicated: this is the creation of new genotypes (Gz). As for the second, it should be pointed out clearly that no plot, understood as a specific set of phenotypical conditions, can be interpreted as a static unity. In the medium and long run they can be improved, precisely because they are the subjects of the farm labour process itself. So progress can be made and new experiences can be gained: through the cycle of observation, interpretation, evaluation and manipulation, the scope of the *art de la localité* is enlarged, which enables the farmer to obtain new insights, and so on.

LOCAL KNOWLEDGE AND THE ORGANIZATION OF TIME

The indicated mechanisms of change and development that are inherent to the dynamics of the local knowledge system, do not usually lead to an unstable state of affairs. Changes are more likely to be an accumulation of all kinds of minor adaptations (which are 'invisible' for the normally trained agricultural scientist). Besides, even these minor changes often take place according to a 'calendar' which spans great lengths of time. From the 'discovery' (or obtainment through exchange) of a slightly different cultivar, via the first tests in different plots, its multiplication, to a substantial harvest will take at least five or six years. Moreover, every successive step carries certain risks, risks that are to be evaluated among other things against the particular situation the farming family finds itself in. Indeed, there is a lot of magical belief that prevents farmers from risking too much at once. But contrary to those who associate attitudes like these with stagnancy or circularity, I think they are crucial exactly for the opposite reasons: magic is – at least in the Andes – essential for achieving progress within the framework of the *art de la localité*. Precisely because the magico-religious interpretation of the world reduces the risk to acceptable proportions; so the experiments and 'the dreams' (as farmers say) are made possible (see Herrera 1980). Tradition and transformation are not at odds – at least on this level. It is precisely 'traditional' magic, with its built-in explanation and fear of the natural world, which makes possible renewal and transformation. Magic delineates, that is, it reduces the space for experiments to socially acceptable proportions. So tradition is converted into the necessary self-defence against the potential turbulence and destruction implied by every experiment. And magic becomes converted into the required set of symbols that guides the experimenter into a still unknown world.[5]

SCIENTIFIC POTATO BREEDING

According to a now widely accepted scheme in which rural development is seen as mainly dependent on technological change, the introduction of new, so-called 'improved varieties' in the Andes farming systems is being promoted in several programmes[6] (state-controlled or run by international experts) as a crucial lever for 'development'.

These improved varieties are the result of scientific plant breeding, partly done in the Lima-based Centro Internacional de Papa

(CIP), which is one of the institutions belonging to the international CGIAR network. The scientific knowledge system on which this plant breeding is based as well as the subsequent diffusion of its results is in many respects, such as its inner logic, its scope, its dynamics as well as the very role of the farmers, quite different from the *art de la localité*, the local knowledge system discussed earlier.

The process of scientific plant breeding typically starts with the formulation of an 'ideal plant type' (see Oasa 1981). One of the frequent specifications of such 'ideal types' is that they must be 'superior' (mainly, but not only, in yields) to the 'traditional' varieties. This is deemed necessary in the first place to create a 'breakthrough' as traditional agriculture is seen as having reached its limits, which cannot be extended through internal processes. Additionally, such a 'superiority' is seen as one of the main factors that may induce farmers to accept the improved varieties.

Then, after the definition of an ideal plant type, the second step is the creation of a new genotype that contains as much of the desired characteristics as possible. In potato breeding this is known as 'building in new characteristics' (which is, as far as potatoes are concerned, a relatively easy procedure; however, the following selection becomes very difficult). In the third step, and this again is typical, the phenotypical conditions which will render the newly formed genotype effective, are derived, specified and tested in experimental stations. In synthesis, the construction of a new genotype essentially follows a course that differs basically from the one entailed in local farm practices. In the Andean highlands the given phenotypical conditions are – within the framework of the *art de la localité* – interpreted as starting points for the selection and adaptation of genotypes, whereas in the scientific knowledge system the genotype is the point of departure for the specification of the required phenotypical conditions. One of the consequences of this drastic change is that the new genotype will only prove to be an effective and rational innovation in so far as these required conditions can be effectively repeated in the fields. This complication is presented in Figure 10.2, which indicates at the same time that to 'innovate' is not just the simple adoption of a recommended object ('a miracle seed'), but – as far as the farmer is concerned – a highly complex reorganization of several farming routines.

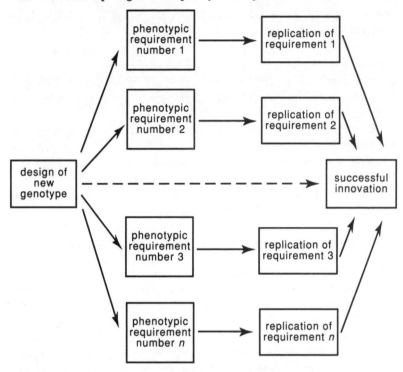

Figure 10.2 The structure of scientific potato selection

SCIENTIFIC KNOWLEDGE AND THE RESTRUCTURING OF TIME

Another important consequence of this (mostly invisible) reorganization is the implied redefinition of the 'calendar'. Whereas the local practice of potato selection and amelioration allows for a step-by-step improvement of different phenotypical conditions (steps that in their turn can follow, for instance, the demographic cycle within the farming family or the logic of patterns of co-operation within the communities), scientific plant breeding demands a sudden and complete repetition of specified requirements in farmers' plots. Let us take, just to illustrate this briefly, an 'ideal plant' definition that is based on the possibility of converting available sunlight into a daily caloric growth of the tubers three times greater than is the case in traditional cultivars. This demands a highly nitrogen-responsive genotype, from which in turn the phenotypical requirements are derived e.g. the amount of nitrogen in the subsoil is to be such and such a quantity. To avoid burning, this amount is to be distributed as fertilizer according to a precise time-schedule, derived in its turn from the specific genotypical cycle. From this, water regulation requirements can be derived, and so it continues. However, the point to note is that these specified requirements must be repeated in the fields, as an integral whole. Even if all the specified conditions except their exact distribution over time are followed, then the 'innovation' fails.

Thus time is converted from a basically indiscrete into a discrete category. And the labour process changes from the skill to confront and exploit specific circumstances, to the skill of applying general and standardized procedures to circumstances that are to be seen as more adverse the more they are specific.

SCIENTIFIC KNOWLEDGE, CONTROL AND POWER

The different requirements are specified in scientific language. Taken together they compose a nomological model: if requirements 1 to n are all fulfilled, then (and only then) genotype X will function. This model is formulated on a global level, that is, within the abstract 'synthetic nature' constructed by science. And the terms it is build on are to be highly standardized, quantifiable and not subject to subjective interpretations. It is through such a model, its language and its terms that the necessary control, manipulation and supervision over the experimental situation is established. Once tested the model can be converted into a means for the external prescription and sanctioning of farm labour. This is exactly what happens in the context of 'planned' or 'induced' rural development.

Artefacts produced by agribusiness (such as fertilizer, pesticides, herbicides, irrigation equipment, tractors and implements, storage facilities and the like) conform pretty closely to the crucial condition of being standardizeable. So it is only logical and – within the world of carefully controlled experiments – also quite efficient to develop the model (or 'scientific design') along the lines of these available and standardized elements. The requirement of a certain amount of nitrogen in the subsoil is then expressed as a certain dose of a specified chemical fertilizer. In practice, however, such a necessity is in no way evident on local farm plots managed with the corresponding *art de la localité*. The amount of nutrients can be augmented, their composition can be changed, by using dung, or through the use of natural fertilizer (such as clover, alfalfa, etc.), or by techniques such as inter-cropping, changes in the cropping and rotation schemes, etc. However, the outcome of such methods cannot be exactly predicted. Nor can the necessary methods for reaching pre-established levels be prescribed in detail. For farmers this is no problem whatsoever (indeed, these were the methods that made fertile large parts of the Netherlands, especially the poor sandy soils of the eastern part).[7] But regardless of the advantages such methods can offer in a situation managed through local knowledge, in a scientific design they cannot be integrated, simply because they are insufficiently adaptable to the necessary standardization. Local methods (and therefore the *art de la localité*) fall outside the scope of scientific design. And consequently, farmers as active and knowledgeable actors, capable of improving their own conditions, also fall outside the scope of scientifically managed rural development.

The foregoing implies that the introduction of 'improved varieties' initiates the creation of several chains of new dependency patterns. New artefacts (namely those specified in the scientific design) must be bought, new procedures must be followed, new circuits (several markets and the banking circuits) must be entered and new expertise (ability to decipher scientific and bureaucratic language) is to be mobilized.[8] In Figure 10.3 some of these chains and their mutual interdependencies are indicated. One of the consequences is that the farming enterprise is to be managed along a relatively new logic: the newly emerging monetary costs are to be balanced against monetary benefits. In itself such logic – although differing radically from the logic normally used by Andean farmers in running their enterprises – is not hard to understand.[9] It is, however, hardly understandable and hardly applicable where markets (and therefore price-cost relations) are highly unstable and often show completely irrational tendencies. The more so, where these markets are considered as 'arenas' where 'others' (brokers or *intermediarios*) are the first to benefit, and where, finally, the effects of market tendencies are, to quote Cole and Wolf 'anti-ecological' (1974).[10]

FROM THE MARGINALIZATION OF LOCAL KNOWLEDGE TO THE INVISIBILITY OF MEN

Local knowledge, or *art de la localité*, is, under these conditions, rapidly becoming not just a marginal, but more than anything, a superfluous or even a counter-productive element: 'a hindrance to change'. Without being able to prove this in a scientific way, I am convinced that the many stories I was told in the Andes, stories

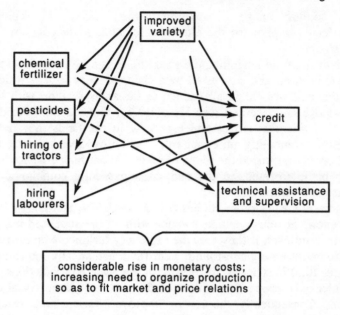

Figure 10.3 Interlinkages as established in the process of innovation

that often centre on a phenomenon which at first sight is only 'magic', namely the 'invisibility' of man,[11] are strongly rooted in and confirmed by farmers' experience with the diffusion of 'improved varieties'. Invisibility means, in these popular stories, that although you do exist in a physical sense, you are not seen by anybody. People treat you as if you do not exist as an individual, and as if you are indeed invisible as a social being. They direct themselves to you but in such a way that anybody or nobody could be in your place. You only exist if others (technical advisers, bank bureaucrats, etc.) are so kind as to remember that you are there – which most often is not the case. That is how invisibility as daily experience is reproduced. Invisibility seems to become especially reinforced when all your careful attention and love for the land are at once declared insignificant by the introduction of general schemes to be followed in production and by the introduction of 'miracle seeds'. Maybe that is why farmers in their turn mystify their own past: they talked to me on quite a number of occasions about 'those times [i.e. the Inca period] when we grew gold, pure gold on these grounds'.

This popular image of invisibility then, is, in my opinion, a perfect metaphor for the effects of scientific knowledge on local knowledge.

Right from the beginning the scientific design of 'improved varieties' is inspired and structured by a claim of 'superiority', which is a claim omnipresent in all science as far as its relation with local knowledge is concerned (see Hesse 1978). Outside the immediate scope of scientific circles and especially in the fields they indeed appear as something quite magical, the improved varieties seem to hold promises outside the scope of reality. What happens, however, is to be interpreted, in the end, as a particular combination of failure and reification.

Farmers are, as other studies (by Dewalt 1979, Hardeman 1984) also show, obviously unable to cope with all the supposed requirements. And even if they are, then the very technico-administrative environment emerging around them (as schematically indicated in Figure 10.3)[12] excludes by means of its own contradictions and turbulency, a proper 'repetition' of the required phenotypical conditions. Consequently, the new or 'improved' varieties are degenerating quickly. Within three of four years they became incapable of generating even low levels of production. The new stock is 'done' or, as farmers in the highlands state, 'Ya no tiene fuerza' (It has no power any more). That is to say, the claim of 'superiority' provokes a reaction that is equally formulated as a magico-religious statement: the power which was once claimed turns out to be rather ineffective (to be lost).

In more general terms this implies that the increasing influence of science in the world produces just the opposite effect, at least under the circumstances described: myths, vagueness, poly-interpretability and a certain subjectivity in the relation to nature are not superceded through heavy inputs of applied science, but rather, reinforced and extended to farmers' relations to science itself!

BACK TO THE POTATO FIELDS

Let us then finally return to the simple business of counting potatoes and measuring plots (which was, after all, my job). In the farming systems I studied in the Andes, farmers reached yields of up to 25 tonnes per hectare, 'simply' through their *art de la localité*. The mean production was, of course, much lower: around 10 tonnes per hectare. The intriguing aspect of the programmes for rural development was that (1) in their ex-ante assessments it was stated that mean productivity was just 5 or 6 tonnes per hectare (Haudry 1984). Thus parallel to the scientific design of a 'new' superiority, a systematic (and quite functional) component of ignorance is created.[13] Or to put it more bluntly, it really seems that ignorance of the local knowledge systems, their dynamics and their scope, is a crucial precondition for the diffusion of the scientific knowledge system.

Finally two questions remain to be answered. What are in the first place the reasons farmers in the Andean highlands are increasingly exchanging their own potato seeds for these 'improved varieties'? And second, what is happening on the interface between the two knowledge systems and their main agents: farmers and technicians?

'Magic' and 'misery': these are the clues that explain the increasing adoption of improved varieties by Andean farmers. 'Magic': because a cultivar intentionally constructed to be superior, effectively functions as a spell. It is introduced and perceived as an emanation from another, more powerful world. The new varieties are also represented (and accepted) as a gift; this association is made especially at the level of direct encounters between technicians and *promotores* on the one hand and farmers on the other. The problem is only that after some time the gift seems to have lost its power. But then, in the mean time other things have changed too. Through the adoption of the gift, the genetic stock normally conserved carefully by these farmers, may have been eroded. And then the 'misery': it is worth noting that, at least in the communities where we did our field-work, it was not the richer farmers who changed completely to the 'improved' varieties. It was mainly the so-called *medios*, farmers having sufficient land but lacking (for whatever reason) the means to cultivate it. They needed credit, but credit forms part of the formula of 'integrated rural development'. It is handed out in kind, in the form of improved varieties, fertilizer, etc. All this of course does not imply that farmers do not now and again withdraw from such 'schemes' and 'formulas'. The point is, however, that after such a withdrawal their material position makes it even more difficult for them to structure their farm labour process along the lines they consider to be the correct ones.

The above-mentioned contradictions are reflected in the interface between the agents of the scientific knowledge system on the one hand and farmers on the other. Distrust combined with dependency versus the 'other' characterize the uneasy position in which both groups are placed. A systematic creation of a sphere of ignorance is indeed one of the answers the lower-level technicians come up with as they are time and again confronted with farmers who try to convince them of their particular situation which, according to them, requires a particular solution (a divergence from the ideal scheme illustrated in Figure 10.3). The technicians however are unable to react adequately to these requests, let alone to respond to the rationality such requests might contain. At a higher level such programmes need and therefore create a great deal of ignorance (cf. the already mentioned systematic underestimation of the productivity of local farming systems); in the fields too, this ignorance is systematically encouraged. At the same time farmers are unable to continue with their local cultivars and are therefore placed in a position that makes it impossible for them to reproduce their local knowledge. They become incomprehensible. But that does not matter: knowing their views, opinions or experience is not relevant anyhow. In the end farmers are made identical to the image ascribed to them in modern agricultural science: invisible men.

NOTES

1 I am grateful to Mark Hobart for his detailed comments on an earlier draft of this paper. I also want to thank the Dutch potato experts D. E. van der Zaag, J. Parlevliet and T. Laudy for their detailed comments and criticism.

2 *Chacrita* is literally 'garden'. However, it suggests an attitude of affection in the speaker to the particular garden in question.

3 Throughout this text I use the terms genotype and phenotype in a rather loose way. Strictly speaking, from an agronomist's point of view, it is even incorrect. The phenotype is the result of the interaction between a particular environment and a particular genotype. A genotype then can only be known through its different phenotypical expressions. However, when it is realized that 'phenotypical conditions' can be read as 'environmental aspects', then there should be no danger of confusion.

4 Of course the production of new genotypes follows the lines of sexual reproduction. Contrary to north-west European conditions, both the Andean eco-systems and the way potato growing is organized by the Andean farmers lead to a rather high chance of success in the production and survival of seedlings (or 'true seed' as it is called nowadays). Plots are small (which implies that there are a lot of 'surroundings') and highly diversified as far as the number and distribution of cultivars is concerned. Insect life is abundant and insecticides and pesticides are hardly used. Apart from all these favourable conditions leading to a spontaneous production of new genotypes, some farmers collect seedlings in a goal-oriented way to develop them further. This is done particularly in the so-called *chacritas*. In the Netherlands this practice was realized by farmers at the beginning of this century. Since then, however, the necessary knowledge has been lost. Now most farmers

and scientists even believe that the production and utilization of 'true seed' is only possible under laboratory conditions.

5 Of course, the foregoing discussion does not imply that *art de la localité* is to be equated with 'the best knowledge ever possible'. The dynamic character of local knowledge – as outlined here – excludes such pretensions from the beginning: what is considered as 'good' today, can turn out to be a mistake tomorrow. The point is that the criteria for such an assessment are also continuously evolving, as I pointed out earlier. 'Each error indeed is the beginning of new knowledge, because every frustration forcefully led to reflexion, to a new mediation on the very conditions of practice' (Herrera 1984: 10). In more general terms this dialectical interrelation between practice and theory in craft-based agriculture (as opposed to the science-based agriculture now emerging in Europe and America) is discussed by Boserup (1965) who relates demographic growth to the creation of new insights resulting in an ongoing intensification, by Slicher van Bath (1960) who studied the same interrelationship in north-west European history (focusing more than Boserup on the development of local knowledge systems), and by Hayami and Ruttan (1985), when discussing the agricultural history of Japan.

6 It certainly reflects a good deal of arrogance towards farmers to denominate new varieties as 'improved' varieties. Such a qualification should be the result of farmers' evaluation and not an ex-ante assessment by international research stations themselves, as Dr D. E. van der Zaag made clear to me (personal communication, January 1987).

7 As described recently by Hofstee (1985) and van Zanden (1985).

8 This role is usually ascribed to the local-level technicians or *promotores*.

9 See for a full description of these 'logics' van der Ploeg 1985 and van der Ploeg 1986.

10 Cole and Wolf here seem to follow Polanyi who stated – much earlier – that 'all along the line human society had become an accessory of the economic system. . . . But while production could theoretically be organized in this way, the commodity fiction disregarded the fact that leaving the fate of soil and people to the market would be tantamount to annihilating them' (1974).

   We found indeed that those Andean potato farmers who were more than others obliged to follow the 'commodity fiction', increased the share of potato culture in their cropping scheme by up to 50 per cent, which is, in agronomic sense, disastrous within a few years. Soil fertility and pest resistance are completely destroyed in such a way (see Bolhuis and van der Ploeg 1985: 308).

11 The image of invisibility is omnipresent in the prose written by Manuel Scorza, once a lawyer working with farmers' unions in the Andean regions (see especially Scorza 1977). The origins of this particular image, however, can be traced back to the *conquistadores* of the Inca empire in the sixteenth century. In this respect Wachtel's study (1976) still stands as a masterpiece.

12 See, for a further elaboration of this theme, Benvenuti's work on the Technological-Administrative Task Environment (1982).

13 Hibon (1981) proved that such an underestimation of the productivity of local farm systems is indeed a structural (not to say, a chronic) feature

in Peruvian agricultural policies. As can be derived from other, recent agronomic studies (see Fresco 1986) the same applies to typical peasant crops such as cassava in Africa.

REFERENCES

Benvenuti, B., Bolhuis, E. and Ploeg, J. D. van der (1982) *I problemi dell'imprenditorialità agricola nella integrazione cooperative*, Bologna: Associazione per l'Istruzione Professionale in Agricoltura.

Bolhuis, E. E. and Ploeg, J. D. van der (1985) *Boerenarbeid en stijlen van landbouwbeoefening*, Leiden: Development Studies no. 8, Leiden: University of Leiden.

Boserup, E. (1965) *The Conditions of Agricultural Growth, the Economics of Agrarian Change under Population Pressure*, Chicago: Aldine.

Bourdieu, P. (1980) *Le Sens Pratique*, Paris: Editions de Minuit.

Brush, S. B., Heath, J. C. and Huaman, Z. (1981) 'Dynamics of Andean potato agriculture', in *Economic Botany* (35)1: 70–88.

Cole, J. W. and Wolf, E. R. (1974) *The Hidden Frontier, Ecology and Ethnicity in an Alpine Valley*, New York: Academic Press.

Darré, J. P. (1985) *La parole et la technique, l'univers de pensée des éleveurs du Ternois*, Paris: L'Harmattan.

Dewalt, B. (1979) *Modernization in a Mexican Ejido: a Study in Economic Adaptation*, Cambridge: Cambridge University Press.

Fresco, L. O. (1986) *Cassava in Shifting Cultivation, a Systems Approach to Agricultural Technology Development in Africa*, Amsterdam: Royal Tropical Institute.

Hardeman, J. (1984) *Selectieve innovatie door kleine boeren in Mexico*, series: Bijdragen tot de sociale geografie en planologie, no. 8, Amsterdam: Vrije Universiteit.

Haudry, R. de Soucy (1984) 'Situación del programa de credito Proderm al 31/XII/83 y propuestas de acción', internal document of the PRODERM programme, Cuzco.

Hayami, Y. and Ruttan, V. (1985) *Agricultural Development: an International Perspective*, Baltimore, Md.: Johns Hopkins University Press.

Herrera, A. de (1984) *Agricultura General (1513)* ed. Servicio de Publicaciones del Ministerio de Agricultura y Pesca, Madrid: Servicio de Publicaciones del Ministerio de Agricultura.

Hesse, M. (1978) 'Theory and value in the social sciences', in C. Hookway and P. Pettit (eds) *Action and Interpretation: Studies in Philosophy of the Social Sciences*, Cambridge: Cambridge University Press.

Hesse, M. 'The cognitive claims of metaphor', in Van Noppen, J. P. (ed), *Metaphor and Religion, theolinguistics 2*, Study Series of the Vrije Universiteit Brussel, Brussels, 1983.

Hibon, A. (1981) *Transfert de technologie et agriculture paysanne en Zone Andine: le cas de la culture du maïs dans les systèmes de production du Cusco (Perou)*, tome I et II, Toulouse: Université de Toulouse.

Hofstee, E. W. (1985) *Groningen van grasland naar bouwland 1750–1930*, Wageningen: Publicatie en Documentatie Centrum.

Koningsveld, H. (1986) 'Wat is landbouwwetenschap? Op zoek naar een identiteit', in *Landbouwkundig Tijdschrift* 98(9).

Lacroix, A. (1981) *Transformations du process de travail agricole; indcidences de l'industrialisation sur les conditions de travail paysannes*, Grenoble: Institut National de la Recherche Agronomique.

Mayer, E. Y. (1981) *Uso de la tierra en los Andes*, Lima.

Mendras, H. (1970) *The Vanishing Peasant: Innovation and Change in French Agriculture*, Cambridge: Cambridge University Press.

Morgan, G. (1986) *Images of Organization*, Beverley Hills, Calif.: Safe Publications.

Oasa, E. K. (1981) *The international rice research institute and the green revolution: a case study on the politics of agricultural research*, Honolulu: University of Hawaii.

Ploeg., J. D. van der (1985) 'Patterns of farming logic, structuration of labour and the impact of externalization; changing dairy farming in Northern Italy', *Sociologia Ruralis*, vols XXV–I.

—— (1986) *La ristrutturazione del lavoro agricolo, gli effetti dell'incorporamento e dell'istituzionalizzazione sullo sviluppo dell'azienda agraria*, Rome: REDA, edizioni per l'agricoltura.

Polanyi, K. (1957) *The Great Transformation*, Boston Mass.: Beacon Press.

Scorza, M. (1977) *Garabombo, el Invisible*, Caracas: Monte Avila Editores, CA.

Slicher van Bath, B. H. (1960) *De agrarische geschiedenis van West-Europa (500–1850)*, Utrecht, Antwerp: Het Spectrum.

Wachtel, N. (1976) *Los Vencidos: los indios del Perú frente a la conquista espanola (1530–1570)* Madrid: Alianza Editorial, SA.

Zanden, J. L. van (1985) *De economische ontwikkeling van de Nederlandse landbouw in de negentiende eeuw, 1800–1914*, Wageningen: Landbouwhogeschool, and in Utrecht: HES Uitgevers BV.

Name index

Abel, R. 130n
Agawu, K. 68
Alatas, S. H. 22
Allott, A. N. 120
Ames, D. W. 65
Apthorpe, R. 38
Arce, A. 11, 15, 39
Aristotle, 24n
Attali, J. 66
Aziz, S. 161

Bailey, F. G. 8
Bailey, J. 157n
Bakhtin, M. M. 24n
Banga, P. M. 60n
Barnett, A. D. 163, 164, 177n
Barth, F. 8
Bassett, T. 65
Baudrillard, J. 25n
Baum, R. 168
Bedaux, R. M. A. 44
Beek, W. E. A. van 4, 18, 45, 52, 60n
Bellman, B. 73, 74
Benda-Beckmann, F. von 5, 14, 24n, 40, 116, 119, 123, 124, 126–30, 130n, 131n, 141–2
Benda-Beckmann, K. von 123, 124, 126, 128, 130, 130n, 131n, 141–2
Benvenuti, B. 225n
Bhaskar, R. 6, 8
Bierschenk, T. 158n
Bolhuis, E. E. 225n
Boserup, E. 225n
Bourdieu, P. 17, 66, 210
Bourdon, R. 158n

Breitborde, L. B. 71
Breman, J. 141
Broeke, Y. ten 141
Brokensha, D. W. 11, 17–18, 22n, 27
Brush, S. B. 213
Burghart, R. 17, 20, 25n, 39

Carlos, M. 179
Chambers, R. 22n, 63, 66, 68–9, 75, 158n
Chanock, M. 130n
Ch'en Po-ta 161
Chen, J. 177n
Chesterton, G. K. 70
Chomsky, N. 80
Cohen, A. P. 4, 19–20, 32, 34, 35
Cole, J. W. 220, 225n
Collier, J. 119, 121
Collingwood, R. G. 4, 10, 21, 25n, 101
Comaroff, J. L. 131n
Croll, E. 14, 26n, 60n, 168, 177n

Darré, J. P. 210–11
de Schlippe, P. 69, 72–3
Dewalt, B. 222
Dieterlen, G. 45
Dilley, R. 23n
Dove, M. R. 122
Durkheim, E. 24n

Elwert, G. 158n
Erler, B. 158n
Evans-Pritchard, E. E. 4, 73

230 An anthropological critique of development

Wallace, A. F. C. 11
Watts, M. 66–7, 74
Weber, M. 32
Werbner, R. P. 121, 122, 123
Wilkinson, P. 130n
Williams, D. V. 121
Wilson, B. 10

Winch, P. 4
Wolf, E. R. 220, 225n
Woodman, G. R. 130n
Worden, J. W. 102

Zaag, D. E. van der 225n
Zanden, J. L. van 225n

Subject index